Great Bordellos
of the World

Turkish Bath, 1862
Jean-Auguste-Dominique Ingres
1790–1867
LOUVRE MUSEUM, PARIS/PHOTO BY
EDDY VAN DER VEEN/COLORIFIC

Great Bordellos
of the World

An illustrated history

Emmett Murphy

Quartet Books

London   Melbourne   New York

First published by Quartet Books Limited 1983
A member of the Namara Group
27/29 Goodge Street, London W1P 1FD

British Library Cataloguing in Publication Data

Murphy, Emmett
    Great bordellos of the world.
    1. Prostitution—History
    I. Title
    306.7'   HQ111
    ISBN 0-7043-2395-8

Designed by Namara Features
Typeset by M.C. Typeset, Chatham, Kent
Printed in Italy – SAGDOS – Brugherio (MI)

To Tom and Fan and Jo
who made it possible

CONTENTS

Great Bordellos
of the World

Nana, 1877
Édouard Manet 1832–83
HAMBURGER KUNSTHALLE,
HAMBURG

INTRODUCTION

IN THE MID-1970s, in America's largest city, in the entertainment capital of the world, a plan was hatched to open the biggest and most luxurious bordello in the United States.

It was to be located just a stone's throw from Times Square, an area visited by an estimated sixteen million visitors each year, tourists and conventioneers whose presence generates an annual turnover of $5 billion. The Luxor Baths at 121 West 46th Street, long a popular gathering place for homosexuals, was to be totally refurbished and converted into the nation's biggest, fanciest and most expensive 'massage palour'.

As news of the project leaked out, the building became a battleground between the city government and the developers: politicians and clergy on one side, real-estate interests and organized crime syndicates on the other. Allied with the city's mayor were concerned businessmen and religious leaders who comprised the membership of the New York City Midtown Law Enforcement Coordinating Committee who were sworn to spearhead a holy war against crime, to hit hard at pornography and at prostitution.

Then, lo and behold, subsequent investigations showed that the owner of the building that was to become a landmark bordello was a prominent member of the mayor's own Crusading Committee bent on driving such poorly disguised whorehouses out of the area, and out of the city entirely, if possible.

After much pushing and shoving, after much legal fol de rol with charges and countercharges blackening the already sooty air, the committee man resigned his position, the clergy was mollified, the Luxor Baths reverted to their original condition, and organized crime went its way opening credit card 'health spas' in other parts of Manhattan. After all the hoopla, for the great City of New York it was business as usual.

This case is cited because it is so typical and so neat. Most of the elements seen in the history of bordellos since their inception are here: real-estate and religious interests, politics and crime, and, by extension, war, conspiracy and betrayal. Moreover, ultimately, continuity and tradition are preserved.

The case of the Luxor Baths is doubly interesting because it occurred shortly before the opening on Broadway of the eminently successful musical comedy *The Best Little Whorehouse in Texas*.

Even the usually fastidious *New York Times* saw fit to lower its standards to accept for the show full-page advertisements which featured a pair of extraordinarily long stocking-clad legs. Prospective theatre-goers were assured that there was 'nothing dirty going on here'. Not only clean-minded New Yorkers and nostalgia-smitten Texans flocked to the theatre: the majority of the customers in an average audience came from the other forty-eight states of the Union.

If the city administration and its puritanical supporters were not ready to accept openly the presence of the planned 'Best Big Whorehouse in New York', the people of the United States were clearly willing to acknowledge the existence of such establishments and, subsequently, on motion picture film, to embrace the concept in the national consciousness.

The word 'whorehouse' is only middle-aged. Earlier we had *dicterion* and *lupanarium*; later, bordel and brothel-house, bagnio and stew, crib, cathouse, parlour- and sporting-house. Whatever the house is called, however, what makes the bordello of extraordinary interest is the way it mirrors the society in which it exists. As much as music or painting or literature, the bordel's architecture and furnishings, the servants, the food and drink, all portray the culture of the era. And, above all, of course, society.

Among them we find the whore who becomes empress; an empress a whore. And queens of the stage aspire to whorehouses of their own, too. Courtesans who model for immortality and trollops who set the course of nations. There are nymphomaniacal cocottes and lesbian *filles de joie*. The bawds we'll consider include masterful thieves, mass murderers and suicides galore. They're a variegated lot, as perverse and evil, as righteous and noble as the whole of mankind.

As for their owners, sponsors and patrons, what a remarkable parade they present: emperors and impresarios, crazed capitalists and sweet killers, movie stars and monks, cut-throats and kings, bold knights and bastard knaves, mountebanks and bankers, footpads and fops, pimps and princes, drug-pushers and pauper dukes, saints and spies, sadists and sodomites, popes and poltroons, philosophers and procurers, generals and degenerates, priests unholy and defrocked, mad painters, hoary politicians and men of genius.

With such a crew shaping the history of the bordello it's not strange, then, that the institution does not exist in most primitive societies. It is a product of civilization.

Previous page:

Decadent Romans, 1847
Thomas Couture 1815–79
LOUVRE MUSEUM, PARIS

CHAPTER ONE

GODS, GRAVES AND HARLOTS

THE TIME IS 1200 BC. In Asia the Chinese are publishing a 40,000-character dictionary. In Asia Minor the Greeks are besieging Troy. In the Mediterranean the Phoenicians are the leading commercial power. In Egypt the first laws regulating the sale of beer are enacted. And in the Holy Land Joshua is about to attack the town of Jericho.

On the advice of the Lord, Joshua sends a pair of spies into the city where they find sanctuary in the house of Rahab, the harlot. In return for the intelligence she supplies them, the men promise her and her family that their lives will be spared by Joshua's army. After much marching about the town and blowing of trumpets and shouting, the walls of Jericho come tumbling down and Joshua and his troops 'utterly destroyed all that was in the city, both man and woman' – all but Rahab and her kin. This indiscriminate slaughter of a city's inhabitants was customary, a thousand-year-old tradition in these parts.

To spare Rahab may not have been unprecedented, but Joshua's marrying her was rather unusual. Granted, Rahab's beauty was proverbial and because of the nature of her business she was probably well-informed about civic affairs. Still, she was a common whore whose house was a simple sun-dried mudbrick affair about fifteen feet deep perched over the space between Jericho's double walls.

To provide the story with a happy ending, Rahab marries Joshua and becomes the ancestress of Jeremiah, Huldah and Ezekiel, among other prophets. In this early account of the bordello's place in history we find four of our elements of continuity. There is no doubt that Joshua was after real estate. His religious fervour carried the day, then and many times thereafter. War, spying, conspiracy and betrayal and the resultant massacre complete the picture.

The Israelites were by no means the only tribes bringing their brand of civilization to others by forceful means. At this same point in time the Aryan nomads were invading India from their homelands somewhere in southern Russia. Like Joshua they were constantly inveighing against the inhabitants of the towns and calling upon their gods to destroy them. Once the conquerors settled

Three Whores Awaiting Customers
Roman architrave *c.* 100–150 AD,
  found in Algate
MUSEUM OF LONDON

down and built their own cities they developed the most elaborate form of temple-prostitution the world has ever seen.

These Aryans were not the first, however, to establish this peculiar form of whoredom. Long before one-woman, freelance prostitution like Rahab's became firmly established, the trade was deeply religion-oriented. At the height of the Sumerian Empire in the fourth millennium BC a temple-bordel was run by the Sumerian priests in the city of Uruk.

The *kakum*, or temple, was dedicated to the goddess Ishtar, lustful daughter of chief god Anu, and housed three grades of women. The first group performed only in the temple sex-rites, while those in the second class had the run of the sanctuary grounds and catered to the visitors interested in combining fornication with religion. The third and lowest class of harlots lived on the temple ground but were free to scour the streets and byways for customers, and they enjoyed a very bad reputation indeed. In years following, this same classification of working girls spreads east and west to Greece, Rome, India, China and Japan.

Isis Jug, *c.* 100 AD
Found in the Thames off Bankside
MUSEUM OF LONDON

One of the best accounts of sacred prostitution is given by the Greek historian Herodotus in the fifth century BC. He had very negative feelings about the later Babylonian custom whereby 'every woman who is a native of the country must once in her life go and sit in the Temple of Mylitta and there give herself to a strange man'.

All women, high and lowborn, were obliged to follow this curious rite. The docile women sat in the precincts of the temple with bands of plaited string around their heads 'and a great crowd they were', he reports, 'what with some sitting there, others arriving, others going away'.

Once a woman had taken her seat in the temple she was not allowed to leave until a customer had thrown a silver coin in her lap 'in the name of the goddess Mylitta' and then had his way with her in a temple alcove. For the more attractive women, evidently, the ordeal was shortlived. But some poor ill-favoured girls might spend months waiting for a compassionate client. As the Babylonian Empire expanded, women of conquered tribes became increasingly available for commercial purposes and the temples then became slave-marts. All revenues, of course, went into the temple treasure chests maintained by the priests. Centuries later the slave-markets persisted in the East, while in the West the fiduciary role of the Babylonian priests would be played by noblemen and princes of the Church.

Even before Babylon and Rahab, stories concerning the relationship between kings and harlots entered literature. *The Gilgamesh Epic*, written around 1200 BC, told the story of the rule of the King of Uruk (Erech), circa 2750 BC. Annoyed by the resistance of the freedom-fighter Enkidu, Gilgamesh sent one of his temple harlots to sap the strength of the young shepherd warrior. For six days and seven nights Enkidu went to the harlot in her tent and slept with her; at the end of that time when he again took up his pursuit of gazelle hunting his knees failed him and he was enfeebled. Although the sheepskin tent carried by the unnamed woman employed by Gilgamesh hardly qualifies as a bordello, her mission does establish her as the first call-girl on record. All of this, of course, predates the more famous liaison between Samson and Delilah by many hundreds of years.

It is the peripatetic Herodotus, too, who gives us the best look at the institution of harlotry in Egypt. By his account even the pyramids were built with the proceeds from prostitution, with the Pharaoh Cheops the biggest beneficiary of them all. The Pharaoh's daughter herself was pressed into service and this hapless princess was able to build herself only a small pyramid near her father's giant tomb with stones donated by sympathetic clients.

Pharaoh Amasis, patron of the arts and Grecophile, was much enamoured of the slave girl Rhodope, but her fame was surpassed by Archidice, whose greed was never surpassed. After turning away a customer when she found his purse too light, she learned that he had later had a dream in which he possessed her.

Statue from Assur Bel Kala bearing
the inscription 'Woman Designed
for Pleasure', 1050 BC
BRITISH MUSEUM

Woman Holding Her Breasts,
  8–9th C BC
Assyrian ivory
BRITISH MUSEUM

The Lady at the Window, c. 8th C
  BC
Assyrian ivory
BRITISH MUSEUM

Archidice took the loudmouthed fellow to court with the complaint that she was entitled to her customary fee. Although the claims court recognized the merits of her charge, the judges ruled that because the defendant had only dreamed of enjoying her body, she should go home and dream that she had been paid.

Although the courtesans from Greece seem to have enjoyed a special status in Egyptian society, for the most part the temple harlots were commandeered from other tribes and were forced to serve as slaves. As late as the third century BC women ranked with cereal, oil and wine as a leading export item from Israel to Egypt according to Zenon, King Ptolemy II's business manager.

The temple bordels understandably were often the focal points of community life. With religious, sexual and commercial elements combined, the facilities served the same function as latter-day baths, inns and pubs. Great devotion was shown in the construction of these Egyptian brothels and they were frequently ornamented with sculptures, frescoes, precious stones and trophies taken from defeated enemies on the frontiers.

On special religious occasions, the sex carnivals were taken to the provinces where specially erected tent-cities were established, a custom that persisted into nineteenth-century Egypt.

In pre-Rahab days, the Semite *zonah* were forbidden to set up shop within the confines of cities and were forced to conduct their business in makeshift tents. They favoured spots where caravan trails crossed or on the busy roadsides leading to the city gates. It was in just such a setting that Tamar set her snare for Judah and where she lifted not only his staff and jewellery but got him to sire her twin sons, Pharez and Zarah.

Following the Biblical line from Tamar's tent, then to Rahab's elevated hut, the tradition leads to Jezebel's palace in the ninth century BC.

This Phoenician princess brought with her into Israel customs that were not only cruel but sensually revolting even by contemporary standards. Moreover, in her court there were more than 400 priests of the nature-god Baal on the dole, freeloaders all, like the poets in the courts of later Celtic kings.

Jezebel and her friends were under the impression that Baal's consort, Astarte, demanded at her annual festival the gift of virgins in her sacred orchard. After marrying the unlucky Ahab, King of Israel, Jezebel set up such a grove adjacent to her palace and reportedly supervised the deflowering rites herself. Steadfast virgins were disposed of by the wicked Jezebel, usually by beheading.

Not until Catherine de' Medici, in the sixteenth century, did another woman enjoy quite so unenviable a reputation, with the possible exception of the Byzantine Empress Theodora, in the sixth century, who at least had a few supporters. Not so Jezebel, who ended by being devoured by pariah dogs, rather a singular demise even for someone in such a line of work.

As much as Queen Jezebel was hated, so King Solomon was beloved of his people in the tenth century BC despite his grandiose lifestyle. Much has been made of his wisdom in the baby-splitting decision, but it's rarely noted that the two disputing women were harlots occupying the same premises who might easily confuse their children as well as their clients.

For his own part, Solomon took himself 700 wives and enjoyed the company of 300 concubines. Or so the story goes. For someone with a stable of 40,000 horses, this doesn't seem too exaggerated though it might have tested his endurance.

More to the point is the fact that his famous temple, decorated with a wide variety of phallic devices, was dedicated to the alien deities of Mesopotamia. Less

Cult Scene of a Questionable
   Nature, *c.* 1750 BC
Old Babylonian stone
BRITISH MUSEUM

broadminded observers have described it as little more than a high-class brothel-
house harbouring common harlots and sodomites, offering odd entertainments
that might have given even Jezebel pause.

In humouring his various wives and their multiplicity of religions, Baal,
Moloch and Astarte among them, good King Solomon was forced to turn a blind
eye to many of the awkward practices denounced by the Sacred Books. It's
extremely unlikely that on his frequent visits to the temple he was in search of
spiritual stimulation alone.

Whatever he found there, whether in temple or palace, it certainly wasn't a
bed. This piece of furniture was never regarded as the ideal place for rest or

pleasure either in Israel or in the ancient East in general. It was considered a foreign contrivance, while its cousin, the divan, was favoured with its arrangement of pillows during the day which could be removed at night.

Now, whether visiting wife, concubine or temple harlot, what sort of woman would be awaiting the King? Certainly someone highly decorated and aromatic. No matter how much the prophets decried their use, they were never able to drive the perfumes and makeup kits from the boudoir. Favourite fragrances were myrrh, aloes, cinnamon and cassia, imports from such exotic lands as India, southern Arabia and eastern Africa.

Addicted to perfumes, the ladies of the day were also exceedingly fond of decorating themselves, the hair with the purple sprays of the loosestrife plant. They were even fonder of the orange powder extracted from the bark and leaves of another shrub, and dyed their hair, their fingernails and their toenails with henna.

The women in Solomon's household and lesser houses tinted their eyebrows and eyelashes with the bluish-grey crystals of galena, a lead sulphide. Powdered lapus lazuli shadowed and deepened their eyes. And dried insects provided the ingredients for the counterpart of today's lipstick, the crimson to paint a seductive mouth.

All this painting and perfuming and decorating was going on while the prophets fumed. Listen to Isaiah: 'And it shall come to pass, that instead of sweet smell there shall be stink; and instead of well-set hair, baldness; and instead of a stomacher, a girdling of sackcloth; and burning instead of beauty.'

It is evident that some form of venereal disease was known to the ancient moralizers, though it is unclear whether or not they thought the cosmetics were directly responsible for the discomforts their users might suffer.

For maiden or temptress seductive perfumes and cosmetics were not the only weapons. The mandrake root is mentioned both in Genesis and the Song of Solomon, and at least until the seventeenth century it had a widespread reputation as an aphrodisiac. In Hebrew mandrake translates as *dudaim*, cognate of *dudim*, the pleasures of love. In the history of the world's bordellos aphrodisiacs rank just behind women and beds or divans.

The Greeks, too, were very keen on the properties of the mandrake root. Mathematician and philosopher Pythagoras named it after the male private parts in the sixth century BC and the physician Dioscorides reported that it was a key ingredient in love potions. There is a much stronger bridge of tradition between the cultures of Asia Minor and the Mediterranean than the questionable mandrake root, however. In early Greece, as well, prostitution was the handmaiden to religious worship. In the temple-bordels the priests were the managers. And as the state's financial experts, the money received by the women for their services naturally fell into the coffers of the priests. The huge temple of Aphrodite Porne

Slave-Market of Girls Destined for
   Greek *Dicterions*
Sir Edwin Levy
NEW YORK PUBLIC LIBRARY

in Corinth was staffed by a thousand or more women who catered to the needs of the sailors frequenting Greece's second largest seaport. The revenues from the temple supported the city's wars against Athens and helped establish colonies on the Adriatic coast.

Chances are that the advent of the secular Greek brothel did not take place until the system of regulated prostitution in accordance with religious rites had broken down, while the demand for the prostitute's services continued. This falls in with the rejection of religious 'voices' and the attendant rise of 'rational' thinking and modern behaviour patterns. As the old deities were discarded and the establishment continued to function, it did so with a single purpose. Prostitution lost its religious connection to become totally secular.

With the Greeks discovering or inventing just about everything under the sun in the arts and sciences, it's not surprising that they also came up with the first municipal bordello. In the sixth century BC the great statesman, Solon, undertook more than sweeping economic and constitutional reforms. On the whole, Solon regarded the influence of women in Athenian society as pernicious. Under his miscellaneous reforms he ordered that wealthy wives would not be tolerated; no bride was allowed to bring more than three changes of clothes and a little light furniture to the house of her new husband. More important, all brothels were put under stringent state control.

Solon confiscated existing buildings and converted them to *dicteria*. He limited these houses to certain parts of the city and their occupants were placed under various other restrictions. They were compelled to wear distinctive dress and, far from being connected with religion, they were forbidden to take part in religious services. Each of the *dicteria* displayed its own emblem. The identifying red light over the front door was still a thousand years in the future; now carved and painted phallic symbols hung outside the houses so that there was no doubt about the nature of the business conducted within. Athenaeus of Naucratis gives a fair description of what a visitor found behind the priapean sign:

> Take a look at everything; their doors are wide open. Price: one obol. These fillies, built for sport, stand in a row, one behind the other, their dresses sufficiently undone to let all the charms of nature be seen. Any man may pick out the one that pleases him – thin, fat, roundish, lanky, crooked, young, old, moderate, mature.

With prices low enough to meet the most modest entertainment budget, and a variety of merchandise sufficient to appeal to any taste, Solon's primary concern, clearly, was with tax revenues. Anyone who paid the state tax – the *pornikotelos* or whore tax – was entitled to open his own *dicterion*. As with the cities of today, Athens was always in the middle of some fiscal crisis. Because any decrease in the number of houses operating would reduce the city-state's income, the women of the houses were forbidden to leave the city limits unless they could post a bond guaranteeing that they would return to work.

A century later, courtesans in Corinth were so numerous that the Greeks often used the word *corinththiazomai* as a synonym for harlotry. Then, as now, the Olympic games were not as pure as some supposed. On one occasion a prominent Corinthian athlete promised to supply the Temple of Aphrodite with fifty new *hetaerae* if he were to be crowned with the laurel. Even the pious lyric poet Pindar found nothing unseemly in this offer to commercialize the games. Additions to the staff would hardly have been noticed by the patrons because as the geographer and grammarian Strabo pointed out at about the time of Christ, 'The Temple of Aphrodite was so rich that it owned more than a thousand temple slaves, courtesans whom men and women had dedicated to the goddess. And therefore it was also on account of these women that the city was crowded with people and grew rich; for instance, the ship captains freely squandered their money here.'

For seafarer or shepherd, in religious shrine or back alley *dicterion*, the baths and anointing rooms were important features. No Greek would consider sexual relations without first enjoying a rubdown with olive oil, which Galen the physician, in the second century AD, felt was essential to good health. In addition to the baths and oils, in the private *aphrodisions* patronized by the wealthy citizens, there were rare perfumes, expensive furniture and erotic sculptures and paintings to provide mental and physical stimulus.

Food appropriate to the occasion was also available in these grand houses. A customer with a small problem in rising to the occasion might dine on a dish containing ground pepper, nettle-seeds, onions, wild cabbage and eggs. A step up on the love-potion scale might be a mixture of shellfish and the pitch from a branch of the pomegranate tree. For someone needing a real lift, animal testes were recommended by the house, particularly those of the wild ass, which enjoyed a great reputation for virility.

In addition to the common *dicteriades* who laboured in the municipal houses, the Greeks also supported two other classes of women, the *auletrides* and the top-class *hetaerae*. The first were primarily musicians and dancers and worked the party circuit, playing flutes and drums, juggling and performing acrobatics, and singing popular songs before mingling with the patrons. Lesbianism was popular in their ranks, but some became the lovers of famous men, such as Lamia who became the mistress of King Demetrius Poliorcetes in the third century BC.

Standing far above the housegirls and partygirls were the élite courtesans who frequently influenced the lives of prominent statesmen, generals and artists. Socrates in the fifth century BC enjoyed their company, as did Solon, despite his low regard for women in general. Some of these high-priced *hetaerae* achieved great political power, while others achieved a notoriety comparable to that of today's motion picture stars thanks to their liaisons.

Probably the most famous of these was Aspasia, who eventually became the mistress of Pericles, statesman in the fifth century BC. Her charm, wit and varied talents won her an important place in the intellectual society of the day. The comic poets represent her as the senior political advisor to Pericles and credit her as the cause of half the wars of Athens, probably something of an exaggeration. Shortly before the outbreak of the Peloponnesian War, Aspasia was accused of impiety, a capital offence at the time, and it was only Pericles' tears and entreaties before the court that secured her acquittal.

In the fourth century BC the notorious Phryne would run foul of the law as well. At one point in her life she had acquired so much wealth that she offered to rebuild the walls of her home town, Thebes, on the condition that they be inscribed with the words: 'Destroyed by Alexander, Restored by Phryne the Courtesan', thus establishing a whore-and-wall tradition that was to crop up repeatedly in the centuries ahead. Phryne sat as the model for Apelles' great portrait of Aphrodite Anadyomene. She was also, according to the best authorities, the model for the Cnidian Aphrodite by Praxiteles. Popular legend has it that her breasts were the most beautiful in all of Greece. This remarkable bosom was so much admired that its exposure to the trial judges on one occasion earned her acquittal on a charge of heresy.

Two ladies, both bearing the name Lais, rank high on the list of most famous and favoured Greek courtesans. Lais of Corinth counted the philosopher Aristippus among her many lovers, while Lais the Sicilian became the very good friend of the immortal general Alcibiades and may or may not have helped him to plan some of his more successful military campaigns in the fifth century BC.

In one man's opinion, Athenaeus, the Corinthian Lais 'appears to have been superior in beauty to any woman that had ever been seen'. Painters and sculptors by the score begged her to pose for them but always met with refusal until the great Myron, in his old age, prevailed upon her to sit for him. As the story goes, when Lais disrobed, the white-haired Myron was so smitten that he offered her all he possessed to spend just one night with her. The haughty Lais walked out on him. Greece's greatest artist of his age, Myron the sculptor visits his barber, his beautician, his tailor, his jeweller, has his aged frame cast in a new image and seeks out the imperious Lais to declare his undying love. 'My poor friend,' she replies, seeing through his metamorphosis, 'you are asking me what I refused to your father yesterday.' A late variation of this tale, dating from the Elizabethan age, concerns Sir Walter Raleigh.

Despite her shabby treatment of Myron, Lais did not refuse herself to poor but handsome lovers while amassing a great fortune. She is reported to have demanded 10,000 drachmas from the statesman Demosthenes for a single evening's pleasure; but she gave herself to Diogenes for a single obol because it pleased her to have a philosopher at her feet. She spent her wealth generously on temples and public buildings, a tradition to be carried on in Byzantium at a much later date, and when she died she was honoured with 'a splendid tomb as the greatest conqueror that the Greeks have even known'.

Whether or not Aspasia was the brain behind Pericles, or Lais for Alcibiades, is not really too important. The fact that their contemporaries thought they were, however, is, because it reflects the feelings of the Greeks about their bordellos and their occupants. Despite their elevated status, the *hetaerae* were known to work in the common houses from time to time, usually when they were between patrons or when they found themselves in difficult financial straits. Because of their uncommon beauty and reputations as the associates of the political bigwigs of the day, they were able to command great prices. With the new treasure accumulated they were able to make grandiose gestures like Phryne's for refortifying Thebes, one of the first examples of 'the whore with the golden heart' which became so much a part of mythology.

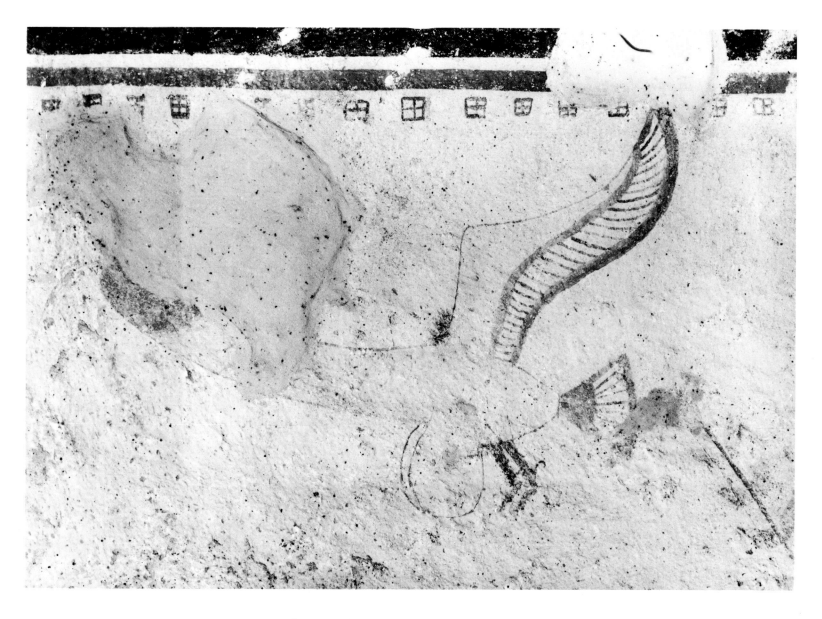

Large Flying Penis
Wall painting in the Tomba del
Topolino, Tarquinia
PHOTO BY LEONARD VON MATT

In the coastal cities of Greece most of the bordello districts were on or close to the waterfront as in Athens and Corinth. But Athens also had a second district, the *ceramicus*, where the houses were situated adjoining the potters' quarters, an area which stretched from the central marketplace to the double gate on the northwest perimeter of the city. Even in these early times government officials apparently felt that there was a strong affinity between the life of the artist and that of the bawd.

In addition to the simply functional public bordels and the sumptuous houses, there was a third class of accommodation which catered to travellers. Greek wayside inns, more often than not, were run by women and were held in low regard by men like Plato who felt that they undermined the state's morality by offering heterosexual pleasures to the common traveller, native or foreign.

It was a different matter for the aristocracy, however. Wealthy travellers did not need the services offered by the proprietors of these inns of dalliance. Many brought their trains of whores and courtesans with them. King Demetrius Poliorcetes, patron of the *hetaera* Lamia, at one point quartered his entire entourage of dancing girls and promiscuous women in the Parthenon. This was a practice later to be adopted by the Crusaders who seemed to feel that the horde of trollops marching in their wake would somehow assist them in crushing the heathen in the Holy Land. It was the same Demetrius who levied a tax of 250 talents (£700,000/$1,500,000) upon the citizens of Athens and gave the money to Lamia with the explanation that the lady needed it to buy soap. Needless to say, the Athenians were forced to remark what a dirty woman she must be.

By the time of Menander, the fourth century BC, Athenian life was portrayed in the theatres as a long succession of seductions, adulteries and bordel visitations. Wantonness in the Hellenic world moved from the confines of city houses and rural lodgings. The wandering historian, Strabo, observed that 'on the canal which runs from Alexandria to Canopus the traffic of ships journeying to and fro never ceases by day and night. Men and women dance, totally unembarrassed, with the utmost licentiousness which seems to make for riotous proceedings.' Two thousand years later foreign observers in China would be equally aghast at the licentiousness found aboard the junks in Chinese coastal waters. Following in the tradition of Corinth which had the reputation of leading all the other Greek cities in the numbers of its bordels, the centre of Greek sexuality was moved to Alexandria. 'It is the house of Aphrodite,' wrote Herodotus, 'and everything is to be found there – wealth, playgrounds, a large army, a serene sky, public displays, philosophers, precious metals, fine young men, a good royal house, an academy of science, exquisite wines and the most beautiful courtesans.' It was the complaint of statesman-historian Polybius – in the second century BC – that the finest private houses in the city belonged to loose women.

During the period when Greek culture was at its height in the Mediterranean world the lot of the common harlot varied. The sons of the Athenian ruler Pisistratus at one point gave the freedom of the city to the *dicteriades* and for a while the women from the brothels were even invited to sit at banquets as the guests of the city's foremost citizens. By the time the pendulum had swung and the reaction against such violations of the old standards set in, the women had organized themselves into corporations for self-protection, much as the medieval harlots of western Europe were to do with their Magdalene guilds.

In general, the status of the brothel-house in Greece was created by the fragmented view of women's place in society. The multiplicity of goddesses provides the key: Artemis for chastity; Hera, the faithful wife; Demeter, the figure of fertility; and Aphrodite, the object of sexual desire. The Greek outlook on love itself was significant too. Thanks to the three leading philosophers – Socrates, Plato and Aristotle – the most exalted love was that between men. As a result, homosexual love cast a pall over all the possibilities of anything but carnal love between the sexes, at least in theory.

Courtesans
Wall painting in the Villa dei
  Misteri, Pompeii
PHOTO BY LEONARD VON MATT

Dancing girls and singsong lovelies might be welcome at the Greek feast but the wives rarely were. As late as the second century BC the Greek historian Polybius was astounded to see during a visit to Rome that patricians included their wives at social events. Like the Greeks the Romans also seem to have had a divided attitude toward the place of sex in human affairs.

On the one hand, the Romans combined a pride of race like that of the Jews with a regard for decency like that of the Greeks. On the other, they mixed pragmatism with a standard of austerity that was remarkably severe in comparison with late Grecian standards. The whores of Rome were registered with the police authorities, had to wear distinctive dress, were required to dye their hair or wear yellow wigs and were subject to a variety of other civil restrictions. Where the Greeks were responsible for changing the bordel from a religious to a secular municipally-operated institution, the Romans must be given credit for creating the first international chain of brothel-houses.

The conservative politician Cato the Elder (195 BC) gave the business its rationale quite simply: 'It is right for young men driven by lust to go to the bordellos rather than to molest other men's wives.' Given the ubiquity of the Roman houses, the population was, clearly, a lustful one.

The institution of the *lupanarium* goes back to the founding of Rome itself, to the she-wolf Lupa, who suckled Romulus and Remus, and its naming corresponds to the unlikely notion of later Americans calling their whorehouses Washingtonia. At the period when the Etruscans were moving into Italy, Joas was King of Israel, the Greeks were establishing colonies in Sicily and the Celts were invading England. The Etruscans introduced horsedrawn chariots to the land, Romulus divided the year into ten months, and some unrecorded entrepreneur opened the first *lupanarium*, staffed by girls who may have enjoyed being called *lupae*. One of Rome's foremost harlots later adopted the she-wolf as the logo for her advertisements, a symbol of simplicity rarely matched since.

While writers like Petronius, Catullus and Juvenal preferred the traditional word *lupanarium*, Martial, Livy and Horace used the term *fornices*, which originally referred to the arches supporting the outer walls of public buildings like the circuses and public baths. It was under these arches that in the first century BC the streetwalkers made their arrangements or, indeed, sometimes conducted their business, to the amusement of the casual observer.

The number of pleasure-houses proper, as opposed to sidewalk accommodations, can be estimated from the number of prostitutes on the official police rolls. Around the Year One the figure was 32,000 for Rome alone, and this was obviously the minimum census figure for the women thus employed. This compares favourably with the number on record (35,000) in New York City in the 1890s.

The bordellos fell into two general categories: the licensed lupanars and those places where sex was for sale as an adjunct to the primary business: taverns, inns and the notorious public baths. As a rule, the lupanars were found around the marketplaces, circuses and theatres, a tradition later followed in Paris and London.

Sexus Rufus is the first writer under the Republic (133–29 BC) to identify a Roman bordello and even names the owner, the *Senatulum Mulerium* (The Little Senate of Women) run by one Heliogabalus, possibly a Greek. Heliogabalus, however, is not by any means the first bordel operator identified by name. That distinction belongs to Kal-Ba, a Babylonian in the seventh century BC. During the reign of Nebuchadnezzar a rich merchant called Nau-Akhe-Iddin rented his

Erotic Scenes
Wall painting in the Tomba dei
  Tori, Tarquinia
PHOTO BY LEONARD VON MATT

slaves to the brothel run by Kal-Ba. No mean businessman himself, Kal-Ba turned back only twenty-five per cent of his profits from the skin trade to the slave-owner.

That the bordello business was highly profitable in Rome is seen by their number and widespread locations. The houses of lowest class and most

frequented were in the Esquiline and Circus Maximus districts. The most elegant were in the fourth region which included the Temples of Peace, Love and Venus. In the Mount Coelius area a great number of houses surrounded the marketplace and the barracks housing the foreign troops.

Phallic Insignia
Stone carving outside a brothel,
  Pompeii
PHOTO BY LEONARD VON MATT

Scene in a *Lupanarium*
Wall painting above the entry to
 one of the rooms of a brothel
 along the Vico del Lupanare,
 Pompeii
PHOTO BY LEONARD VON MATT

Just as at Corinth and the Piraeus the sexual needs of the Empire's sailors were not neglected. At the ancient port of Misenum the ruins still survive of the *centum camerae* (House of a Hundred Rooms) which once catered to the seamen of the Roman fleet.

A house of such size, however, was the exception rather than the rule, with the average brothel offering from six to a dozen rooms. As with most things Roman, the best example of a lupanar is found at Pompeii. The story that the original excavators found a mummified couple *in flagrante delicto* is probably apocryphal. Nevertheless, the brothel-house is there to be seen on the corner of Vicolo del Balcone Pensile.

From the street the visitor enters a wide corridor which runs for about twenty-five feet through the middle of the building and ends at a toilet area fronted by a shoulder-high screen, an accommodation not unlike those found in public lavatories today. Doorways on both sides of the central hall lead to the performance rooms themselves.

Above the doorways to the cells are murals which portray the different kinds

of entertainments which can be anticipated beyond the threshold. It was an early nineteenth-century German researcher and classifier who reported that exactly ninety different positions were assumed by the Romans for conducting sexual intercourse. Although this figure is far below that listed by the Arabs and Indians, it is not to be derided because most modern experts recognize only thirteen different basic configurations. Perhaps mankind has lost some of its ingenuity over succeeding centuries.

In the Pompeiian murals most of the standard methods of intercourse are shown, including the ever-popular *soixante-neuf* position. No two of the paintings are alike and each conceivably portrays the speciality of the room's occupant.

Erotic Scenes
Wall painting from a brothel in
  Pompeii
NATIONAL ARCHAEOLOGICAL
  MUSEUM, NAPLES/PHOTO BY
  LEONARD VON MATT

A Man Raising a Wine Horn to
  Toast His Courtesan
Wall painting, Herculaneum
NATIONAL ARCHAEOLOGICAL
  MUSEUM, NAPLES. PHOTO BY
  LEONARD VON MATT

Each room in the house at Pompeii has a stone couch projecting from the wall at the far end which when in use was covered with rugs and cushions. The walls are marked with interesting graffiti: the number of guests entertained on a given night, the amount earned by the occupant, the initials of clients, or timeless sentiments, '*Marius Piavonius Honoria semper amat*' and the like.

There was no missing the business of the house from the street. A stone phallus set in the wall above the door or carved in the paving on the street in front of the door immediately identified the place during the day, while at night a large hanging lamp with bells in the shape of a phallus was hung out as a beacon for the wine-soaked local or confused tourist from the provinces. This handy guide disappeared from the bordels after the fall of Rome in AD 476 and did not reappear until the fourteenth century in France when the Papacy had fled Rome for Avignon and the custom of the 'redlight' then returned by edict.

When the average Roman house opened for business each day, the girls put their charms on display in front of the building and when the first customer arrived they lined up in front of their respective rooms for closer inspection while they gave their sales spiels. Printed signboards above each door gave the girl's working name and listed her prices for different kinds of entertainment. On the reverse side of the sign was the word *occupata*, which served the same purpose as the Do Not Disturb notices on today's hotel rooms.

The bordellos themselves came in many different shapes and sizes. For the patricians there were, of course, spacious and elegant houses. These were built around the traditional Roman courtyard with its central fountain and with the *cellae* or rooms opening from the four sides. In these four-star bordels a large number of paid servants and unpaid slaves kept the premises running smoothly. The *ancillae ornatrices* watched over the toilettes of the working girls, keeping their clothes in order and assisting them with their hair and makeup. The *aquarii* moved about serving wine to inflame the limpid or to refresh the exhausted. The *villicus* acted as a combination of bouncer and chief steward, and it was he who took the dinner orders in the upper-class bordels where meals, if not food orgies, were the order of the day.

Aphrodisiacs, naturally, were in great demand by jaded customers. When one considers the popularity of health-food stores and vitamin emporia today some of the ingredients favoured by Roman sportsmen do not seem particularly outlandish. Some of the ingredients favoured by Latin lovers were the intestines of various birds and fishes, parts of reptiles and frog bones. Deer sperm was highly valued as was the penis of the wolf and hedgehog. Among a wide variety of herbs the mandrake root was still at the top of the list.

Some of the aphrodisiacs sold in these houses were unquestionably dangerous and often caused temporary illness, attacks of madness or, in some cases, even death. Senator Lucullus and Lucretius, author of *De Rerum Natura*, both died from partaking of poisonous love potions. Similar quack medicines would

Phallic Hanging Lamp
Bronze, Pompeii Museum
PHOTO BY LEONARD VON MATT

A phallus insignia outside a brothel
  in Pompeii
PHOTO BY LEONARD VON MATT

achieve the same magical but lethal effects in nineteenth-century America where opium-laden tonics were available at the friendly neighbourhood apothecary's.

What the *dicteriades* were to the Greeks, the *meretrices* were to the men and women of Rome. Although the costumes of the women inside the lupanar varied, one article of attire was required on the street, the yellow wig which distinguished her from the raven-haired Roman patrician maid or matron. Within the bordello the *meretrix* dressed as colourfully as she pleased, or dressed not at all. Gilded breasts or nipples were favoured by some and these were exposed over a diaphanous skirt.

For a people so dedicated to law and its processes it's not surprising that Roman harlots and their trade were so finely sorted and regulated. While in India the entire population was classified in different castes, the Romans were busily ranking the entire hierarchy of whoredom. The *meretrices* were the women whose names were kept on the public rolls by the district registrar. The *prostibulae* escaped the standard city tax which licensed the trade and did their business wherever they could find it.

The *delicatae* represented the counterpart of the Athenian *hetaerae* and today's £200-a-night call-girls. Then, as now, their clients were politicians,

Hermaphrodite and Pan
Wall painting from the Casa dei
   Dioscuri, Pompeii
NATIONAL ARCHAEOLOGICAL
   MUSEUM, NAPLES

military leaders and big businessmen. The *famosae* worked the same side of the street, but these were women of patrician families who turned to the trade for financial reasons, or simply for lubricious tricks. The *doris*, named after the Roman counterpart of Phryne, were renowed for their beautiful proportions, the centrefold girls of yesteryear. The *ambulatarae*, clearly, walked the streets and searched the circus for customers. The *lupae*, moving down in class, inhabited the groves of the suburbs. The *aelicariae* were the bakers' girls who sold the bread rolls called *colyphia*, from the gladiators' slang for penis; they augmented their incomes by selling themselves as well as their bakery goods. The *bustuariae* conducted their business in cemeteries and as a sideline acted as paid mourners at funerals. The curious institution of cemetery-bordel reappears in late fourteenth-century France when the cult of death reached its peak.

With everyone from the lowest labourer to the wealthiest businessmen making use of all these classes of paid women it's not surprising to find the names of Roman emperors among an avid clientele. Among the most prominent are Titus, Vespasian, Vitellius and the much maligned Nero. As for Caligula, that monster of cruelty and vice, the less said the better. The palace of the mad tyrant, Emperor Commodus, has been portrayed as little more than a giant bordelio with more than 300 beautiful girls at his command, a veritable prototype for the harem which the Arabs would later claim they borrowed from the Turkomans. Another 'pervert and sexual monster', Elagabus, has been described as cavorting naked and shameless among his hundreds of naked whores, hardly what we would expect from a head of state. Such unseemly carryings-on, however, were not confined to the obviously sex-crazed males at the top of Roman society.

The omnipresent bordellos of Rome apparently held a peculiar fascination for women of patrician birth as well. For the upper-class women who could afford them, a number of male-staffed houses were opened, but those who made the headlines of the day put themselves to work in the common lupanars. According to Juvenal, Valeria Messalina, the third wife of the Emperor Claudius in the first century AD, had such a predilection:

> She languished in her brothel's stinking covers, seizing that room reserved for her sole use. She bared her painted nipples and kept loose those thighs that birthed the well-born Britannicus.

According to the pundits of the time, Plutarch, Tacitus and Livy among them, Messalina was not alone in her taste for the bordel lifestyle. Julia, daughter of the Emperor Augustus, built such a record of fornication with so many different men that she was banished from Rome for life. According to contemporary reports, Julia's granddaughter, Agrippina the Younger, sister of Caligula, and mother of Nero, 'devoted her life to vice'. When she wasn't busy entertaining the hordes of the palace guard, she found time for the Emperor himself. Says Tacitus:

> On a number of occasions in broad daylight when Nero was tipsy after dinner, Agrippina appeared before him elaborately made up, and acted with the unmistakable suggestion of incest. She kissed him with indecent passion and wheedled him to her criminal purpose.

The well-publicized and now much-imitated Roman orgy was not confined to imperial palace or patrician villa. As in Greece, throughout the Empire wealthy travellers and their entourages found their sexual needs catered to in the inns and taverns at convenient intersections of the highways connecting the various provinces. Fortunately, one such wayside accommodation has been uncovered and restored, again at Pompeii. Here, the owner Aselina and her two popular assistants, Smyrna and Maria, sold not only refreshing drink but themselves as well.

The Roman baths, however, were the most popular places of all for

Priapos the God of Fertility
Wall painting, Pompeii
NATIONAL ARCHAEOLOGICAL
   MUSEUM, NAPLES/PHOTO BY
   LEONARD VON MATT

fornication. Women frequently had to pay twice the normal admission fee of men because they were expected to recoup their expenses and more from male customers inside. Within the sprawling baths the attendants of both sexes offered sexual services as well as massage. As the custom increased in popularity, small cubicles were added to the original designs of the buildings to give a greater degree of privacy. In terms worthy of any contemporary metropolitan mayor, Pliny, in tones of stern disapproval in his *Natural History*, describes the unnatural goings-on in the Roman baths-cum-massage palaces. The bathhouse-bordello trail leads through the centuries from here through the bagnios of Paris and the stews of London to today's international discotheque-cum-jacuzzi.

On one score at least the Romans have not been bettered to this day – the public sex orgy. The *Lupercalia* was originally held on 15 February in honour of Acca Laurentia, wife of the shepherd Faustulus, who reared Romulus and Remus. In time, as an expression of public vitality the *Lupercalia* was put in second place by the festival of *Ludi Floreales*, inaugurated by the popular Flora who gave her accumulated savings in the public treasury for a grand municipal celebration. Over the years, Flora was transmogrified to the goddess of spring and honoured with a six-day festival from 28 April to 3 May. The major event of the programme took place in the Circus Maximus where all the harlots of the city gathered. On cue, a host of healthy young men were let loose into the arena to be entertained as expected for the edification of the rest of the citizenry. By no stretch of the imagination could the Circus Maximus be called a bordello, but here under the open sky plebs and patricians alike could witness just what was going on daily in the *lupanarium* around the corner.

The picturesque customs of Roman harlots and the Roman brothel organization were to have far-reaching effects for centuries. At its height, the Empire stretched from Babylon in the east, the Sudan in the south, to Portugal in the west and to Scotland in the north. When the Romans conquered other tribes and nations they brought with them not only their art and language, their philosophy and law, but institutionalized prostitution as well.

Wherever the legions of Rome marched and finally encamped *lupanaria* would be established to meet the needs of the troops. The average term of enlistment for the foot soldier was two years, during which time he was forbidden to marry. To keep the men from becoming too restless, women were secured for bordel service from the local population – if any survived. (By his own account, Caesar slaughtered 1,685,000 Gauls, the equivalent of all French casualties suffered during World War I.) Pressed into service in the military bordellos, the women who survived the massacres were called *putae*, from *puteus*, a well or tank, which gives a fair idea of how they were thought of and treated.

After subjugating the Belgae, Aquitani and the Celtae and informing his countrymen that '*Gallia est omnis divisa in partes tres*', in 54 BC Julius Caesar

looked across the Channel and saw that the island beyond looked to be a green
and pleasant land and should make an agreeable addition to the Empire. Because
of the reputation for savagery enjoyed by the Picts and Brythons in residence at
the time, it was almost a hundred years, AD 43, before the Divine Emperor
Claudius, sometime husband of Messalina, decided that civilization should be
brought to the barbarians of Britain.

What the Romans probably thought of as an incursion, rather than the
old-fashioned invasion, was to have a profound and lasting effect on the island
society. Under old Celtic law there existed a general parity of rights for men and
women. It was Queen Boadicea who is credited with leading the revolt in AD 61
when 70,000 Romans and collaborators were massacred and the marketplace of
Londinium and major towns were burned. With the Queen's ultimate defeat and
the destruction of Celtic beliefs, the systematic exploitation of women was
introduced and the Roman-style bordello was established as a social institution.
As Londinium recovered and began to thrive, the brothels, unknown previously,
began to attract native customers as well as men of the occupying forces. At first,
these bordels were just that: little houses built of boards. But gradually they were
refined to resemble the familiar lupanars at home and the brothel lifestyle eventually reached the castles of dukes and kings.

To augment the warm bodies available among the local inhabitants, slave-
traders brought women up the Thames from every corner of the Empire. Roman
victories in North Africa, the near East, and the trans-Danube area meant that
hordes of slaves were available for export. The Emperor Titus, one of the
conquerors of Britain, uprooted the entire population of Palestine in AD 71 and
sold the inhabitants into slavery. As a result, tens of thousands of Jewish women
found themselves in army brothels, many in this alien island of 'rocks, caves,
lakes, fens, bogs, dens and shades of death'.

The Roman military garrison was encamped on the south side of the Thames
opposite the market town called Londinium, and comprised some 600 to 1000
men. As with any military machine, the Roman troops were supported by many
times their own number of service personnel. In addition to the bordels, the
infantrymen found amusement in wine shops, taverns, gambling houses and
other games enjoyed by foot soldiers when not in combat.

The earliest military bordellos here were simple affairs, little more than
wooden huts with thatched roofs, standing on clay foundations. Instead of stone
benches covered with pillows and blankets as at Rome and Pompeii, the customers had to be satisfied with straw-covered wooden bunks. In the higher-
priced houses the boards would be covered with sheepskins, obviously officer
country. Contemporary accounts depict long lines of infantrymen queueing up
in front of these huts on payday and then moving through on an assembly-line
basis, a scene to be repeated nineteen centuries later in the whorehouses of
Honolulu.

As is usually the case on any frontier, living conditions improved and the amenities in the bordellos kept pace. Around AD 150 the Romans built a permanent fort in Londinium's northwest quarter and, inevitably, another bordello community sprang up around it. Instead of wooden shacks, the women now worked in terraced brick houses with tiled roofs. These were built Roman-style around courtyards and boasted plastered walls decorated with the standard whorehouse murals designed to stimulate and inform the waiting clients. On the front of the house a painted sign or piece of sculpture plainly identified the business. A stone architrave found recently in London shows three women, two reclining in supposedly seductive poses, while a third prepares some kind of food, possibly an aphrodisiac.

With the sex business so much a part of everyday life it's not surprising that a whole pantheon of fertility gods found their way to Britain through Rome from Greece. Hermes, Priapus, Dionysus, all had their celebrants, and, as usual, an enormous penis was the god's salient symbol of potency. This same fascination with the king-sized male member appears repeatedly in the oriental phallic-worshipping cultures, particularly in Japan. The Chinese are much more realistic, or less ambitious, in their depictions.

Reminiscent of the Athenian aphrodisian rites, the women of the Roman settlements in Britain on Hermes' Day reportedly cavorted through the streets, offering themselves freely to the male revellers, garlanding the god's enormous organ with wreaths. Firminius Lanctanius reports that: 'They worshipped the sexual organ, calling it God.'

Thanks to these wine-inflamed revels and the periodic uprisings of the conquered peoples, the bordello communities of Londinium were repeatedly burned to the ground just as Japan's Yoshiwara districts were a thousand years later. They were rebuilt each time, however, and business resumed as usual. There was too much money to be made to let the industry lie idle; and as long as the Romans kept taming the barbarians, there was no shortage of women to staff the houses.

In time, the road from the Dover coast to Londinium was dotted with inns and taverns of varying degrees of comfort for the different classes of travellers commuting between Britain and the continent. All of these were stocked with women to warm and comfort the seasick visitors from abroad.

As Londinium grew commercially and industrially, supported and financed by the legions of Rome, her bordellos flourished mightily. The original slave inmates gradually disappeared and were replaced by Brythonic and Gaelic women who were reduced to the trade or found the bordel life more rewarding than carding wool or milking goats. Although the Romans brought law and order of a sort to barbarian Britain, they also brought legalized, institutionalized prostitution.

The Celtic people, who had been annihilated in Gaul, squeezed in Britain into

Cornwall, Wales and Scotland, then pushed off the island itself to Ireland, were to have their revenge, however, in a most peculiar way. Towards the middle of the fourth century, the bulk of the London traffic began to flow in the opposite direction, from Britain to the continent, from Londinium to Rome. The Empire was crumbling and the legionnaires were needed at home to stem the barbarian tribes from the north and east.

Towards the end of the fourth century a man called Arthur was born, and he grew up to be the general of the native armies fighting in the south of Britain against the remnants of Roman rule. The legends that grew up about him and his lieutenants, the high-minded lancers and swordsmen of the Round Table, were to shape the history of Europe for the next thousand years. The tales of their questing as exaggerated around the campfires would create the codes of chivalry responsible in large part for ten centuries of savagery, and, with today's hindsight, lunacy. The Greek ideals of love, the Roman worship of the matron, both were scratched in favour of the visions of the parfait knight and his ladylove atop a pedestal. Both of these romantic figures, of course, were supported, more realistically, by a bordello life that has never been surpassed for hypocrisy and universality. Welcome to the so-called Dark Ages.

CHAPTER TWO

KNIGHTS ON THE ROAD

FOR CENTURIES the Roman frontiers on the north and east have been threatened by the Germanic tribes. Their warlike and nomadic spirit, their burgeoning population, and the magnetism exercised by a culturally flourishing empire provide the motives for tribal migrations. During this same period the Chinese have been putting pressure on the Hung-nu of Mongolia. The domino theory, so popular with statesmen in the twentieth century, is forcefully illustrated when these Mongol Huns move westward and conquer the Ostrogoths, setting off a chain reaction. After Attila's death it is Gaeseric and the Vandals who sack Rome and overrun the Roman colonies in the regions north of the Alps. During this period of Barbarian Migrations, the Jutes, Angles and Saxons invade Britain and fill the power vacuum created when the Roman legions retreat to defend the homeland. For a period the great city of Imperial Rome is entirely abandoned; reportedly, no living creatures remain but the rats. In a time of ceaseless migration and constant bloodshed few records survive. The institution of the Roman *lupanarium* is wiped out, to be replaced for the most part by rape and slaughter. The barbarians find it difficult enough to feed their own people regularly without looking after hostage women.

There is evidence, however, that the bordello continued to exist even in these dim times. The word itself comes from the medieval French *bordel*. Originally, the bordel was a place, a small house of boards; the brothel a person. Eventually, 'brothel's house' was shortened and became synonymous with Ben Jonson's 'burdello' and Milton's 'bordello'. If the job of the whore is the oldest profession, it is also one of our oldest cognate words, going back to *car* in Indo-European, *cara* in Celtic, *hóra* in Old Norse, then *hore-cwen* in Anglo-Saxon for adulteress or dirty woman. Oddly enough, *cwen* split to become the queen of royalty and the quean of whoredom.

    As for sexual relations, in the fourth century St Augustine, Bishop of Hippo, could see little difference between *copula carnis*, between husband and wife, and *copula fornicatoria*, between man and whore. Both were sinful in his book. On

Nude Banquet (predecessor of what was later to be known as *le petit souper*)
Medieval illustrated manuscript
BIBLIOTHÈQUE NATIONALE, PARIS

candum etia ma   continuation foit xaifonnable se
lum. Translateur.   xeut apxuoir qui confidex les
En cefte partie sa   matieres des song pxccedens. Car
fettue commence le   ou premier il a traittie du cultz
iiie liure qui eft de sitz et des   uent suuiy. On second il a deter
fais dignes de memoire de la   mine des chofes qui apxaticnent
citc de romine et des eftrangiers a la vertu de prudence siconme
Onquel apxez ce que valerius ce   font les inftitutions des ancienc
oiii liures precedens a determ   sa difaipline de chevalerie ou

the other hand, in his *Confessions*, he suggests that if prostitution were suppressed, 'capricious lusts will overthrow society'. Even the savage Visigoths
disapproved of prostitution. In AD 450 tribal custom dictated that whoring
women be publicly scourged and their noses slit, an unpleasant practice that
persisted in England as late as the eighteenth century. As far back as AD 100
Tacitus reported that the punishment of the Teutones for prostitution included
disembowelment or suffocation in excrement as favourite forms of execution.

For these Teutones, whoring was not sinful, just very bad form. However,
once converted from their pagan ways to Christianity, things began to change
radically for this cottage industry. Where it survived, the Church of Rome
forbade relations between spouses during certain periods of the year: the forty
days before Christmas, the forty days before Easter and eight days after
Pentecost; the eve of great feastdays, Sundays, Wednesdays and Fridays; during
the wife's pregnancy and until thirty days after giving birth if it was a boy and
forty days if it was a girl. And five days before taking communion. Small wonder

Brothel Outside Medieval City
Drawing from the *Master of the
House Book*, 15th C German
COURTAULD INSTITUTE OF ART,
LONDON

that the wooden shack at the edge of the wood was so popular.

The most radical change, however, came from an unlikely source. At some time during the seventh century someone invented the plough. This led to cooperative farming and to the creation of villages. In turn, this meant more productive agriculture, better self-defence for the people and centralization for the women of the bordels. For the first time since the fall of Rome the bordello once again was an urban institution. During the next century a second great change took place. Beds became popular in northern Europe. The ancient Germans lay on the floor of forest or hut on beds of leaves covered with animal skins, or in a kind of shallow chest filled with leaves and moss. Later they laid carpets on the floor or on a bench against a wall and on them placed mattresses stuffed with feathers, wool or hair. These were generally wide enough to accommodate a single sleeping occupant at a time; but, with the addition of legs, the sleeping platform could be widened to support two or more bodies simultaneously. A modest kind of luxury was returning to the trade.

As usual, the upper classes enjoyed more luxuries of every kind. Charlemagne, whose reign marks the transition from the Dark to the Middle Ages, possessed five queens and an equal number of beautiful concubines. The lubricious happenings at his court were known far and wide. Nevertheless, it was his unamiable practice, from time to time, to have the resident whores stripped naked and made to run through the streets while the townsfolk were encouraged to curse them and pelt them with filth. As this failed to discourage them sufficiently, he banned the business entirely in 801 with threat of more severe punishments.

The degree of success achieved by Charlemagne is revealed by the fact that when his son, Louis the Pious, took over the royal palace at Aix-la-Chapelle, he was obliged to do a thorough housecleaning. A capitulary in the year 820 forbade whores and whoremongers in the palace and houses nearby: 'Any man in whose house prostitutes have been found must carry them out on his shoulders to the marketplace where they will be whipped: if he refuses, he will be whipped with them.' Conditions were so bad that Louis was later forced to send his sisters into a nunnery. However, twenty years later, Charles the Bald adopted a more lenient attitude. When he and his men were besieging the city of Neuss he provided one prostitute for every four of his soldiers.

Within the Church itself the problem of sexual licence was a grave one. Starting with the pontificate of Gregory I (590–604), for some 400 years the Holy Fathers sought to stem the sexual excesses and marriages of the clergy, all with a startling lack of success. Even the Papacy itself was not free from taint. In 904 a high papal official's daughter, Marozia, had her lover crowned Pope (Sergius III). Smarting from this ploy, ten years later Marozia's mother had *her* lover installed as Pope John X. Keeping this grand tradition alive, Marozia's grandson, John XII, the first teenaged Pope, was tried by an ecclesiastical council on charges of incest and adultery with his father's concubine. Around the Holy City, obviously, a good share of the population could call the Pope 'father' in both a literal and theological sense.

The confusing of church with bordello was not confined to the Vatican. The Bishop of Liège found time between masses to father sixty-five illegitimate children, while an energetic abbot at St Pelayo had both the time and money to support seventy mistresses. Things reached such a pass in Switzerland that in order to keep their wives free from priestly ministrations, the husbands petitioned that every priest be allowed to keep at least one concubine in the rectory for diversion. Clearly, the Church would not be able to stamp out whoredom in the towns when it could not keep its own house clean.

Another great change was brewing, however, to keep the public's mind off the problems of licentiousness. In 1094 there was pestilence from Flanders to Bohemia; a year later famine in Lorraine. During the previous decade all of

The Fountain of Youth
Woodcut from the *Master of the
Banderoles*, 15th C German
COURTAULD INSTITUTE OF ART,
LONDON

western Europe had been hit by floods, drought and famine. Seven hundred years after the Huns surged into the West the tide would be reversed. On and off for the next 195 years the nobles and peasants of Italy, France, England and Germany would be trudging back and forth across the face of the continent. Along with much of the population, the bordello took to the road.

The Crusades were launched in 1096 when Pope Urban II offered remission from temporal penalties for taking the Cross, and total forgiveness of sins for death in battle. At the same time, he contrasted the impoverished condition of many nobles with the prosperity they could enjoy after conquering new fiefdoms in eastern lands. 'It is God's will!' he proclaimed. The Huns and the Goths had been pushing westwards. It was time now to push back. The agitation was carried on by preachers, prophets and visionary hermits. Urban had pointed a way to solve the socio-economic problems created by pestilence and famine. Rich or poor, men felt that if they could only reach Jerusalem and capture it, they would enter a blessed life, either terrestrial or celestial.

Whole families moved with children and chattels piled on their carts, following in the grand wake of the haughty dukes, pugnacious knights and sometimes loyal foot soldiers. Making up these great migratory waves, in addition to the military forces, were common adventurers and plain crooks, bankrupts and fugitive monks, escaped villains and respectable wives. In the baggage trains, too, there were the lesser women: cooks and washerwomen, soothsayers and whores.

William of Malmesbury described the Norman nobility as 'given over to gluttony and lechery', and exchanging concubines with one another lest fidelity dull the edge of sword or husbandry. At the siege of Acre in 1189, the Arabic historian Imad-Eddin reported that 'three hundred pretty Frenchwomen . . . arrived for the solace of the French soldiers . . . for these would not go into battle if they were deprived of women'. Impressed by this conduct, the Moslem horsemen demanded the same kind of inspiration. It is not surprising, then, that all Christendom was littered with illegitimate children. The heroes of countless medieval sagas were bastards – Arthur, Chuchulain, Gawain, Roland and William the Conqueror, among them.

On the way to Jerusalem there were whores to be found in the host cities. And there were the women found by foragers who were added to the baggage trains, whores by force. Business was conducted in tents, in and under wagons and in fields under the sky. With so many men off to war in search of salvation and booty, on the home front the women were little better off than those accompanying the ill-fated Crusaders. Here it has been calculated there were seven women for every man. The number of destitute women was also increased by the ecclesiastical laws ordering married priests to put away their wives and to practise strict celibacy. These abandoned women had no other choice than to become *focarii*, or ambulatory whores, with neither priestly spouse nor home. Many of the wealthier women went into nunneries, but because they entered from compulsion and not from conviction and were in the main sophisticated women, many of the religious sanctuaries became quasi-bordellos.

What had started as an expression of religious fervour, of course, soon turned into little more than a real-estate takeover. Gold and land and new serfs to rule were the objectives. If not many of the camp-followers had hopes of becoming women of property, they probably could count on some of the riches filtering down to them. The general assumption grew from experience that a Crusader would never return home. Although many did return, usually worn out, bankrupt and diseased, most ended in graves in the Holy Land or by the roadside en route or while returning.

The Abyss
Woodcut from *The Dance of Death* series by Hans Holbein the Younger, 1523
COURTAULD INSTITUTE OF ART, LONDON

Some of the things those who did return brought with them were to change greatly the look of the brothel-house in the centuries ahead. The doughty pilgrims lucky enough to survive familiarized Europe with new foods, new manufactures, new colours and new fashions in dress: maize and sugar, the glass mirror and face powder, damask, muslin, silk and cotton, even the rosary itself; all these things came to medieval Europe, in part, from the poorly conceived and ill-starred Crusades.

When Godfrey of Bouillon and Bohemund I landed in Asia Minor with their small armies they found a society totally alien to their Norman backgrounds. Instead of cold, damp stone towers they found imperial palaces where fires were kept burning all year round to brew the perfumes required to deodorize queens and princesses. Robert of Clari estimated that Constantinople contained two-thirds of the world's wealth. Another chronicler of the era reported: 'If Constantinople surpasses all other cities in wealth, it also surpasses them in vice.' The women of Byzantium were famous even in backward Europe both for their licentiousness and their religious devotion. The practice of castrating children to serve as eunuchs in the harems shocked the first Frankish visitors, but they were on familiar ground when they found that among the sprawl of gambling halls and taverns there were countless bordellos, many 'at the very church doors'. These houses were unlike any they had encountered at home, however.

For the troops the accommodations were little better than the *lupanaria* at Pompeii, but for the coarse nobles from northern Europe there were labyrinthine villas of marble decorated with mosaics and murals, curtains of silk sliding on silver rods, doors inlaid with silver or ivory, ornate tapestries on the walls, colourful carpets on the floors. The impression these sumptuous whorehouses made on the untutored minds of the first Crusaders was enormous. Its influence would be seen throughout the Western world for the next 800 years and more.

By the time of the Fourth Crusade, 1202–4, the defenders of the faith had grown accustomed to the place. They turned on their Greek allies, who mistakenly had called upon them for aid in the first place, and proceeded to pillage and plunder Constantinople. To show their contempt for their victims, the crusading Northerners placed a whore in the patriach's chair in the Hagia Sophia cathedral. It is doubtful that this was done from a sense of history, although it does mark the second time that a prostitute sat on the throne in the capital of the Church's eastern empire. The first occasion was nearly 700 years earlier when the whore's name was Theodora.

Her bordel-to-palace success story is certainly not unique. Jezebel before her turned Ahab's palace into a brothel, while later Nell Gwyn would lie close to the English throne, but few other whores ever attained Theodora's influence and elevation. She was born in AD 508 in Constantinople, later Byzantium, Istanbul today. At the time, the Saxons were first occupying England, the Franks were conquering France, the Visigoths held Spain and the Ostrogoths ruled Italy.

There was not a courtesan worth mentioning in all of Europe. However, the Byzantine emperors in the East considered themselves the rightful heirs of the Caesars and even then Constantinople was certainly the centre of the known civilized world and deserved someone of the stature of Messalina.

The daughter of a circus performer, Theodora entered the bordello life in the Byzantine capital at the age of twelve. From the start she displayed a great talent for the trade and caught the eye of the city's most prominent madam, Antonina, who took the girl under her wing and groomed her into a courtesan of the first rank who entertained only rich and powerful clients. Happily, one of these was appointed a governership in Libya. He persuaded Theodora to accompany him to North Africa, but she soon tired of the provincial life and started a long and arduous journey home through Egypt and Syria, somewhere along the road acquiring an illegitimate son. Once back in Constantinople she met Justinian, the nephew of the Emperor, Justin. Theodora herself promoted the story that he discovered her in a modest house in the suburbs where she was spinning cotton while praying to the saints. However, the court historian, Procopius, a malicious gossip from her point of view, reported that she had gained an audience through a letter supplied by an actress in a travelling troupe which had employed Theodora briefly during her journey home. Even then, throughout the Mediterranean world, the word actress was synonymous with whore.

How the two met is irrelevant because, shortly after, Theodora was instructing the prince, a former shepherd boy from Bulgaria – which incidentally gave the world the word buggery – in everything he wanted to know about sex. More important, he was counting on her for advice on political affairs because of her knowledge of the world outside the Byzantine court, the sort of tradition established by Rahab and carried on later by Holland's Margarete Zelle, known to us as Mata Hari.

Now that the young prince found her indispensable both in and out of bed, he set Theodora up in a charming little house of her own called Homisadas which was connected by a secret stairway to the royal palace. From this well-appointed upper-class bordel Theodora conducted her campaign for marriage to the prospective Emperor. There were several obstacles in her way, not the least of which was a law which explicitly forbade the nobility of Byzantium to marry either actresses or prostitutes. Theodora's record, Procopius was quick to point out, proved that she was both. Undaunted, Theodora pursued her course. Fortunately for her, the antagonistic Empress died. She turned her charms then on the Patriarch, the Eastern Pope, and convinced him that she was simply a misunderstood girl with deep religious convictions. Then, conveniently, the Emperor Justin also died, but not before Theodora had persuaded him to change the marriage laws so that it was now possible for a man of any rank to marry any woman of his choice, regardless of her occupation.

So, from being down and out in Alexandria a year earlier, at the age of nineteen the harlot Theodora became the Empress of Byzantium, crowned and anointed in the basilica of St Sophia. Shortly, seeking to make amends for her past, and possibly as a public relations gesture, she turned her attention to a project for the reclamation of fallen women. This was perfect material for snide historian Procopius who wrote:

> It was but natural that the Great Queen should exert herself in favour of her former colleagues. Five hundred prostitutes who used to ply publicly for trade around the Forum for a modest fee have been compulsorily invited by the Empress to join a new convent, 'The Repentance', on the far shore of the Bosporus, as a well-deserved retreat for meditation. It appears, however, that monastic meditation is not entirely to the taste of such women, and many of them have chosen to cut short their chances of redemption by jumping at night into the sea.

The idea of a whore-queen on the throne of Byzantium did not settle well in the minds of the general population. Rumours spread that Theodora had given the Emperor a venereal disease and rendered him impotent. Other reports had her parading about the palace quite naked but for a ribbon about her waist, a concession to the laws against total nudity. An eyewitness account of a servant had her entertaining ten young noblemen on a single night, while servicing their thirty servants the following day. In the wake of such unfavourable reports, street mobs burned and pillaged the homes of the wealthy and surrounded the palace, urging that the Golden Brothel be burned.

Using the traditional Roman ploy, Theodora promised bread and circuses to placate the angry citizens. She ordered that the Hippodrome be made ready for a spectacular offering of chariot races, gladiator games, free bread and wine – everything to attract as large a crowd as possible. When the last event was over, the Palace Guard of mercenaries marched in and the slaughter started. Thirty thousand spectators lay dead at day's end. So much for the idea of burning down the Golden Brothel.

After this triumph, things took an awkward turn for the imaginative Theodora. Justinian discovered that her private lute player was her illegitimate son, John, and ordered the execution of the young man. Her spirits declined thereafter and she spent her remaining years building religious memorials to herself. When she died at the age of forty-one her last request properly reflected her earlier lifestyle: 'Bathe my body in oil of roses and sprinkle it with rare perfume.'

The Orthodox Church raised Theodora to sainthood. The same cannot be said of Jezebel or Nell Gwyn. Emperor Justinian carried on bravely after her death. His General Belisarius, paramour of the madam Antonina, went forth to retake North Africa from the Vandals and defeated the Ostrogoths to return Rome and all Italy to the Empire. Succeeding emperors maintained Constantinople as the cultural and commercial centre of the world until the arrival of the Crusaders and the enthroning of the mock-Theodora at St Sophia.

Those militant pilgrims fortunate enough to return to their homelands from the Eighth Crusade at the end of the thirteenth century found their countries

Brothel and Gymnasium
Woodcut from the *Master of the
Banderoles*, 15th C German
COURTAULD INSTITUTE OF ART,
LONDON

changing radically. Between 1150 and 1300 the population of western Europe tripled; slavery, that great reservoir supplying the bordellos, diminished as serfdom increased. However, south of the Alps, Moslems and Greeks were kidnapped by slave-traders along the shores of the Black Sea, western Asia and northern Africa for sale as farmhands, domestic servants, eunuchs, concubines and prostitutes in both Islam and Christendom. The slave trade flourished, especially in Italy, probably due to its proximity to Moslem lands, which could be preyed upon with good conscience as fair revenge for the raids of the Saracens. Naturally, oriental luxury and sophistication in the bordellos appeared first in Italy and gradually spread northwards from France to Germany and then westwards to England. One of the most recent and visible imports to England from the East was silk, which was now being manufactured across the Channel in France. No longer confined to court, silks began to appear in the apparel of the stewhouse occupants and the girls of the street. London's first recorded street solicitation was described thus: 'Seated on a jaded mule, her hair hanging over her shoulders, holding a little gilt rod in her hand, dressed in indiscrete clothing, she excited the travellers' attention in many ways.' The indiscretion was probably some display of leg or bosom; when the whores took to silks, the public sense of decency would be much offended.

In the thirteenth century refinements included bedsteads made of wood which were much decorated with inlaid, carved and painted ornaments. Curtains were hung from the ceiling or from an iron arm projecting from the wall. In the fourteenth century, the tester bed made its first appearance. The canopy was an innovation brought from the East and combined with the curtains developed into a room within a room. Such privacy for bedroom behaviour had never been known before, either in the baron's suite or the better brothels.

Now that all the able-bodied men no longer marched off to further the vainglorious ambitions of the nobility, there was more leisure time for the bishops and dukes. Marketday became an institution, money replaced barter, and the fair was a welcome occasion for nobles and peasants alike. From at least the end of the eleventh century onwards the royal grant of a licence to hold a fair seems to have implied also a licence to hold a court of summary jurisdiction for offences committed at the fair itself. In England these were known as Piepowder Courts, from the French *piedpoudreux*, 'dusty feet'. From all reports, complaints against whores and bawdy women constituted the major business of these kangaroo courts, suggesting that a tester bed was not essential to the conduct of business.

During this period the two-ton knight-and-horse combination was the dreadnought of battle. The kings and dukes of France too often put too much faith either in their horses or their saints with disastrous results. Climate and terrain were rarely considered. If the king decided to attack the Swiss in their Alpine strongholds he invaded during the winter snows. If the dukes decided upon an incursion of North Africa, they made their landings under the blazing summer sun. At the close of the Crusades, with no infidels to run down or skewer, the idle knights took to combating one another. Later, during the medieval period in Japan, the unemployed Samurai would develop customs akin to the European that would deeply affect Japanese bordello life. In the West, the tournament became much like the day the circus comes to town, with much drunkenness and brawling, entire hamlets and villages going up in flames after the last knight was unseated. These were winner-take-all contests, with the loser handing over his horse, his armaments and whatever money he had wagered on himself.

These war games were a mixture of play-fantasy and gambling enterprise. They were first devised on the Continent and flourished in Burgundy, Flanders and Champagne. Like today's athletes, champions could make a good deal of money. Gradually, the sport grew less violent and blunted lances were used. The joust entered into romance as a chivalric activity linked with the devoted love of a lady. The fantasy appears full-blown in the thirteenth-century *Fulk Fitzwarin* where 'all valiant knights who tourney for love' were invited to attack one another for a lady's hand and favour. The reality of the business was quite a different matter.

It is more than likely that the idea of chivalry had far more influence upon men and women of later ages than it did in medieval life. The legendary King Arthur, chief of the Brython nobles, held court in the early 500s. Sir Thomas Malory's *Morte d'Arthur* was published by Caxton a thousand years later, in 1485, but it firmly established the Arthurian legends. To latter-day psycho-analysts the sexual symbolism of the Grail itself is obvious. As a chalice or cup it represents the food-bestowing breast, on one level, the uterus of the mother goddess on another. In the Christianized version of the myths the Grail contained the blood of Christ, and so, presumably, represents his mother, the Virgin Mary. Just as in the late eighteenth and early nineteenth centuries the Romantic Movement was followed by the Age of Reason, so in the Middle Ages the confusion and turbulence of the Dark Ages was succeeded by the Age of Chivalry and the Cult of the Virgin.

The picture of feudal life given by Sir Walter Scott's nineteenth-century novels differs markedly from medieval reality. The celebrated jousting, for example, was a sign of the decay of knighthood when an attempt was being made by the frivolous nobility to glamorize the past. Scott picked up the banner from Malory which in turn was taken up in this century by Cecil B. DeMille and CinemaScope, Inc. When the castle layabouts were diverting themselves with tournaments the ladylove of their desire was, more often than not, in the whoring trade. If not, then she was a member of the lesser nobility in need of money because of the spendthrift ways of a dimwitted husband. The coins from the winner's purse went to the 'lady' for a brief encounter in the nearby tent or pavilion which had been set aside for the purpose. In any event, the tradition of the tent-as-bordello established during the Crusades when men fought to kill or maim was warmly preserved.

The vagabond women who travelled throughout the land from tournament to fair and trooped after the king's court, which was usually on the move with his bed in the baggage train, were a common sight during the Middle Ages. They moved in all-women bands or sometimes teamed up with *vagrantes*, unemployed clerics in search of a parish. The decline of *l'amour courtois* is readily seen when the first and second halves of *Le Roman de la Rose* are compared. The first part was written by Guillaume de Lorris before 1240, the second finished by Jean Chopinel de Meung around 1280 in a totally alien style. What started as a poetic rhapsody to the female sex ended as a harsh attack upon all womanhood. The 'rose', the object of pursuit, is ultimately revealed as the pudendum, much to the shock or amusement of different readers.

Another class of independent women lived more settled lives and had their houses of business in the towns and cities. They worked at their trade under the protection and regulation of the town councils and are most frequently described in medieval writings as 'the daughters of joy'. At different times and in different places they were either allowed to operate openly and freely or were condemned and harassed. Under the most favourable circumstances they functioned under the guild system which enforced its own codes of conduct and sought to suppress competition from the roving vagabond bands. The monk Jacques de Vitry described the scene in the Latin Quarter of Paris in 1230 thus:

> Fornication counted as no sin. Prostitutes dragged passing clerics to brothels almost by force, and openly through the streets; if the clerics refused to enter, the whores called them sodomites. . . That abominable vice (sodomy) so filled the city that it was held a sign of honour if a man kept one or more concubines. In one and the same house there were classrooms above and a brothel beneath; upstairs masters lectured, downstairs courtesans carried on their base services; in the same house the debates of philosophers could be heard with the quarrels of courtesans and pimps.

When royalty went a-visiting the town council often put its best foot forward by giving new dresses to the local bordello workers. When King Sigismund visited Ulm in 1434, the city fathers provided new velvet dresses for the bawds and filled the streets with torchholders to light the way to the bordels for the members of the royal court. During the visit of Frederick III to Nuremberg in 1471 he was met in the streets by the entire bordello population. And when Charles V visited the same city later, the brothel women turned out en masse clad only in garlands of flowers. As late as 1516 in Zurich it was the custom for the mayor, the sheriff and *les filles de joie* to dine with visiting ambassadors, a custom practised at times by the Athenians.

Labour relations between the workers and the court were not always smooth. At whim, kings issued edicts to moderate this presentation of 'joy' and orders were given that special clothing should or should not be worn, just as in Imperial Rome. From time to time, the women were also forbidden to wear jewellery and silk, although such costuming was generally considered to be part of the profession. During the reign of Charles VI, the bordello women called a strike after the fashion of Lysistrata and refused to perform in bed until they were no longer required to wear a nun's white habit when in public.

As usual, it was the poor among the harlot population who suffered most under the changing attitudes and laws. Sentences such as hanging, drowning and being buried alive were not uncommon. Barbarian customs died hard. Life was not easy, however, for the more successful and wealthy light-ladies either. Generally, these women were segregated, taxed and forced into municipally-supervised areas to practise their trade. In 1234 the first official redlight district was established at Avignon, a landmark decision in the history of this most ancient of institutions. The lewd women of Avignon were forbidden to wear veils and the whorehouses had to be identified by red lanterns placed over their doorways. The aroused citizens were guided while the pious or unwary were

Medieval Scene of Dissipation Drawing from the *Master of the House Book*, 15th C German
COURTAULD INSTITUTE OF ART, LONDON

warned, a sensible step by the French who pride themselves so much on their logic. The house with the red light became an international symbol for vice even in remote lands such as Asia where the colour often contained other meanings.

Meanwhile, in Toulouse, 200 miles to the west of Avignon, there had been successful bordellos in operation as far back as anyone could remember. In 1201, the year after Cambridge University was founded, the already well-established University of Toulouse in conjunction with the burghers embarked on an interesting experiment. The jointly-owned bordello was moved outside the city walls to the suburb of Grant L'Abbye where it flourished until 1389 when anti-war rioting broke out in the city. The widely unpopular Hundred Years' War was in its fifty-second year, so the protest was understandable. Possibly because soldiers were known to frequent the bordel at L'Abbye, it became a prime target for the anti-war rabble. The unprovoked attacks in 1389 against the house in the suburbs had an unfortunate effect on the business, and the University and merchant shareholders faced the prospect of a sharp falloff in dividends. The academics and the tradesmen appealed for help from the King, Charles VI. In response, the King had his official fleur-de-lys emblem set in the stonework over the building's portcullis. The royal stamp proved to be no deterrent at all. To save the business, the bordello had to be moved back within the city walls. Three years later, in 1392, Charles VI was officially dubbed Charles the Mad and his brother Louis, Duke of Orleans, took over the distribution of the fleurs-de-lys.

At about the same time, in Milan, there were so many bordellos operating that Bernabo Visconti, Prince of the City, decided to tax them for revenues to maintain the city's walls, another example of the link between sex and public protection that goes back to Phryne the Courtesan. Just as in earlier times the business of sex and the Church were closely intertwined. Harlotry was so widespread under Pope Innocent III that he established a chain of Magdalene houses in an effort to try to turn the occupants to other industry. All too often this meant taking the women out of one establishment to have them return to the old profession in the new location. Again, in Avignon, when it was the alternate Papal City, Queen Johanna established a bordello for Christians only and called it 'The Abbé'. Not to be outdone, Pope Julius II in the sixteenth century founded a similar house in Rome. Whether of First or Second Estate, Church or Nobility, the coffers always needed filling to keep an economy healthy for the administration.

With the Church at its most powerful point during the Middle Ages, it is hardly surprising that in addition to their guild the prostitutes of Paris had, like the other professions, a patron saint of their own. Quite naturally they chose Mary Magdalene. They burned candles before a stained glass picture showing *Sainte Marie L'Egyptienne* about to board a boat, her skirts hiked up to reveal a pair of inviting thighs; the inscription read: 'How the saint offered her body to the boatman to pay for passage'.

Because of the decimation of the male population during the Crusading years, a surplus of women naturally developed. With no outlet in marriage, many of the hapless women of the period were forced to embrace the religious life and literally went to live in the church. They lived in a small room over the church porch or in a cell built up against the outer wall. Other recluses confined themselves to small buildings in the churchyard. Most of these women were from the upper or wealthy classes and were helpless unless someone looked after them. There had to be at least one servant to cook for them and look after their clothes and toilette. Although these recluses were expected to keep busy to escape the lures of lust by sewing, reading and praying, the kindest charge against them by the townsfolk was that they gossiped. Although with the sanction of the local bishop they were committed to spending their lives in a small cell, they none the less did entertain guests at times when they could afford it. It is no surprise, then, that they produced hordes of illegitimate children. 'Who has more facility to commit wickedness than the false ancre [anchoress]?' asks one commentator of the period. If a queen or mother superior can own her own luxurious bordello, he might as well have asked, who would deny a lesser lady her own small bordel if it keeps her mind and body alive?

On the Continent, in the thousand years between the fall of Rome and the Renaissance, the bordello passed through three clearly defined stages. First, near-extinction as the barbarian waves moved from East to West; then a travelling roadshow as the Crusaders rampaged from West to East in successive waves; thirdly, thanks to the development of the guilds and the support received from royalty and the Church nobility because of the welcome revenue, the bordels grew into accepted and even highly valued institutions such as those enjoyed in Greece and Rome.

Across the Channel a parallel but distinctive development was under way. In 1066 the Goths added the stirrup to their horses and won at Hastings for the Normans against Harold's Saxons. The spear-wielding foot soldiers could not unseat William's horsemen. As a result, some historians feel that the stirrup was the greatest contribution of the Goths to mankind. Others argue that it was the bathhouse, in England at least, where the institution of the 'stew' gave the bordello a new look and flavour.

CHAPTER THREE

NYMPHS TO THE BATHS

WHILE ON THE mainland of Europe kings and emperors are turning bordellos over to city management, in Britain kings and prelates are legalizing them for their own great profit. From the time of the final Roman evacuation in AD 410 until the middle of the twelfth century the whorehouses on the south bank of the Thames at London exist in a state of benign neglect, at least by Court and Church. Then, in 1161, Henry Plantagenet II issues the 'Ordinances Touching the Government of the Stewholders in Southwark'. This landmark document was also signed by the Archbishop of Canterbury and his deacon, Thomas à Becket. With its signing start almost 400 years of Church- and Court-promoted whoredom on the site of the original Roman bordels, on the south riverbank between the Blackfriars and Southwark bridges, half a mile west of London Bridge. The only other comprehensive history of a bordello community of similar magnitude is found in Japan's Yoshiwara. In many ways their histories are similar. In China, explosives are already in use in warfare. In Spain, the Arabs are manufacturing paper, and civilization has reached such a high degree in Iceland that fire and plague insurance policies are being issued. In England, chess has caught on as a popular pastime and is played, among other things, in the baths.

London's 'stews' descended from the Roman *thermia*, the hot baths, which were synonymous with brothels at the height of their popularity. They were heated by what the Latins called *stufa*, the old Dutch *stoven* and the Saxons *stuves*. The equipment used to heat the water in London's bathhouses thus came to identify the place and its business. Until the end of the last century many social historians argued that the stews were nothing more than community washrooms, but illustrations of the facilities of the time show clearly that much more than soap and hot water was available. Although he evidently wanted to regulate the stews, Henry II's primary concern was with taxation.

Dating pictures of the stews is simple. Those with latticed windows predate 1180 when the first glass windows were introduced in England and thereafter proliferated, until Francis Bacon was moved to observe irritably that in new

A Medieval Stewhouse
Drawing from the *Master of the
House Book*, 15th C German
COURTAULD INSTITUTE OF ART,
LONDON

houses it was impossible to escape either sunlight or draughts. Later, with the royal coffer in mind, William III in 1696 decided to institute a window tax and in the first year collected over a million pounds; the common folk immediately cut down on their use of glass and their homes reverted to the gloom and odour enjoyed during the Dark Ages.

Certainly there were no glass windows in the bordels when the last Roman departed, but within a thousand or so years, many refinements had been added to the houses in the Borough of Southwark and in the clandestine bordellos on the other side of the river in London proper. Edward the Confessor had developed his tastes in France and although forks were not yet in use, he did introduce carpets and tapestries to his court and eventually such niceties inevitably filtered down to grace the bordel floors instead of the traditional rushes. Edward himself had large landholdings in Southwark, including several plots in the Bankside.

This did not prevent Edward's canonization in the same year that Henry issued the Stewholders Ordinances.

When the latter took the throne in 1154 he kept alive the tradition established by Charlemagne 400 years earlier. This second ruler in the Plantagenet line was not content with wife alone, but kept also at least six mistresses and sired sixteen illegitimate children. With such a cavalier outlook on Henry's part it is obvious that he was motivated chiefly by avarice when he had the ordinances drawn to regulate business in the Bishop of Winchester's Liberty of the Clink in the ancient Borough of Southwark. Some of the sixty-four laws set forth:

> No stewholder or his wife should let or stay any single women to go and come freely at all times when they are listed.
> No stewholder to keep any woman to board but she go abroad to her pleasure.
> To take no more for the woman's chamber in the week than fourteen pence.
> No stewholder to receive any woman of religion or any man's wife.
> Not to keep open his doors upon the holy days.
> No single woman to take money to lie with any man except she lie with him all night till the morrow.
> No stewholder to keep any woman that has the perilous infirmity of burning nor to sell bread, ales, flesh, fish, wood, coal or any victuals.

If the laws were followed to the letter, the boarding women would have been far better off than the slaves who populated the Roman bordellos and baths. Although no women of religion were to be permitted, it did not prevent nunneries from owning whorehouses – and many did. The reference to the 'perilous burning' shows that venereal disease was well recognized at the time. Although it looks good on paper, it is doubtful that the regulation concerning the all-night stay was designed to promote lasting attachments. Rather, it was probably made law to prevent the woman from throwing the customer out in the middle of the night when he could fall prey to the countless footpads and cut-throats who infested the black and narrow lanes and byways.

There were eighteen boarding-house stews covered by the original ordinances, each occupied by approximately twenty women. The houses were thatched with rye straw, or, occasionally, were roofed with wooden shingles. Walls were of wattle and daub or cob, with timber framing. According to contemporary surveys, each bordel had a garden at the rear stretching as far back as Maiden Lane. Generally, the buildings consisted of two storeys with the upper one projecting. Street signs and advertising boards projected, too, so that the already crowded streets were full of obstructions. Later, it would be ordered that all such houses be painted white. The house-names would then be written in large letters that could be seen from the embankment on the far side of the Thames.

By the thirteenth century the bordels were built of boards and plaster, then covered in part by wooden shingles. The floors in these places, as in most of the private homes in the land, were covered with rushes which were changed twice a

A Medieval House of Prostitution (with a bordello on the ground floor and a theatre on the first floor)
Woodcut, late 15th or early 16th C Italian
BBC HULTON PICTURE LIBRARY

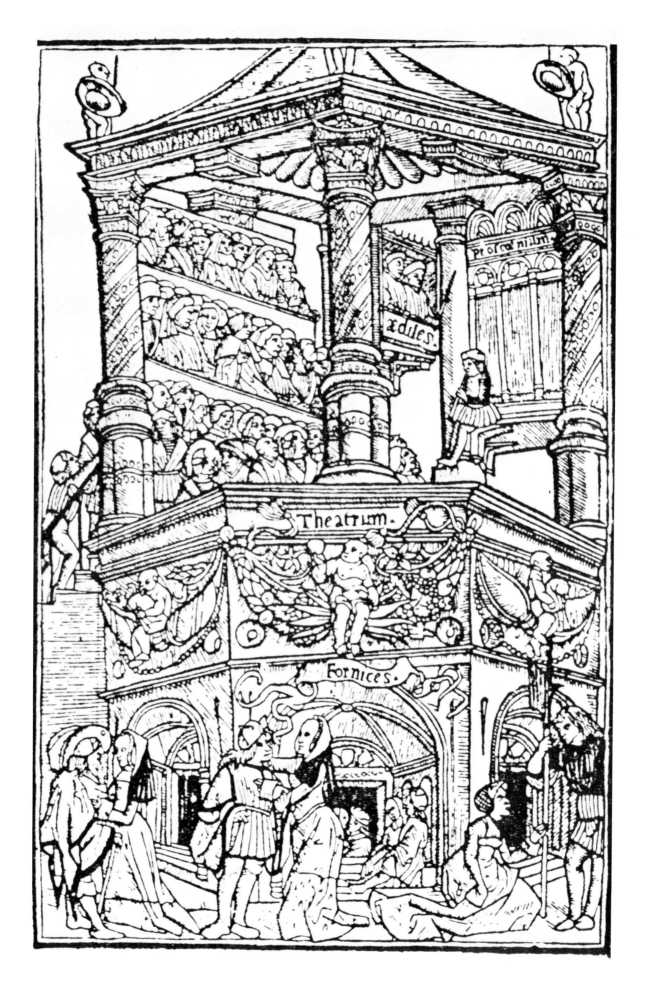

year. Later, sweet herbs and flowers would be used to dilute the stench. A Dutch physician visiting one such house in 1560 was surprised and pleased to find bright and sweet-smelling flowers in both bedrooms and privies. By this time the four-poster bed had replaced the box-bed and was hung with curtains; comfortable pillows were increasingly coming into use. In the better houses of accommodation tapestries were hung on the walls, more to keep out the draughts than to decorate.

In the rooms of the better-off harlot, in addition to the bed, there would be a stool, possibly a basin and ewer and a chest for keeping the woman's clothes and personal possessions. Sometimes the chest had arms or even a rail along the back to transform it into a rudimentary settee. The chest was usually a heavy plank construction with butterfly hinges and was painted in bright colours and touched up with gilding for the more successful of the stewhouse residents. Every bedroom was equipped with a chamberpot, usually of pewter, or silver in the first-class bordels. The rooms for the most part were heated by burning wood and when that was scarce, turf and dung fired the stoves up until 1233 when coal was first mined in Britain, at Newcastle.

It was in the thirteenth century, too, that jesters were first introduced in the courts of Europe, and leprosy was brought home by the Crusaders. In the redlight districts of Southwark and London tiles began to replace the thatched or shingled roofs of the bordels. Inside, the first linens appeared and glass mirrors began to be commonplace. For the first time since Roman rule major improvements in the ambience of the bordellos were being made, while simultaneously the general standard of living was deteriorating.

Municipal records show that in 1287 the Dean of St Paul's Cathedral, which was visible directly opposite the Bankside on the north side of the Thames, held properties in Cock's Lane which were let out to boarding prostitutes. Like the dean, the King was also pressed for funds. In his efforts to extract money from his subjects in every conceivable way, Edward I sold knightships for £20 each. Even the most notorious whoremongers were being dubbed knights. It was during Edward I's reign (1239–1307) that the name Gropecunt Lane appeared, identifying the district where thrill-seekers collected who could not afford the entrance fee to even the meanest of the houses. Clearly, these were hard times both for royalty and common citizen.

There is a simple explanation for the peculiar relationship between Crown and Church on the one hand and the brothel institution on the other. While the theologians were swayed by the traditional Christian hostility towards sexual activities in all their manifestations, there were also strong economic and political pressures pushing the Bishops and the King into cosy coexistence with the thriving bordello business. It was not coincidence that during these years the stews were often called 'abbeys' housing their 'abbesses' and 'nuns'. There were other advantages enjoyed by stewholders who conducted their business on

The Procuress, 1656
Jan Vermeer, 1632–1675
STAATLICHE KUNSTSAMMLUNGEN,
GEMÄLDEGALERIE, DRESDEN.
PHOTO BY EDDY VAN DER VEEN/
COLORIFIC

church-owned properties, not the least of which was that they could not with impunity be accused of carrying on the commerce of the devil.

When Edward was not busy knighting brewers and stewholders he was worrying about the accusation made by certain scandalmongers that his son, Edward Junior, to succeed him in 1307, was a flamboyant homosexual. Whatever, Edward II's compassionate nature led him, after his ascent, to open the Lock Hospital in Southwark which was devoted to the treatment of 'lepers'. Syphilis and leprosy were frequently confused at this time. When the distinction was finally drawn, the Lock Hospital specialized in venereal diseases. Later, in Japan's Yoshiwara, the same sort of institution would be called the Lock Hospital. For outpatient care, John of Gaddeson suggested that the disease could be best treated by 'running, jumping, inhaling pepper, tickling the vagina with a feather, washing with roses and herbs boiled in vinegar'. The Japanese, too, would later favour similar prescriptions.

At the start of the fourteenth century a disease far more serious than leprosy or syphilis was on the horizon. While the Crusades had ended in 1291, their after-effects would be felt for centuries. Starting in 1347, the Black Death spread across Europe with fearsome speed. The plague originated in the Issyk-kul lake area of central Asia years earlier before sweeping across the Mediterranean and upward to northern Europe. In the single year 1347, one-third of the population of England perished. Between 1347 and 1351, 75 million Europeans died from the bubonic plague. (For comparison, during World War II when the world's population was much larger, there were 55 million civilian and military deaths in Europe and Asia.)

Before *Bacillus pestis* took its unprecedented toll, particulary high in Southwark, business was growing fast in the Bankside. The first named stew is mentioned in 1306, *The Bull's Head*. Fifteen years later it was recorded that a papal agent, Cardinal William de Testa, as a Church investment bought a bordello and called it *Aulus Comitis*, 'The Social Club'. Three years later, whatever his sexual proclivities, Edward II built a retreat for himself on the south bank of the river, named it *La Roserie*, and engaged in some sort of high jinks he clearly did not want observed at Court. By 1337 a stew called *The Barge* was owned by the nuns of Stratford, evidence that these devout ladies knew a good real-estate investment as readily as did the gentlemen of Church or Court.

Not surprisingly, during the epidemic years of the plague, both attendance and profits were up for the stews in Southwark and the fancier houses across the river. The prevailing fatalistic attitude advocated that you should eat, drink and make merry in the whorehouse because come dawn, like as not, they will be dropping your corpse in the street for the cartman. With life and death in such stark profile, there was little time for euphemism. During this period, in addition to the original Love and Maiden Lanes, new designations like Slut's Hole, Codpiece Lane, Whore's Nest and Cuckold Court appear to identify the streets where the strumpets worked and strolled. The notorious bottom-of-the-line Gropecunt Lane remained on the tax assessor's lists until the middle of the fourteenth century when the Grope had become Grape, the lane a street, and the *queynte* of Chaucer had been lost entirely. Later still, the grape became grub to give us Grub Street which persists in the language as a synonym for the meanest hack-writing – and thus maintains some of its original implication.

Ribaldry reached such a pass in the public thoroughfares before the plague petered out that the City of London issued an ordinance in 1351 concerning 'The Dress of Common Women within the City' – reminiscent of the Roman code concerning the dress of that city's *ambulatarae*. Because it was becoming increasingly difficult in London to distinguish the ladies of noble houses from the 'lewd' or common women of the bordellos, the latter were barred from wearing hoods on their cloaks or garments that were either trimmed with fur or lined with silk. At the same time, perhaps because the origins of the plague were connected in the public mind with the filthy conditions in many of the stews, health inspections by

Customers Arriving at and Leaving a Brothel (one of the earliest illustrations of a bordello extant) The Romance of Alexander, 14th C BODLEIAN LIBRARY, OXFORD MS. BODLEY 264, FOLIO 91 VERSO LOWER RIGHT

Car li rois alixand ne vuet mie targier
A·v·cens cevaliers a fait aprimiyer
Acabzuns fu armes ⁊ ot le cuer legier
Son hardement volra prouuer ⁊ assaier
Le ceual point ⁊ broche des esperons dormier
⁊ a brandi la lance dont li fers fu dacier
En lescu tholom feri le cop premier
Lanste fu de rosel tout li fist pechoier
⁊ tholom fiert lui qui duit fu du mestier
Si espies fu trenchaus ⁊ lanste de pomier

the legal authorities were stepped up. By today's standards their efforts could be described only as cosmetic, for the first water closet would not be designed for another two and a half centuries.

Following the plague, towards the end of the fourteenth century, more and more bagnios were bought by respectable guildsmen and merchants of London, breaking the monopoly held earlier by the Church and Crown. With their strict new dress laws, the city fathers evidently were trying to keep the line drawn between their wives and their employees. Despite the new competition, the Church was not without its resources; it continued to draw taxes from its own. Through the custom of *couillage*, a Roman invention, priests were taxed for the 'hearth girls' they employed to look after their domestic and human needs. It was not by accident that one of the Bankside's most popular stews was called *The Cardinal's Hat*. Other famous houses opening during the fifteenth century bore names such as *The Antelope, The Bell, The Castle, The Crane, The Cross Keys, The Elephant and Lion, The Fleur de Lys, The Swan* and *The Unicorn*.

Taxed by the owners of romantic-sounding houses on the one hand, the women of the stews were not immune to annoyance by the citizens of their own class on the other. From the time of the peasants' revolt lead by Wat Tyler in 1381 onward, 'whorebashing' became a gruesome pastime of the people of the street. Thanks in part to the plague and enhanced by the ravages of the Hundred Years' War the number of vagabonds became a matter of grave concern to the burgeoning middle class. It was estimated that in London alone there were 12,000 'begging poor', almost one-tenth of the population. Every year as many as 400 unfortunates who tried to supplement begging with thieving were 'eaten up by the gallows'. As well as the city's streets all of the country's highways were haunted by the homeless and the lawless. None the less, there was some charity. Bethlehem Hospital for the insane, later Bedlam, was opened in 1407. Although it was more a place for confinement than rehabilitation, its existence did show some public awareness that the rope was not the answer to all social problems. Forty years later, new laws taking some recognition of the cause of the plague's wide sweep called for new public sanitation efforts and quarantine measures were instituted. Nightly bonfires became popular because it was noted 'the virtue that a great fire hath to purge the infection in the air'.

The French and English had evidently not purged their fighting souls with the endless campaigns of the Crusades; following generations were given a chance to prove their mettle and foolishness with the longest of all wars which lasted even longer than the Hundred Years ascribed to it (1337 to 1453). Despite all the hardship and cruelty imposed by this conflict between benighted knights and barons, some beauty and sensibility remained alive. The Bohemian Baron Leo of Rozmital was most forcibly struck by the great beauty of the Thames and the London landscape when he visited England in the middle of the fifteenth century. He was also much impressed by the gardens attached to the houses of the great

The Peasant Dance, c. 1568
Pieter Bruegel the Elder, 1525–69
KUNSTHISTORISCHES MUSEUM,
VIENNA. JOHN HILLELSON
AGENCY/MAGNUM

merchants and guildsmen, particularly the goldsmiths', and he was awed by the apparent love of flowers demonstrated by the entire population, noting that even the poorest houses were adorned with flowerpots. In this case, the poorest houses were the Bankside stews, revealing that the occupants were not unfamiliar with the joys of horticulture.

Having survived the Great Plague of the previous century, the citizens of England now suffered a crippling epidemic of syphilis. This fifteenth-century scourge was believed to have been transmitted by French soldiers who contracted it in Naples. Henry VII ordered all the bordellos closed, blaming this latest plague on 'the winds from Winchester' and 'the Winchester geese', connecting once again the Bishop with the atmosphere and the women in 'the Bishop's Liberty of the Clink' in Southwark.

It was this same Clink that gave the prison its name. With her place of employment shut down, it was not uncommon for a Winchester goose to find herself in the clink where the first word she heard was 'garnish'. She would be forced to pay the keepers of the gaol for her upkeep, an amount based on her alleged crime and probable ability to pay. If she had money she could buy food and drink and be visited by friends. If poverty-stricken, as most were, she would be stripped of all her possessions and thrown into a dungeon where only a merciful God could spare her from starvation. The Clink was neither better nor worse than its other famous contemporaries, the Fleet, the Cage, the Marshalsea and the King's Bench, where it was said, 'prisoners are lodged like hogs and fed like dogs'.

The criminal laws were terrifying, the list of felonies enormous and the penalty more often than not was death. It was death for conspiracy against the Crown, of course, but it was also death for transporting horses into Scotland. It was death for stealing a hawk's eggs and for taking the possessions of a dead man. It was death to take a horse by violence, but only a fine for obtaining a horse by fraud. Minor offences against the law were punished by public penance, the offender being made to stand in the pillory or being hauled through the streets tied to a hurdle with a description of his crime written in large letters for all to see. A special pillory for women, known as the *thewe*, was provided for female lawbreakers. Lucky was the offending stewmaid who found herself in the pillory rather than on the 'ducking stool', with which she would be dunked in the river until she was properly penitent or unhappily drowned. Even the ducking stool was a pleasanter instrument than the earlier 'cucking stool' on which the unfortunate woman was suffocated in excrement.

Despite Henry VII's order to close them down, a few months after his edict a dozen of the Bankside's most famous stews reopened. When his turn came, Henry VIII gave Cardinal Wolsey instructions to clean up the Bankside as early as 1519. Of Wolsey it was said by chroniclers of the day: 'He has no wife, but whores who be his lovers.' One of his illegitimate daughters was the Abbess of Salisbury. Perhaps because his heart was not in it, Wolsey's men rounded up only fifty-four 'vagabond and loose women' from among the thousands of women who might have been affected by the King's edict.

Some twenty-five years later, in April 1546, Henry VIII ordered a genuine crackdown. All houses, high and low, were to be shuttered. It could not have been for Puritanical reasons because the King's private life was no less licentious than most of his ancestors. Just when and from whom Henry VIII contracted syphilis is unknown, but certainly it affected his mind as well as his body. After all, Stephen Gardiner was the Bishop of Winchester at the time and it was he as the King's pimp who delivered the geese to order. More than likely it was simply a part of Henry's plan to seize all of the Church's property, denying all the bordellos to other entrepreneurs and preserving them for his own enrichment.

Henry's wild scheme was small inconvenience to the stewholders, however, because in the same year Edward VI succeeded to the throne, and soon the reconstruction and revitalization of the Bankside was under way. To enliven things further, bear- and bullbaiting came to Southwark. Here Edward had built the Paris Garden which seated at least 1000 spectators. Later, a second and larger ring was constructed exclusively for bullbaiting and large crowds flocked to it until Parliament banned the grisly games in 1642. As late as the end of the seventeenth century there were reports of tiger-baiting in London, but these exhibitions were available only to the upper classes.

For their outdoor entertainments the girls in the stews had to count on public executions which drew enormous crowds, especially when their other pleasures were curtailed by whimsical monarchs. These burnings, hangings, mutilations and decapitations thrilled the fun-loving London crowds and most members of the audience could easily project themselves into the role of the victim without much trouble. An added pleasure was obtained when one of the girls witnessed the despatch of one of her less popular customers.

For milder entertainment in the sixteenth century cards replaced dice as the most popular form of gaming. A sure sign than gentility was on the rise came with the introduction of pocket handkerchiefs. Although sedan chairs were in general use, the coach also appeared for the first time, borrowed from the French who called it *coche*, in turn having lifted the invention from the citizens of the Hungarian town of Cosz where the first horsedrawn carriage appeared. There was no public outcry when the better-off women of the stews moved about the town in sedan chairs, but when they put on airs and presented themselves in coaches the moral majority became incensed. The argument about what form of transport harlots were entitled to, often turning into battle, would last for centuries, and was not confined to England. Whereas once a whore's or courtesan's clothing was the major matter of debate, the issue later revolved around her means of transportation.

By the time of Elizabeth I's reign (1533–1603), London was still only a large town or a small city, with a population of 180,000. Within the century between the reigns of Elizabeth I and Charles I the population of Britain doubled and the number of bordellos kept pace, but with a difference. Because of French and Spanish oppression in the Netherlands, there was a flood of Dutch refugees to England where they opened or took over the management of many stews. Sir Walter Raleigh's son, Carew, told the story of his encounter with a discriminating whore from Holland: 'She thrust me from her and vowed I should not take her, for your father lay with me but an hour ago.'

Many of the elder Raleigh's contemporaries doubted the virginity of his erstwhile good friend, Queen Elizabeth. One of their accounts had her travelling incognito by ferry for an assignation with the Earl of Leicester at *The Three Cranes*, one of the better-class stews in Southwark. If true, she would have found things much less sanitary than at home. A water closet had been installed in her palace at Richmond by Sir John Harrington, courtier and author, in 1596, but on the whole this invention was not taken seriously by the general population. Nor would it have been feasible because water was still carried to the houses in buckets from the nearest public pump. As to personal cleanliness, it seems that men and women of the late Tudor and Stuart times washed neither extensively nor frequently and made less use of public baths than in former days.

When his turn came, in the early seventeenth century, James I did little to help improve conditions. What William III later did with his window tax, James I now accomplished with his ownership of the commercial soap manufacturing monopoly. Where the one cut down on sunlight for the average citizen, the other reduced any fondness for cleanliness. On the other hand, cosmetics and beauty aids were, as always, popular with good wives and harlots alike. Just how great the dependence was is illustrated in Ben Jonson's *The Silent Woman* when the husband says of his wife: 'All her teeth were made in Blackfriars, both her eyebrows in the Strand, and her hair in Silver Street. . . She takes herself when she goes to bed in some twenty boxes.' Having divested herself of her various artificial bits and pieces the Jonsonian woman would put on or off her 'night-rail' which she wore under her nightgown before entering the bed.

During the reign of James I nothing was done to stop the proliferation of the London brothels. Quite the contrary, because his own visits to the most notorious bordels of the day were widely advertised. The broadcast information that 'James Stuart slept here' was enough to triple a stew's business overnight. One such house to win almost instant acclaim was *The Holland's Leaguer*. Some time in 1603, when Shakespeare was completing *All's Well that Ends Well*, a lady from the Continent doing business under the name Donna Britannica Hollandia moved into the Manor House in the Paris Gardens district and opened a bordello that was several cuts above any of the others in the area. Providing only upmarket food, drink and girls, Mother Holland was soon counting James and his favourite at court, the Duke of Buckingham, among her classy customers.

Thirty years later, the Holland house panache had begun to fray and Charles I sent a company of soldiers to shut it down. The crafty madam waited until the royal soldiery were massed on the drawbridge before lowering it precipitously into the foul waters of the surrounding moat. The occupants of the house then proceeded to empty their chamberpots on the men thrashing about in the shallow water. The beleaguered house was thereafter known as *The Holland's Leaguer*.

Surviving records from these stirring times show that a woman in a first-class stew might entertain ten to twelve men a night. In the lower-class houses thirty customers was the average, although one industrious wench reportedly chalked up fifty-seven lusty fellows during a single tour of duty. To increase their stamina male customers relied on lambs' testicles as an aphrodisiac. Coming and going between the stews, all but the most peaceful gentlemen wore swords, while merchants got along with mere knives. Apprentices and yeomen had to be content with heavy cudgels. Except in the very best neighbourhoods, a visit to the brothel could be a very dangerous affair. If the customer did not have his wallet

Holland's Leaguer
Woodcut, Southwark, early 17th C
MARY EVANS PICTURE LIBRARY

lifted while engaged, he stood a good chance of being waylaid or even murdered on his way home through the dark, stinking lanes and alleys. The first street-lighting did not appear in the heart of London until 1684, and not in the Bankside until much later where both footpads and wayward husbands preferred the cover of night.

During the interregnum following the Civil War, (1642–52), Oliver Cromwell and his Roundheads severely curtailed public entertainment and temporarily put an end to Stuart extravagance. What kind of people would tolerate a monarchy that managed to double a war debt during five years of peace? During the Long Parliament frivolities like dancing and sports like cricket were denounced. More serious activities like cockfighting, duelling and adultery were banned, the last punishable by death. However, neither Cromwell nor his supporters had the temerity to shut the bordellos. Nor did the righteous Lord Protector deny himself the pleasures of the flesh. He shared his bed with one Bess Dysart, a notorious whore and a probable nymphomaniac who was later to become the Duchess of Lauderdale.

By the time of the Restoration in 1661 it was estimated that there were 100,000 whores in England, or one in every ten women in the relevant age group. Under the rightminded Protestants business was better than ever on the Bankside. Now the clergy of the Reformation came under attack. 'The Beggar's Petition' of the day asked: 'Who is she that will set her hands to work to get three pence a day, and may have twenty pence a day to sleep an hour with a friar, a monk or priest?' Certainly not another renowned Bess. The foremost quean in the better circles was Bess Broughton; it cost the client £50 for dinner alone with this lady, post-prandial entertainments as high as the market would bear.

The name of Charles II, reigning from 1660, soon became synonymous with lechery. Married to a barren queen, he enjoyed the attention of a dozen mistresses and recognized fourteen illegitimate children, none of whom had to worry about the 'bar sinister' on their escutcheons as a sign of bastardy. In heraldry there was no such thing. The 'bar' was dreamed up by Sir Walter Scott for his fictions more than a century later. In Charlie's court lubricious behaviour was equated with loyalty. When the Earl of Sandwich openly took a mistress, Samuel Pepys noted that he was only doing what everyone else at court was doing. The Earl of Rochester best described the life of the rakish courtier in Charles's court:

I rise at eleven, I dine at two.
I get drunk before seven, and the next thing I do,
I send for my Whore, when, for Fear of the Clap,
I come in her hand and I spew in her Lap.
Then we quarrel and scold till I fall fast asleep;
When the Bitch growing bold, to my Pocket doth creep;
She slyly then leaves me – and to Revenge my Affront
At once she bereaves me of money and cunt.

I storm and I roar and I fall in a Rage,
And missing my Whore, I bugger my Page.

As the King's gentleman of the bedchamber Rochester had firsthand knowledge of his subject. The envy of rake-hells like George Villiers, Charles Sackville and George Sedley, John Wilmot (the Earl of Rochester) was Charles's frequent companion in wantonness. On the night that the Dutch sailed up the Thames and cheekily burnt the English fleet, the King was revelling with Lady Castelmaine, while Rochester was dallying with Mrs Malet, the heiress, whom, when seduction failed, he married. Like his ribald monarch, he 'was soon cloyed with the enjoyment of any one woman, though the fairest in the world, and soon forsook her'. Years before the King's death in 1685 the witty and oft-banished Wilmot wrote *Epitaph on Charles II*:

Here lies our Sovereign Lord the King,
    Whose word no man relies on,
Who never said a foolish thing,
    Nor ever did a wise one.

By whatever standard, of all his mistresses, Charles was fondest of Nell Gwyn, the beloved, legendary child of the slums who – according to the Victorians – rose from the gutter to climb into the King's bed and who died repenting her licentious ways. As best can be determined she was reared in stews and was successively employed as a pothouse wench, orange-seller, actress, whore and King's paramour. Either she was a great wit or had wits enough about her to employ a clever courtier like Rochester to prepare her ripostes. When Louise de Querouaille was created Duchess of Portsmouth, Nell appeared before her wearing a new gown. The recently elevated courtesan remarked patronizingly, 'Nelly, you are rich, I believe, by your dress; why, woman, you are fine enough to be a queen.'

'You are entirely right, madam,' Nell shot back, 'and I am whore enough to be a duchess.' On another occasion, having been called a whore by one of the titled court ladies, Nell reportedly objected only because the remark was made by one who 'was an old notorious whore even before whoring was in fashion'. Whatever she was or may have been, Mistress Gwyn prided herself on being the King's 'Protestant whore' and somehow managed to keep Charles's affection for seventeen years despite formidable competition and widespread criticism of their relationship. In the tradition of Theodora, in her later years Nell became a born-again Christian.

Some of the critics of the régime saw God's punishing hand in two great events which occurred in the middle of Charles's reign. The Black Death returned in 1665. It was unrivalled in its sudden spread and its deadly effects. Nowhere did it hit harder than in Southwark. On a single day in September, 7000 plague deaths were recorded. Normal life was thrown completely out of gear. Shops closed, theatres and all places of amusement were shut and royalty and the wealthy fled to the countryside. The speed with which the contagion spread is accounted for by two factors: the open sewers in the middle of the streets; and a failure to isolate the victims. Their clothes and belongings were thrown into the streets where they were seized upon by the wretched and the poverty-stricken.

'In such plagues we poor people have mickle good,' says the beggar in William Bullen's *Dialogue Against Pestilence*. 'We beggars reck nought of the carcase of the dead body, but do defy it; we look for old cast coats, jackets, hose, caps, belts and shoes, by their deaths which in their lives they would not depart from, and this is our hap. God send me of them.'

Such good fortune brought death to 68,596 souls among all classes. Once again the Bankside was decimated. Then in the first week of February of the following year, 1666, even before the plague had abated, the Great Fire of London broke out. Half of the city disappeared, including London Bridge. The fire consumed eighty-nine churches, 400 city blocks and 13,000 private homes. The Bankside could not survive these successive crippling blows. As the centre of English whoredom it did not disappear completely, but it became only an enfeebled shadow of its former self.

Stews levelled by fire, customers sorely reduced in number and circumstances, the Winchester geese took flight, or at least those who could afford to. Some sailed for America, others to France, more to Italy where their fair complexions and rosy cheeks, gossip had it, were greatly prized. Transportation as punishment for crime had been introduced by Elizabeth I in 1597; better to flee voluntarily than to be exported to some stockaded village in the New World. In Renaissance Italy prospects for a skilled strumpet were glorious indeed, or so many thought.

CHAPTER FOUR

A FINE ITALIAN BAND

The insular position of England, combined with the nature of the English character, has always allowed that country to feel shocks of change on the Continent tardily and usually without too much discomfort. And so it was with the Renaissance. While the history of the bordello in Britain is traced through the Bankside with the stews and bawdy houses named after exotic animals, or identified by their madams as with *The Holland's Leaguer*, in Italy the tradition is traced through the names of the great courtesans who established their popular residences in the various great city-states under the Viscontis, the Sforzas and the de' Medicis or in Rome within walking distance of the Vatican. When the victims of the London holocaust reach Italy they arrive 150 years behind the Golden Age of the Bordello. On other cultural fronts, the first ballets are developing in Italian courts, Botticelli and Ghirlandajo are painting frescoes in the Sistine Chapel and Leonardo da Vinci is designing submarines and flying machines. And a census taken in Rome in 1490 reports the presence of 6800 registered prostitutes in a population of 90,000.

The common order of *cortigiane di candela* had barely earned much more distinction than the harlots of London by the end of the fifteenth century. As wealth and refinement in the Italian duchies grew, however, so did the demand arise for women with some degree of education and social grace. This new class was called *cortigiane oneste*, cultivated women with fine manners, finer dress and remarkable piety. To keep up with the new humanists whose favours they sought, until the shoe was on the other foot, they adopted classical names like Camilla, the allegedly immoral Faustina, Penthesilea (Queen of the Amazons killed at the siege of Troy) and Polyxena (sacrificed for Achilles' death). The elevated position of these ladies is reminiscent of the *hetaerae* of Athens; perhaps there is something in the nature of the city-state which has a refining effect on the profession. Rome's famous Imperia was refined to a point where she learned to compose sonnets under the tutelage of Domenico Campana. In Milan, Bandello was acquainted intimately with the regal Caterina di S. Celso who was noted for her musical accomplishments. In his classic sixteenth-century chronicle *Ragionamento del Zoppino*, Pietro Aretino reports of one stellar courtesan: 'She knows by heart all of Petrach and Boccaccio, and many beautiful verses of Virgil, Horace, Ovid and a thousand other authors.' This might be taken for hyperbole if it were not for the fact that more recently Peig Sayers (1873–1958), a native of the Blasket Islands off Slea Head in Co. Kerry, Eire, could recount no fewer than 375 narratives, each the length of a contemporary novel.

Whatever the accomplishments of the *cortigiane oneste*, it is clear from the distinguished visitors they received that more than simple bedroom entertainment was expected of them, while they, in turn, were treated usually with some degree of respect and consideration. As the mistresses of dukes and princes of the Church, poets recited their praises, and frequently artists of renown painted their portraits. This was the age of Andrea del Sarto, Michelangelo, Titian, Raphael and Piero della Francesca, most of whom had some contact in one form or another with the *prima cortigiane*. As the feminine counterpart of *cortigiani*, the courtiers who swarmed throughout the ducal palaces of the Italian states, the word *cortigiane* suggests a certain dignity of status quite lacking in the score of variations of the Anglo-Saxon 'whore'.

From 1309 to 1368 the Pope and Curia had resided in Avignon, France, and it was during these years that the city-states were established in Italy. Once the Papacy returned to Rome, subsequent Renaissance popes saw themselves as sectarian princes, artists or scholars and hastened the spiritual decay of the Church which had begun some 500 years earlier when the doors of the Holy See were opened to mistresses of every kind. Certainly what was good enough for the Pope and his cardinals was good enough for the lesser princes and even the average citizen if he had the means to support an expensive indulgence.

The state of morality in the Holy City at the end of the fifteenth century is best illustrated by the stories of two prominent *cortigiane*, Vanozza dei Cattenei and Giulia Farnese. These two ladies were kept, successively, by the remarkable Pope Alexander VI, begetter of the notorious Borgia clan, who started life as Rodrigo de Borgia, a profligate Spaniard benefiting by fraud and murder. Vanozza followed Rodrigo to the Vatican from Valencia and there bore him four children, Cesare and Lucretia among them. Vanozza was provided with three different husbands during this period to disguise her relationship with Rodrigo-Alexander.

When Vanozza retired from service, Alessandro Farnese presented his sister Giulia to the Pope in exchange for pardons for a variety of crimes. At the age of seventeen, Giulia had already been married to a member of the Orsini family for two years. Persuaded by the Pope to leave her husband, she moved into his quarters in the Vatican and there bore him three children. Despite the fact that he apparently loved her, Alexander could not give up his old habits. In 1501 Giulia witnessed one of his frequent orgies where several score of naked ladies of the

Italian Courtyard
Jan Weenix 1642(?)–1526
NATIONAL GALLERY, LONDON

Venus and the Organ Player
Titian c. 1488–1576
PRADO MUSEUM, MADRID

court performed with members of the Pope's retinue and prizes were awarded to the most durable of the participants. Alexander's record is preserved in the Papal archives. Giulia's beauty is preserved for us in Pinturicchio's *Madonna* and Giacomo della Porta's *Truth*, a marble nude decorating the tomb of her brother, Pope Paul III.

The first standards for Italian Renaissance feminine beauty were set forth in the middle of the fourteenth century by the writer Boccaccio, not in his famous *Decameron*, but in the *Ameto*. Here he established what was to become the cult of the *biondo* which seems to have persisted to this day. The ideal beauty, he suggested, had either blonde hair or blonde hair shading to brown. What Boccaccio had set forth as an example, fifty-odd years later Agnolo Firenzuola promulgated as law in his *Dialogo delle bellezze donne*.

As for his qualifications as arbiter, Firenzuola studied law at Siena and later at Perugia where he became a close friend of the licentious Pietro Aretino. He went on to practise law for a time in Rome and eventually settled at Prato as the Abbot of San Salvatore. Here, lecturing the ladies of the city, he pieced together an ideal

A Blond Woman
Palma Vecchio d. 1528
NATIONAL GALLERY, LONDON

beauty from a number of beautiful parts. Not the smallest part of the female anatomy escaped his observation or dictum. The eyes, preferably goddess blue, although lustrous brown was admired, would be large and full. The ears, neither too large nor too small, would be firmly and neatly joined. The chin would be round, a dimple its glory. The leg would be long and not too hard in the lower parts. When speaking or laughing or smiling the beautiful woman would show no more than six of her upper teeth. His precepts would later find the most acceptance in Venice where the *biondo* fashion would reach lunatic proportions. There, while boating along the canals proper, Venetian ladies would point out that the hordes of blonde courtesans populating the city were imports from Germany; many, in truth, were Winchester geese who had flown south.

As for the Italian courtesans themselves, most entered the profession while in their adolescence, usually introduced by a mother or an aunt. If the young girl appeared to have the requisite promise of good looks and the wit to realize that she could become both famous and rich if she employed her charms properly, there was no telling how high or far a talented girl might go. Catherine de' Medici, the bride of Henry II of France, cunningly used prostitution as an important arm of diplomacy. Long before the intelligence services of the East and West employed the device, Catherine was ordering her maids of honour to bed down with foreign diplomats and there on the silk sheets to learn of state secrets which she could turn to her own ends.

Among the most famous of the grand courtesans were Beatrice, Corsette, Fiammeta, Grechetta, Imperia, Massina and Tulia. As with today's models and film stars in most cases the names were assumed. Their careers are linked not only with popes and cardinals but the wealthiest traders of the day as well. The rewards for their services were looked upon as gifts rather than crass payment.

The most publicized of the group was Imperia who was born in Rome in 1481, the same year work on the frescoes of the Sistine Chapel was started. Probably it was she whom Raphael took as his model for the Sappho of his *Parnassus.* Made exceedingly wealthy by her patron Agostino Chigi, Imperia de Cagnaris gathered around her a flock of scholars, artists, poets and churchmen. While a grand palazzo was being built for her in the Borgo Leonino she occupied a house near the church of St Lucia in the Via Giulia. The ancient Roman tradition of the city house and the country house was revived during the Renaissance as soon as the wealth and culture of the people allowed, and this ideal was always prominent in the dreams of the leading courtesans. Although Imperia achieved ownership of both palazzo and villa, in addition to masses of jewellery and coffers of gold, she apparently was an unhappy woman. She was the only *cortigiane* of note to take her own life and the poets of the day went wild in their recognition of the event. Today, a comparable tragedy would bring forth a flood of books and television shows to meet the public appetite for scandal in the world of celebrity. Despite her suicide at the age of twenty-six, she received an

Two Venetian Ladies on a Balcony
Vittore Carpacio 1460–65(?)–1526
MUSEO CIVICO CORRER, VENICE

Allegory of Love, III
Veronese 1528–88
NATIONAL GALLERY, LONDON

honourable burial in the church of San Gregorio with a marble tomb engraved in the finest lapidary style.

Vying in popularity with Imperia was Beatrice. She lived and worked in a fine house adjacent to the Osteria dell 'Orso, then Rome's four-star hotel. Many of her clients were foreign travellers staying there. Beatrice also was reportedly an

The Toilet of Bathsheba
Style of Giordano
NATIONAL GALLERY, LONDON

intimate of Raphael. Descriptions of her correspond with the painter's *Fornarina*, the nude half-length courtesan in Rome's Barbarini Gallery so that it is highly likely that Beatrice was the model.

Almost as renowned was Tulia d'Aragona, daughter of a courtesan and a cardinal. Admired for her flaxen tresses and sparkling eyes, her generosity and carelessness with money, her courtly mien and witty conversation, she moved in the ducal circles of Naples, Rome and Florence like a visiting princess. The Mantuan ambassador at Ferrara in a letter written to Isabella d'Este described his first meeting with her in 1537:

> I have to record the arrival among us of a gentle lady, so modest in behaviour, so fascinating in manner that we cannot help considering her something divine. She sings impromptu all kinds of airs and motes. . . There is not one lady in Ferrara, not

even Vittoria Colonna the Duchess of Pescara, who can stand comparison with Tulia.

Her portrait was painted by Moretto da Bescia, in which she projects all the innocence of a schoolgirl. Unfortunately, Tulia had the misfortune to outlive both her beauty and her wealth. She died in impoverished circumstances in a small house on the banks of the Tiber, but she kept her lute and her harpsichord with her to the last. She left also a book she had written entitled *On the Infinity of Perfect Love*.

Of all the grand *cortigiane* Nana was undoubtedly the most famous. In his autobiography Benvenuto Cellini calls her the most fashionable courtesan of his time. She was the model of Parmigianino's famous portrait which hangs in the National Gallery of Naples. Among other things, Nana was noted for the number of times she sold her virginity, a not uncommon practice among her contemporaries. Nor was she above robbing many of her casual clients while they slept, a bordello practice that seems almost universal.

Even when relations between a courtesan and a long-term lover were broken off, the men apparently still wanted to maintain the good opinion of the ladies, which seems to indicate that although passion may have departed, some affection may still have remained. Equally likely, the men may have wanted only to protect their own reputations from the gossipy tongues of the women they abandoned. Of course, no courtesan worthy of the name was happy to see a lucrative relationship terminated, so the women went to extraordinary lengths to keep their clients and patrons tied to them.

A favourite aphrodisiac of the day was the *confarreatio*, a kind of cake which purportedly had magical qualities. The courtesan lay naked on a bench while her maid placed a board across her loins and on the board put a tiny oven. The cake was cooked in the oven while the servant assured the hopeful harlot that the cake was being heated by the heat of her body, the flame of her passion. Small wonder that later when he was fed such a hot cake the vacillating lover or reluctant customer would be unable to refuse any of the inflamed woman's requests. Reportedly, many a papal fortune changed hands thanks to the ingestion of such tasty cakes.

In the world outside the bordello, life was much more sophisticated. During the fifteenth and sixteenth centuries Italian life was probably more polished and ennobled than in any other country of the Western world. In the well-paved streets of the cities riding in horsedrawn coaches was universal. Elsewhere in Europe one rode on the horse's back if one rode at all. As late as 1687 the sedan chair was the most popular form of transportation in the rest of Europe.

Despite the fact that the first-class courtesans wore as much gold as their limbs could bear, much in the fashion of Hindu ladies who wear all the family's wealth on their arms, they did show some refinement of taste in their personal quarters. Their wide four-poster beds were supplied with the finest linens, the walls decorated with charming tapestries, their sideboards sprinkled with vases and silver ornaments, and their dressing-tables covered with numerous beauty aids. In no country of Europe since the fall of the Roman Empire was so much attention given to the skin and hair, despite all the denunciations from the pulpits of the land. False hair was the favourite ornament, made of white or yellow silk. Dyes and other mixtures were used to get the *biondo* effect for the natural hair. On sunny days the courtesans spent hours on their loggias hoping the sun would act as a bleach. Not until the twentieth century when the chemical industry invaded the marketplace did women invest so much time and money in decorating their outer shells.

The case of Caterina Sforza, Countess of Imola, provides an illuminating picture of how seriously cosmetics were considered. Finding her once-famous beauty fading at the age of forty-four, she wrote for assistance to a well-known Roman beautician called Anna. Anna's letter of instruction in return with the consignment read:

> Here is a black salve which removes the roughness in the face, making it fresh and smooth. Apply this at night and allow it to remain until the morning; then wash yourself with pure river water. Next, bathe your face in the lotion called Acqua da Canicare, then dab it with the white cream. Afterwards, take a pinch of this white powder; dissolve it in the lotion labelled Acqua Dolce and apply it to your face as thinly as possible.

Whether because of or despite the beauty aids, the Countess Sforza proved to be not too good a customer; she died just a year after first trying Anna's beauty treatment. It is interesting, and in keeping with present-day merchandising practice, that the prices of all the items listed in Anna's line escalated, each salve and lotion and powder more expensive than the last. When the preachers proclaimed with ever-increasing vehemence that these paints and potions were the Devil's products and the tools of courtesans, so much more did the fine ladies clamour for them.

Both in their fancy carriages and their private chambers the grand courtesans wore dresses of silk or velvet and donned cloth of gold. Thanks to the trade with the East they were adorned with precious stones and pearls. Everything – body, clothing, furnishings – was scented with musk and other fragrant oils. The widespread use of perfumes went beyond all reasonable limits. On feast days and at carnivals even the mules were treated with scents so as not to give offence to the crowds. On one occasion Pietro Aretino thanked Cosimo I for a purse full of perfumed money.

Money, aromatic or not, was everywhere spent lavishly. When entertaining popes, cardinals, princes of state or merchant princes, a courtesan's typical dinner menu might include partridge and pheasant, quail and capons, thrushes and pigeons, all with savoury sauces; various fruits swimming in liqueurs with iced sherbet on the side; all accompanied by red, white and rosé wines. The

entertainments supplied in a first-rank bordello were described in a letter by
Niccolo Martelli to his friend Bernado Buongiolami:

An Allegory of Love
Garofolo 1481(?)–1559
NATIONAL GALLERY, LONDON

> And the royal way in which they treat you, graceful manners, their courtesy and the
> luxury with which they surround you, dressed as they are in crimson and gold,
> scented and exquisitely shod, with their compliments they make you feel another
> being, a great lord, and while you are with them you do not even envy the inhabitants
> of paradise.

It is doubtful that even James I enjoyed such luxury in London's finest
brothel, *The Holland's Leaguer*, when he went to town. But all was not always so
celestial in the Italian houses as this *pasquinade*, a popular rhyme of the day,
warns:

Lassa andar le cortesane   Leave the courtesans alone,
   se non voi disfarte del tutto   if you don't want to lose all you've got.
Come l'altre son puttane   They're prostitutes like the rest,
   na piu caro vendon lor frutto.   but they cost more, for you know what.

The sentiment expressed in this street refrain was popular in Baghdad a thousand years earlier, although the warning in Arabic was given much more forcefully and at greater length. Just as in Baghdad, and the Bankside, in Italy too the customer and his possessions were frequently in jeopardy. While the footpads of Southwark rolled the unwary in the gutters, in Rome the courtesans, even the most prized and publicized, were known to lift a customer's wallet on the sly or even cause his clothes to disappear under the pretext of having them cleaned.

To forestall any noisy intrusion no grand bordello was complete without a host of bodyguards. Jealous lovers or disgruntled customers were inclined to get their revenge through the practice of *sfregia*, face slashing, which not only ruined the courtesan's looks for good, but usually destroyed her means of livelihood as well. A more degrading form of revenge was the *trentuno*, an occasion when the offending woman was raped by upwards of thirty hired men, or the *trentuno reale*, an attack by seventy-five hired thugs. Such gross indignities caused both clients and revenue to fall off sharply.

In addition to the bodyguards who were on hand to prevent such disasters, no notorious palazzo was without its *mezzanos*, pimps and entertainers, and the *ruffina*, a combination hairdresser, talent scout and procuress. No truly successful house was without its *strega*: the most important activities of the *strega* concerned love affairs, and included the promotion of love or hatred – as with the magic cakes, including abortion and even the manufacture of potions. This was a dangerous line of work because convicted witches were burned at the stake. After the Bull of Innocent VIII in 1484, witch-hunting became an increasingly popular pastime, so it was a wise witch who practised her craft secretly. Aretino, however, reveals some of the materials of the *strega*'s trade: human hair, bits of skull, ribs, teeth, dead men's eyes, the navels of small children, the hymens of virgins, slices of skin and bits of clothing stolen from tombs. Supposedly these grisly bits and pieces could be used for good or evil, depending on the *strega*'s disposition and intent. Wax or bronze figures representing the human subject were anointed with holy oil stolen from churches or melted down, depending on the result desired by the passionate mistress. Such dark and dubious carryings-on in the cellars of the bordellos seem mild indeed compared with the villainy often practised in the marble halls of the wealthy lords.

Seldom in world history have there been so many acts of calculated wickedness as practised by the rulers of fifteenth- and sixteenth-century Italy. Their favourite instruments of administration were the poison cup and the dagger in the night. Or, if they wanted to do things with a certain panache, a dose of diamond dust in a rival's dinner would do the trick in his bowels. This practice finds its counterpart in the 'lover's salad' of southeast Asia where finely sliced bamboo shoots serve the same purpose. While a distraught courtesan might have robbed a grave to concoct the right love potion, her devilry did not match the practice of Gian Maria Visconti who fed his hounds on human flesh, turning them loose once they had regained their appetite to track down fleeing prisoners for his entertainment.

The poisonous ways of the Borgias are too well known to need recounting, but Duke Cesare was a man of many parts. He had the habit of roaming the streets at night with his footguards on curious forays which led the Venetian ambassador to write: 'Every night four or five murdered men are discovered, bishops, prelates and others, so that all Rome is trembling for fear of being destroyed by the Duke.' Better to have one's trousers stolen in a homely bordel than to cross Cesare's path after dark. This son of a Pope does not stand alone in his monstrosities. Sigismondo Malatesta, tyrant of Rimini, was convicted in the Court of Rome for murder, rape, adultery, incest, sacrilege, perjury and treason, all committed not once but on several occasions. His attempt to murder his son Roberto was dismissed by his defenders with the proposition that Sigismondo had been misled by the court astrologer. This same theory was advanced in the case of the rape of the Bishop of Fano by Pier Luigi Farnese of Parma, the son of Pope Paul III. Holy orders clearly were no deterrent to sodomy.

The destiny of the courtesans of Rome was ultimately determined by the Vatican's attitude toward their enterprise. When high-living popes were in power they lived well and usually flagrantly. Nevertheless, ideas of moderating their lifestyles went back to the reign of Leo X in the first quarter of the sixteenth century. It was Paul IV in the second half, however, who took active steps to bring the women into line. As a first measure he forbade them to use carriages while moving about in public, believing that such beautiful and expensive conveyances helped to promote their trade while at the same time fostering the public notion that in harlotry existed the best route to a house in town and a villa in the country.

After his election in January, 1566, Pius V dropped a bomb which rocked the entire country. He decreed that within six days all the courtesans of Rome would have to leave the city. The screams of outrage could be heard all the way to the Swiss border. Most of the *cortigiane* had been living on credit. The merchants and shopkeepers were appalled, naturally. How in the world would they be able to collect their debts if the Pope banished their debtors to the hinterlands? The Pope, quite naturally in his turn, was miffed by their attitude which put commerce before morality. The people, Pius decided, would have to choose between him and the harlots. Here indeed was a dilemma of epic proportions.

In an uncharacteristic action for the time, a compromise was reached. Instead of forcing the courtesans to leave the city entirely, the Pope agreed that they might stay, but that they would have to confine themselves to a certain quarter, across the river, to the *trastavere*. The Pope thus succeeded in turning the clock back several hundred years, sending the women back to the ghetto where they had worked earlier. Moreover, he created in Rome the counterpart of London's bordello district, the Southwark's Bankside, also 'across the river'. What was

The Sons of Boreas Pursuing the
  Harpies
16th C Venetian school
NATIONAL GALLERY, LONDON

worse, perhaps, the courtesans were now required to wear a special distinctive dress, a gown stretching from throat to toes; further, a voluminous veil to hide tempting eyes and lips was also required dress. The working women were now not only called 'nuns' but they looked like nuns on the public thoroughfares. However, if the venerable profession had fallen on hard times in Rome, such was not the case in other parts of Italy which, for a time anyway, had not become so reactionary.

Twenty years after the professional companions in the Holy City had repaired to the ghetto, in Florence the historian and social philosopher Scipione Ammirato commented on the great increase in the number of courtesans in that city. Every night he observed large numbers of 'women clad in bright garments' emerging from the crowded quarter behind the Palazzo Vecchio. It is impossible to tell how many of these new faces may have emigrated from Rome, but there was another cause which Ammirato had not considered. In order to keep their estates intact as long as possible, the Florentine landowners were shipping potential wives to the convents and dooming many potential husbands to permanent bachelorhood, thus eliminating almost half the normal number of marriage settlements each year. Before long, the average male, if he married at all, did not do so until he was thirty-six.

When these unattached young men were not amusing themselves with the imported or native streetwalkers of the city they were found in the *Porco*, the *Bertucce*, the *Chiassolino* or other renowned nightspots where 'enormous blasphemies, robberies, cheating, falsehoods and other crimes' were regularly committed over the gambling tables. Crime was not unknown at the most prominent bordellos like the house of La Pisanella or the apartment of La Maiorchina on the Via delle Pinzochere behind Santa Croce. Count Giovan Francesco del Benino was murdered at La Pisanella's by Giulio Rucellai. Earlier, Carlo Rocasoli Rucellai, son of the philosopher Orazio, killed his cousin Giovanni Alamanni after a rousing night at La Maiorchina's. News of such events appeared in the daily gazettes, but the number of homicides among ordinary citizens in the bordellos went unreported and unrecorded for the most part.

Chronicler Ammirato and the Archbishop of Florence did not see eye to eye on the issue of prostitution and the often accompanying bloodshed. The latter had banned notorious women from the church, but Scipione saw them as no greater an evil than beggars or bandits who were a natural part of the cityscape. However, like Pope Paul IV, he did deplore their use of ostentatious carriages which had become more 'superb and sumptuous than ever; they were adorned with noble carvings, curious paintings, exteriors and interiors of gold leaf, rich drapes, and velvets of various colours so that they became portable sitting-rooms'.

As in Rome and in Florence later, when the courtesans were segregated it made life more difficult for both them and the Jews who were often isolated in the same area as a symbol of their degradation. From early times, the Church had been strongly against sexual relations between Christians and Jews, even when marriage was not involved. As late as the seventeenth century a Jewish girl was burned at the stake for having had intercourse with a young Italian noble. Despite the dire penalties facing them, out of the eighty-eight condemnations of Jews in Florence in the fifteenth century, no fewer than thirty-four were for sexual offences.

While Rome and Florence were bringing promiscuity under control, Venice was set on the opposite course. Even in the Middle Ages Venice had had a reputation for sexual liberality. By 1443 things had come to such a pass that a law forbidding transvestism was passed; any man found in female dress in a public thoroughfare was liable to a fine for offering unfair competition. At the same time it was the practice of many courtesans to dress in men's clothing in certain places to have better access to male customers than they might otherwise have had. Much good the law did. By 1480 it was necessary to issue a decree that such practices were to be considered a form of sodomy, a capital offence. Nevertheless, nearly a hundred years later, in 1578, it was necessary to issue another law forbidding courtesans to go *vestite de home* while riding the canals of the city in gondolas. The Church could talk as much as it liked; the Venetians seldom listened.

Aside from the peculiar habit of dressing like men, several other oddities about Venetian women caught the eye of English traveller and diarist John Evelyn in 1643. First were the *choppines*, high-heeled shoes worn by proud dames which were so difficult to walk upon that Evelyn surmised that they were designed to keep the ladies at home. Wearing *choppines* from time to time was prohibited to courtesans, who might have found them restrictive to trade, anyway. Then there was the matter of their hair, and once again the names of Boccaccio and Firenzuola are recalled. On the strange ways of the ladies of Venice, Evelyn reports: 'The truth is, their garb is very odd, as seeming always in masquerade; their other habits are also totally different from all nations. They wear very long, crisp hair, of several streaks and colours which they make so by a wash, dishevelling it on the brims of a broad hat that has no crown, but a hole to put out their heads by; they dry them in the sun, as one may see them at their windows.'

Sharp-eyed Evelyn also observed that courtesans 'cover their bodies and faces with a veil of a certain glittering taffeta, or lustree, out of which they now and then dart a glance of their eye, the whole face being entirely hid with it'. This quaint practice was more the result of Moslem influence in Venice than the Pope's persuasion from Rome. An unveiled portrait of one of the city's leading courtesans, Veronica, was painted by her very good friend Tintoretto. Veronica also had the honour of entertaining Henry III, King of Poland, when he visited the Pearl of the Adriatic, presumably again without benefit of veil.

By the eighteenth century Venice had come to represent a totally permissive society in the eyes of the rest of the world. Every legitimate entertainment and every imaginable vice were available to citizens and visitors alike. The support of kept women was considerable, but still fell short of the demand. Thrifty Venetians and foreign visitors like Jean-Jacques Rousseau banded together to pool their resources in support of a single concubine. Sexual excess had spread from the sixteenth-century *cortigiane* to married women of all classes, many of whom frequented the gambling casinos in which cubicles were provided for assignations.

Nothing better illustrates the dissipation and frivolity of the time than the notorious Carnival of Venice. During Evelyn's visit it was a time for bull-running, athletic contests and masquerading, sort of a combination Halloween and New Year's Eve which lasted a week or so. A century later it had grown quite out of hand according to another observer, Philippe Monnier: 'Six months of the year it lasts, from October to Christmas, from 12th Night to Lent; on Ascension Day it starts again for two weeks and again upon St Mark's Day and whenever a doge is elected, whenever a procurator is chosen, on the least occasion always on the slightest pretext. In masks men and women do business and buy fish, write their letters, pay their visits and plead their cases in court.' Behind their masks the courtesans were free to visit the finest homes in Venice and the city's leading citizens, male and female, were free to visit the bordellos unquestioned.

The mad gaiety penetrated religious institutions where some nuns took to wearing pearls and immoderately lowcut habits. On one occasion the inhabitants of three convents argued bitterly about which religious house should provide a bed companion for the Papal Nuncio. Monnier also reported the scandal of two abbesses who fought a duel with daggers for the amorous attentions of the Abbé Pomponne. A Venetian epigram summed up the prevailing attitude of the immoral majority: 'In the morning a little Mass, after dinner a little gamble, in the evening a little woman.'

And it was in Venice that the curious institution of the *cicisbeo* was perfected if not invented. On a visit there another amazed Englishman, Lord Coke, wrote in the eighteenth century:

> How shall I spell, how shall I paint, how shall I describe the animal known by the name of chichisbee? He is an appendix to matrimony. Within a week of her nuptials a young lady makes a choice of her chichisbee. From that moment she never appears in public with her husband, nor is ever imprudent enough to be seen without her chichisbee. He is her guardian, her friend, her gentleman usher. . . The husband, (believe me, I entreat you, if you can) beholds these familiarities not only contentedly but with pleasure. He himself has the honourable employment of chichisbee in another house; and in both situations as husband and chichisbee neither gives nor receives the least hint of jealousy.

With a lover in every household, one might expect bordello attendance to fall, but quite the opposite was true, as that great eighteenth-century libertine Giovanni Giacomo Casanova de Seingalt took pains to report. Clearly not every *cicisbeo* was content with the company of another man's wife alone, because the number and style of the Venetian bordellos gained them a worldwide reputation. When he was not in the bawdy houses or gambling casinos Casanova claimed to have found time to seduce thousands of women, although only 116 are actually named. His speciality was the seduction of the wives and daughters of friends, often simultaneously. All this must be taken with a grain of salt because he was under the impression that the fifty oysters he ate for breakfast each day were responsible for his potency. The stamina of which he boasted is generally associated with the male performers in sex circuses who are homosexual.

On his part, fortunately or unfortunately, seventeenth-century traveller John Evelyn discovered that every bathhouse was not a brothel: 'I went to one of their bagnios where you are treated after the Eastern manner, washing with hot and cold water, with oils and being rubbed with a kind of strigil or seal's skin, put on the operator's hand like a glove. This did so open my pores that it cost me one of the worst colds I ever had in my life.' Lucky he was not to have caught a malady more lasting.

For Turkish bath or Turkish trade, the infidel had been known to the Venetians from the time of the earliest Crusades. It was the Venetian Marco Polo who in the thirteenth century crossed the Moslem world and opened the way for

St Mary Magdalene
Correggio *c.* 1489–1534
NATIONAL GALLERY, LONDON

trade with far-off Cathay. It was in the latter half of the Renaissance that Europeans were introduced to the bordellos of the Middle and Far East, first through commerce and then through military conquest as they began to exercise power in the lands beyond the shores of the Mediterranean. Words like harem and houri entered the vocabulary of the Westerners. The East and the Exotic became synonymous with the Erotic. More importantly, the influence of Araby on the grandest bordellos in Europe and the New World would be enormous for centuries to come.

CHAPTER FIVE

HAREMS AND HOURIS

DURING NEARLY 200 years of the Crusades – 1096 to 1291 – many Oriental customs and ways of thought begin to find their way to Europe through Italy and southern France. So when the merchants of Venice and other Mediterranean seaports begin to exploit trade with Asia fully during the Age of Exploration, the West is not unfamiliar with the mores of the Islamic world, but many of the institutions prove puzzling. Probably the most confusing discovered is the harem, from the Arabic *harim*, meaning forbidden. Relying on the tales of surviving Crusaders, the Europeans come to believe that these great compounds which enclosed hundreds and even thousands of wives, concubines, female slaves and eunuchs are giant bordellos. What else can be expected of the heathen who believes that paradise, *al-Jennah*, is 'an everlasting brothel providing celestial concubines', seventy fair-skinned houris for every male who makes it to heaven? Although not every harem is a bordello in the strict sense of the word, not every great house of secluded women is a harem. Later, the Turkish word for inn, *serai*, will be accepted in the Islamic world both for hostelry and whorehouse, and become known in the West as the seraglio.

As in earlier civilizations, the Arab institutionalization of prostitution had its roots in the slave trade. Within a period of less than 200 years the followers of Muhammad had burst out of their native peninsula to conquer all of North Africa and most of Spain on their western front and to subdue all of south Asia as far as the Indus river on the eastern side. With so many countries subjugated in such a short period of time, the Arabs were hard-pressed for ways to handle the population. In the early days of expansion, the males were simply slaughtered; later they were neutered. Children were simply abandoned as the nomadic tribes swept on. Captured women became the slaves of wives and daughters or concubines if they proved young and attractive enough for the position. Including the women among his chattels as clear evidence of his worth, the sheikh guarded them all fiercely. A harem was impossible to protect completely while on the marches of conquest, but once the nomads had become citified and gentrified no

Semitic prince or warrior worth his salt would be without his walled seraglio. When the centre of power, the Caliphate, was moved from Damascus to Baghdad, the most popular women used to stock the harems were taken from the Turkish tribes on the northeast frontier. The Turks at the time occupied the lands between Mongolia and the Black Sea. Seven hundred years later the roles of Turk and Arab would be reversed.

One of the earliest Islamic bordellos on record was the house of Ibn Zamin which operated in Baghdad during the reign of al-Mansur, AD 754–775. His name indicates that he was probably of Persian or Indian origin. According to the records it was his practice to buy girls cheaply from the slave-traders coming down from the Turkish borders, and train the girls to sing and dance and play the lute. When they were sufficiently accomplished, Zamin resold the girls at exorbitant prices to the wealthy merchants of the city. Alongside the *serai* of Ibn Zamin was the house of Ibn Zuraiq, a rival entrepreneur. For some time the two men had the reputation for housing not only the best-looking women in Baghdad but in the entire Caliphate. When it is considered that the Moslem empire stretched from the Atlantic to the Indian Ocean, the girls must have been exceptional.

Three women are mentioned specifically in the chronicles as singing-girls in the house of Ibn Zamin and the prices they fetched are listed. Rubaiha, after extensive training in the art of entertainment, was sold for 8000 dinar. Sa'da brought 9000 dinar. Salma Zaraqa, the prima donna called 'blue-eyes', brought top dinar at 10,000, the equivalent of two first-class racehorses. At another auction, Crown Prince Madi reportedly paid 17,000 dinar for one of the singsong girls. Probably she was not only blue-eyed but blonde as well. This preference for the unusual persisted at least through the Middle Ages when the captured Frankish women brought the highest prices in the slave-market.

The author of the *Kitbul Nowashsha* presented an intimate picture of the ways and wiles of the typical trained Arab courtesan. Once she found herself in the company of a wealthy young man she did everything to snare his affections, sending him locks of her hair, clippings from her fingernails, strings from her lute, letters dampened with tears, even fragments from her toothbrush of twigs. Once the poor wretch was convinced that the girl was all but dying for his love, she changed her tune. The requests to her lover give a good idea of what presents were most desired by the women of the seraglio or boarding-house:

> Once in her complete control, she begins asking him for valuable presents such as materials for dress from Aden; curtains from Nishapur; garments from Angog; turbans from Sus; silken waistbands; shoes; sandals from Kanbaja; head ornaments set with jewels; bangles; valuable ruby rings. Not infrequently she feigns sickness. She has herself treated or bled without the slightest cause. All this with one object in mind; namely to obtain presents such as amber-scented shirts; chemises fragrant with musk; expensive lozenges; neckchains of camphor or cloves soaked in wine. Unending are her demands for presents. The lover's purse exhausts itself; money is gone and purse lies empty. Perceiving that there is nothing more to be got, she shows

The Harem Bath
Jean Léon Gérome 1824–1904
COURTAULD INSTITUTE OF ART,
LONDON

signs of impatience and makes her lover feel her change in attitude. She speaks unkindly to him and seeks a pretext for breaking with him.

The Italian lampoon encapsulated the same warning in four lines.

While writing her love-letters or composing her demands for presents, the typical *serai* entertainer occupied a flat-roofed building made of dried mudbricks with a courtyard at its centre. In the middle of the courtyard was a covered cistern into which went all the refuse water of the household. The enclosed surface of the poorer houses was of pounded earth; in the better establishments, mosaics adorned the courtyard. A pleasure-house with mosaics and a garden was indeed first-class. The garden was as prized by the Arab as the country villa by the Roman and to this day green is still the favourite colour in the Moslem world.

The business of the houses was conducted in small, dimly lit rooms facing the courtyard. Windows were little more than slits near the ceiling to reduce the sun's glare. In the poorer houses sheepskins on the dried-mud floors served as beds; in the better places Persian rugs were used with a profusion of silk-covered pillows. Eventually, the divan became popular as influences from the East increased. An essential part of every house was the *hhemmuan*, a bathhouse. The Qur'an (*c.* AD 650) spelled out just when and how the Believer should bathe in the smallest detail. Ablutions (*ghasl*) were required after sexual intercourse (*jima*) or after any discharge of semen through masturbation or nocturnal emission (*ihtilam*). The devout were required to wash thoroughly, making sure that the water reached every portion of the body and every hair of the head. If water was not available, the use of clear sand for cleaning was authorized. Fornication in the bathhouse itself was prohibited: 'Have no connection with women in the bath for its consequence is palsy.' Even the Prophet himself reflects the thinking shared by self-righteous Romans and Londoners: 'Whenever woman enters a bath, the devil is with her.'

The standards of feminine beauty appear to have changed little between Biblical times and those of Muhammad. Plump breasts stand out like hyacinths, the poets report. The neck is like a gazelle's. Her teeth might be taken for pearls, her cheeks for roses. The forehead is like the full moon in the night sky. And a nice Arabic image: 'Her lips are fresh and red like a gory sabre.'

For enhancing one's beauty, the chief concerns were with the hair and eyes. A certain kind of clay, preferably from Qatif, was mixed with rose petals, then softened with water. Next, an egg was applied to the hair, followed by the clay mixture. After removing the egg and clay shampoo, skimmed and melted butter mixed with saffron was applied to achieve that fresh and lustrous look. The second most important item in the Arabian woman's toilet was the makeup for the eyes, with black *kohl* the universally used cosmetic derived from antimony. Pounded almond kernels were sometimes added to a silver-like antimony paste. Among the wealthiest women, powdered pearls were added to the antimony, as Cleopatra was wont to do.

Lady Performing Her Toilet
18th C Mughal Indian
BRITISH MUSEUM

The *mullahs*, of course, constantly inveighed against the habits of the sing-song girls. It was not due to the fact that the religious leaders were indifferent or insensitive to feminine charms, because they had their own well-stocked harems, but outside that enclave they affected a thorough contempt for earthly things and expressed a pious horror at the sinfulness of the world and of women in particular.

The historian S. Khuda Bukhsh places the start of the formal harem system at the time between the end of Umayyad rule (AD 750) and the Caliphate of Harun al-Rashid, 657–788. The fashion of using eunuchs to guard the seraglio came into use presumably in imitation of the Byzantine court or of the Persian kings. The trade in eunuchs was entirely in the hands of the Byzantines. In the beginning, eunuchs may have been employed in the houses of the rich as chattels of luxury to attend the skeikh's women, but with time and the altered state of the expanded harem they became imperious warders and supercilious supervisors. Prior to the Caliphate there was not a single instance of the son of a concubine succeeding to the office of Caliph; after Rashid most of the Caliphs were the sons of Greek or Persian slave girls.

During its period of dominance in the seventh and eighth centuries the entire Arab population lived at the expense of the conquered countries and acquired fabulous wealth through shares of booty and as tax-collectors.

The leading families lived in the traditional way of the nomad, looking upon numerous offspring as the surest guarantee of power and influence. For example, a son of Umayyad Caliph Walid I had no less than sixty sons; and with the daughters and inmates of the harem, male and female attendants, relations and clients, the entire household numbered more than 1000 persons. The household of an Abbasid family numbered 4000. The royal court of Caliph Muqtadir included 11,000 eunuchs alone. Because the Qur'an draws no distinction between the sons of wives or concubines, the fight for pre-eminence among the women in the seraglio was intense. Intrigue was constant, murder frequent; offences against chastity were brutally punished, either by stoning or decapitation.

To escape the risk of punishment, homosexuality became increasingly popular within the harem walls. S. Khuda Bukhash contends that the practice was almost unknown to the Arabs earlier, but that after closer contact with the Persians, and notably after the ascendancy of the House of Abbas, the practice became more and more the vogue, until the sons of the great Harun al-Rashid affected feminine manners and went about the court in yellow female garments.

Another circumvention of the laws of chastity was achieved through the practice of *mut'a*, a sort of legalized prostitution. Several stipulated conditions had to be met before the *mut'a* could take place. These included the agreed length of the quasi-marriage, the size of the dowry (which could be as small as a few dinar), and the recognition by the woman that after the agreed period for the relationship she had no claims on the man. These 'marriages' could be as short as a

Ladies with Their Attendants
18th C Mughal Indian
BRITISH MUSEUM

single night. The custom is similar to the Teutonic 'night-gift' arrangement which was popular at about the same time. During this first period of Islamic power the Anglo-Saxons were conquering the Celts in England and subjugating the Franks in Gaul. With the ascendancy of Charlemagne in Europe around AD 800, Arab power in the rest of the known world went into a decline.

The next great Islamic period lasted roughly from 1300 to 1660 when the Ottoman Empire embraced many of the lands occupied by the Arabs at the height of their power 600 years earlier. This time the Turkish sons of Othman held the reins of power. The success of this state was due to the autocratic power of the sultans and to the effectiveness of the army. Every year 20,000 Russian and North African slaves were imported for military service. Added to this was the 'toll of boys' whereby every fifth Christian male child in the Empire was surrendered to the élite army of the Janizaries. Under the sultans large territories were administered by grand viziers and under them the pashas ruled individual fiefdoms which now included the Balkans. During the interim of the two great Moslem epochs, the Arabs had introduced numerals imported from India, had started the manufacture of paper in Spain and the chemist Abu Nasa Jaffar had invented sulphuric acid, but any customer who might have fallen asleep in a house of joy and awakened six centuries later would have found little change in the surroundings or the inhabitants of the house. The activities, however, had certainly become more sophisticated.

In the middle of this second period, probably between 1394 and 1433, Shaykh Umar ibn Muhammed al-Nefzawi wrote *The Perfumed Garden*, the definitive Arabic how-to sex book popularized by Sir Richard Burton in the nineteenth century. At great length and in full detail al-Nefzawi describes the eleven basic Arab positions for sexual intercourse and reveals that he is familiar with the *Kama Sutra* by explaining the additional twenty-five positions observed in India, pointing out that some of them are evidently physically impossible and must have been included in the Hindu text for purely aesthetic purposes. Among those positions practised by the Arabs were *Neza al-kouss*, the rainbow arch, *al-khouariki*, the one who stops in the house, *Nik al-haddadi*, the smithy's position, and the ever-popular *al-loulabi*, the screw of Archimedes.

To keep fit for visits to the *serai* he suggested that men live on strengthening diets which included spiced fruits, aromatic plants, eggs, meat, honey and other nourishing foodstuffs. As his authority he cites Djelinouss (Arabic for Galen) who extracted plant juices for medicinal purposes in AD 190 during the reign of Marcus Aurelius:

He who feels that he is weak for coition should drink before going to bed a glassful of very thick honey and eat twenty almonds and one hundred grains of the pine tree. He must follow this regimen for three days. He may also pound onion seed, sift it and mix it afterward with honey, stirring the mixture well and taking this while fasting.

The Slave Market
Jean-Léon-Gérôme 1824–1904
STERLING AND FRANCINE CLARK
ART INSTITUTE WILLIAMSTOWN,
MASSACHUSETTS

He also warns against visiting the bordello too soon after eating:

If your stomach is full, only harm can come of it to both of you; you will have threatening symptoms of apoplexy and gout, and the least evil that may result from it will be the inability of passing your urine or weakness of sight.

On the subject of food, it is interesting to note that the internationally famous belly-dance, the *reqs essurreh*, was devised for the convenience of those who over-indulged in heavy foods over long periods of time. Because excessive fat was a sign of great wealth and power, sultans, khans, viziers and even local pashas tended to overeat. However, the gross belly made sexual intercourse in most accepted positions difficult if not impossible. Hence it was the task of the *sehniqeh* to cavort in front of the obese customer until he was aroused and then straddle his thighs in the thirteenth position, called *Daq al-arz*.

In an area of the world that gave the world three of its great religions it is not surprising that the Moslems were greatly concerned with visions and dreams. While the Italians of the Renaissance were preoccupied with astrology, the people of Islam at the same time were inordinately concerned with the significance of their dreams, particularly the girls employed in the *serais* along the caravan routes. Not all of the Shaykh's interpretations in *The Perfumed Garden* would be received unfavourably by Freudians. A dream of entering a window easily, for example, suggested that an effortless business transaction was in the offing. A narrow window in a dream implied that a difficult business deal lay ahead. Dreams could tell the sleeper when to visit the bordello or when to avoid a trip to a specific house or a particular woman. For all their contributions to science and medicine, when it came to the business of sex, the Arabs were every bit as superstitious as their European contemporaries. As for the romanticization of the commerce, both cultures appear to be on a par. The French troubador had his rose, the Arab poet his starling.

As life in the common Moslem bordellos became more diverse the entertainers themselves began to fall into separate classes as they had in earlier civilizations. Common whores were called *kehbehs*. The naked dancers became *shermoodehs*. The equivalent of the Greek *hetaerae* and Roman *delicatae* were known as the *auliemehs*. At the top of all the Arabic courtesans were the *deeleelahs*, probably from the perfidious Delilah who deprived Samson of all his strength. Then, as now, the *gawad* was essential to the success of most houses. Literally, *gawad* means 'one who guides' and the pimps who roamed the narrow streets and labyrinthine alleys in and around the *suqs* and marketplaces did exactly that.

Eventually, after the death and division of the Ottoman Empire, with Lebanon going to the French when the European powers were dividing the area, Beirut became the pleasure capital of the Islamic world. *Le rouge et le noir* décor of the famous Beirut bordellos became internationally modish, with perhaps half the nightspots today in the United States alone decorated with black vinyl and red linen, popularly known as the 'Lebanese Whorehouse Style'.

As Shaykh Nefzawi's *Perfumed Garden* indicates, he was familiar with both the culture of ancient Rome and with the even older civilizations of India. Sea trade between Arabia and the Indian subcontinent had been going on for centuries before the first European states made contact and set about establishing their first settlements there. In the spring of 1498 Vasco da Gama anchored off Calicut and diplomatic relations between Portugal and the Hindu raja were established two years later. By the time chronicler Domingo Paes reached the court of Vijayanagar in 1522 formalized prostitution in India was more than 3000 years old. Paes observed:

> These women live in the best streets that are in the city; their streets have the best rows of houses. They are much esteemed and are classed among those honoured ones who are the mistresses of captains. These women are allowed even to enter the presence of the wives of the king and they stay with them and eat betel with them, a thing which no other person may do, whatever rank they may have.

Before the invasions in 1500 BC of the *arya*, Indo-European-speaking nomads (Iran to Eire) from the northwest, the civilization called Harappa existed along the length of the Indus river. The people were short, black and flat-nosed. They built windowless houses and had a great affection for bathing and perhaps even a religious devotion to the bathhouse, a trace of which can still be found in Indian bathing customs today. The Harappa present a casebook example of how technology can destroy a civilization. Unlike the contemporary Sumerians who built with sun-dried brick, the Harappans and the citizens of Mohenjo-Daro used kiln-burnt brick. To fire the kilns they needed wood and to get the wood they chopped down their forests. As a result they were able to turn a green and fertile valley into a desert landscape. When the Aryans arrived with their innovative chariots, they found a perishing culture. Like the Israelites, the Aryans were herding nomads who looked down on the agriculturists and thought Harappan city life corrupt. And like Joshua they called upon their gods to destroy the city walls. One of these deities was Dyaus-Pitar who would later be known in the West as Jupiter.

The epic *Rig-Veda* portrays in great detail the role of public women in the Vedic society between 1500 and 600 BC which the Aryans superimposed on the Harappan. The Aryan military forces were accompanied not only by craftsmen, labourers, professional singers and spies but by courtesans, as well, who took their place in the relative safety at the rear of the baggage trains. The harsh life of the military campaigns was made more bearable undoubtedly by the presence of the 'public women, open to the visits of all', who wore bracelets of gold and clothed themselves in bright red garments which gave the same signal as the lights in Avignon would 2000 years later.

One institution in Vedic life, the *samana*, apparently encouraged libertinism.

During the *samana*, which was held in conjunction with athletic contests and tournaments, women were present and seemed particularly attracted to chariot-racing. Here young women and widows tried to find husbands while the courtesans found profit in the occasion with young sportsmen avoiding marriage, all of which sounds not unlike the jousting games of the Middle Ages.

When a royal household was on the move, the *Veda* reports, it generally included in its retinue 'chariots, traders' goods and brothels'. As the Aryans gave up their wanderings and pillaging and founded cities of their own, the bordello, *ganikaghara*, became part of urban cultural life. A visitor to one such house described a friend's reception:

> To him came running up quite fifty pleasure girls, splendidly dressed, fair-hipped, young and tender, sweetly scented, wearing thin red garments, decked in gleaming gold, well-versed in speech and honeyed words, skilled in dance and song, smiling, gifted with the knowledge of the heart's stirrings. They washed his feet and marked him for the highest honour. They served him good food and showed him to a couch.

Despite the fact that the courtesans of the Vedic period were much appreciated for the most part, on occasion they were called wenches, streetwalkers, harlots and even less complimentary sobriquets. One poet describes them in terms which have a familiar ring from other periods:

> Like poisoned draughts or robber fell, crooked as horn of stag,
> Like serpent evil-tongued are they, as merchant apt to brag,
> Murderous as covered pit, like Hell's insatiate maw are they,
> As goblin greedy or like Death, that carries all away,
> Devouring like a flame are they, mighty as wind or flood,
> Like Neru's golden peak that aye confuses bad and good,
> Pernicious as a poison-tree the fivefold ruin bring,
> On household gear, wasters of wealth and every precious thing.

Time and again throughout the life of the bordello the ladies in residence appear to be different creatures to the spirited rake and the jaded libertine. What remains constant is the grading of the women. Before that took place, however, the Aryans had first to put themselves in order. So it was that during the second half of the Vedic period the Indian caste system developed. At the top, at the outset, were the warriors, *Kshatryas*; followed by priests, *Brahmins*; peasants, *Vaishias*; mixed and subjugated people, *Shudras*; and those with no caste at all, *Pariahs*. For a people so fond of sorting and classifying it is not surprising to find that the public women are later divided into a dozen orders and suborders, a score of families and subfamilies, a hundred species and subspecies. By that time the *Brahmins*, as usual, would have replaced the military leaders at the top of the social pecking order.

By the time of the Buddha, in the sixth century BC, there is ample evidence of a flourishing and highly organized urban life in great Indian cities like Rajgir, Vaisali and Benares. With urbanization, as always, came an increase in the

Algerian Women in Their
Apartment, 1834
Eugene Delacroix 1798–1863
LOUVRE MUSEUM, PARIS. PHOTO BY
EDDY VAN DER VEEN/COLORIFIC

number and the stability of the bordellos. One of the first houses to be identified specifically belonged to Ambapili, a resident of Vaisali. Her relationship with the Enlightened One predates the Christian story of Mary Magdalene by 500 years. When the Buddha visited the city it was in Ambapili's mangrove garden that he slept and rested. She not only entertained him, but made a gift of her garden to him as well.

With the founding of Pataliputra as the capital of the Magadha Kingdom in the fifth century BC a refined court life devoted to physical pleasure emerged. In the *Dasa Kumara Charita*, 'The Story of the Ten Princes', a mother described the care taken in raising her daughter that might have been written by a courtesan's proud parent in Renaissance Italy:

> From earliest childhood I have bestowed the greatest care upon her, doing everything in my power to promote her health and beauty. As soon as she was old enough, I had her carefully instructed in the art of dancing, acting, playing on musical instruments, singing, painting, preparing perfumes and flowers, in writing and conversation, and even to some extent in grammar, logic and philosophy.

This was written 100 years before Alexander and Hellenism arrived at the

Indus, but it is clear that through the emphasis on grammar, logic and philosophy a common interest is already present. The Greek connection is also already evident in the language. Compare the Greek *kusos* with the Sanskrit *cushi*, both meaning waterditch, which in turn became the Latin *cunnus* and the Old English *queynte*. However, while the Greeks went about reducing their number of gods and ended questioning their very existence, the people of India pursued an opposite course which reached a point where the gods were involved in every aspect of existence, not the least in sexual relations.

To understand the place of the bordello in Hindu life, it must be recognized that sex was considered not only normal and necessary but almost sacramental. It was conceived of as the human counterpart of divine creation and the religious symbolism emphasized this on all levels of expression, from the figures sculpted on the temple walls to the postures and posturings of girls within. The Hindu concept of salvation was of the union of the individual soul with the universal, the merging of the one in the other, so, as a parallel, the union of man in woman, in which the duality was lost, for the Hindu became the symbol of liberation.

In the late Vedic period it became the custom for the first-born female of every family to be dedicated to the tribal god to whom she was supposed to be married and, for him, to be made to serve as a temple prostitute. She was required to have intercourse with the priests and other temple officials and with religious visitors for payment which purportedly would be used for the maintenance of the temple. According to the Brahmins who managed the temples: 'To have intercourse with a holy prostitute is a virtue which obliterates all sin.' No pleasure-house since has been able to boast a better advertisement.

During the height of the Jain period, the fifth century BC, the life of the princes, noblemen and merchants outside the temples became exceedingly hedonistic thanks to the growing riches of the empire. Naturally, the number of wives, concubines and slave girls at hand kept pace. The *Jnatadharma Katha I* lists the remarkable achievements of a first-class courtesan in the city of Champa. In addition to her outstanding physical qualities she was proficient in:

> The seventy-two traditional arts (song and dance and the like)
> The sixty-four erotic embraces
> The thirty-one kinds of sexual poses
> The thirty-two ways of pleasing men

This singular person was also a linguist, conversant in eighteen regional languages. The harried girl must have been so busy studying and practising and keeping her book of numbers up to date that she had little time for her fundamental enterprise on the divan.

Later, Mallanaga Vatsyayana would up the number of positions of intercourse to eighty-four, and the even more learned or imaginative Yusodhra raised the count to a mind- and body-staggering 729.

Women Resting after Their Bath
18th C Mughal Indian
BRITISH MUSEUM

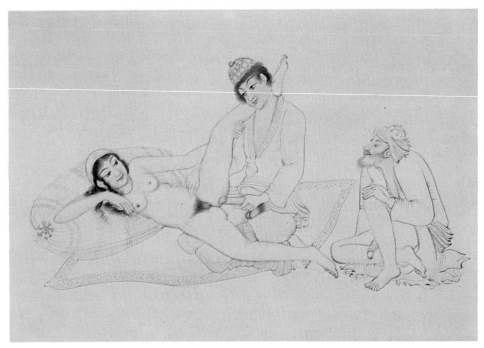

Eventually, the basic classes of public women broke down into three general groups: *kalutas*, common whores; *devadasees*, temple girls; and *ganikas*, courtesans. For the sophisticated Hindu mind, however, this was not sufficient. The *ganikas* alone were subclassified according to their secondary specialities: *tramati*, singer; *pramathi*, dancer; and the top-ranked *malkha bai*, poetess.

Although the business of sex was condoned or encouraged in temple, court and bordel, adultery definitely was not. Manu, the eminent Indian lawmaker, recommended that conjugal infidelity be treated as a capital offence. The *Manu Smriti Samhita* cites 371 separate sex offences calling for severe penalties. An adulterous husband could be burned alive; while a wife guilty of the same offence was to be devoured by dogs, just as was the infamous Jezebel.

By the Mauryan period in the third century BC, the temple entertainers were regarded as employees of the state. When a woman retired as a *devadasee*, she was re-employed by the state as a spinner of cotton, wool or flax. On the other hand, the *ganika*, as a freelance, was forced to pay a monthly tax to the authorities amounting to her average income for a two-day period. When the royal treasury was found wanting, the monthly tax rose to fifty per cent of her earnings. A fourth class of courtesan appeared now, the *rupajiva*, who rated a step up from the *ganika*. This class of woman was allowed entry to the royal court and was frequently employed as a spy. Given the freedom of both the town and the court, the *rupajiva* was able to report to the local raja both on any dissatisfactions or mutinous plans among his troops stationed in the towns and on any plots developing against him among his nobles. Here is a tradition as old as Rahab, carried on by Catherine de' Medici and Mata Hari, immortalized by Ian Fleming,

Erotic Scene
19th C Persian painting
COURTESY OF LAWRENCE E.
GICHNER

Prince Surrounded by Women
  Entertainers
18th C Mughal, India
VICTORIA AND ALBERT MUSEUM,
  LONDON

and practised with varying degrees of success by the Soviet KGB and various administrations in Washington, DC.

Whether the Indian courtesan was engaged in grave affairs of state or simply earning a living in the customary way, she usually lived in a house consisting of two rooms with an open-air kitchen at the rear. The front room was used for entertaining. Here lay a bed-like accommodation, a low pile of perfumed mattresses covered with a white counterpane with silk-covered pillows scattered at head and foot. Built against the adjoining wall and reaching to the height of the couch was a platform on which were placed a box of beeswax, garlands, lotions and perfumes, a box of perfumed powder to remove the odour of perspiration, a jar of lemon peelings and betel leaves for sweetening the breath.

On the open veranda at the front hung several cages containing multi-coloured songbirds. At the rear, beyond the kitchen area, was a garden with a swing hanging from a shadetree and a mosaic-inlaid platform covered with flowers which served as a kind of gazebo for drinking, smoking and sharing aphrodisiacs – all in all an extremely pleasant place to spend an evening or an entire night, depending on the weight of one's purse.

Flowery windowboxes decorated the London stews and stylized flower arrangements made the Japanese bordels like small art galleries, but no other culture approached the Indian when it came to floral ornamentation. The women wore garlands around their necks, flowers in their hair. The customers themselves were garlanded. The religious idols received fresh flowers every day. Even the elephants wore great wreaths of flowers in the festival parades. With sex an integral part of nature and flowers another aspect of nature, the better houses of the period seem to have been half bordello and half florists' shops. Certainly the scents were sweeter than in any house of Europe or the Middle East.

Shaykh Nefawzi wrote his Arabic treatise on sex practices at the start of the fifteenth century AD. Mallanaga Vatsyayana composed the *Kama Sutra* long before *The Perfumed Garden* was compiled, at some time between the first and fourth centuries AD. However, the second book on the behaviour of courtesans in the *Kama Sutra* is attributed to an even earlier source, a writer called Dattaka who wrote his guide on sex at the request of the public women of Pataliputra in the sixth century BC. After telling the courtesan where and when to sit at her window and how best to display her charms, these two Indian originators go on to tell her with whom she should associate to protect her life and property, starting with police officers, court officials and astrologers and ending with barbers and beggars. Next are listed the types of men she should consort with simply for the purpose of gaining money: men of independent income, young men, men who have no ties, concluding with ascetics who are troubled by internal desires and the physician to the king. Clearly the medical profession did not enjoy the prestige then that it does now.

In the years following the publication of the *Kama Sutra*, during the Gupta period which lasted until AD 525, the courtesans continued to play an important part in the royal household and in the king's court. They participated in almost all royal functions and festivals, singing and dancing, playing drums, pipes and cymbals, in addition to their fundamental duties. The start of the Arab incursions in 711 had little effect on the lives of the professional *ganika*, but as the conquest continued many would lose both their customers and all they possessed. And despite the Arab overlay, the essential Hindu sex structure was maintained.

Work on India's most famous temple started at about the same time that the Italians were building the Tower of Pisa and Henry II was doing penance at Canterbury Cathedral for having Thomas à Becket killed. Located at Puri in the

Group of Ladies
18th C Mughal Indian
BRITISH MUSEUM

State of Orissa, this enormous structure was dedicated to Vishnu, Lord of the World, fourteen years after work began in 1176. Its pyramidal shape is about the height of a sixteen-storey building and its main enclosure is somewhat larger than a football field. It was staffed by an estimated 1000 *devadasees* whose first duties were to care for and to decorate the idol of the god and then to entertain the worshippers who visited the shrine. The Hindu cult of fertility was apparently on the same level as that prevailing in Sumer 6000 years earlier.

The most notable Indian examples of sex-in-art are found at the temples at

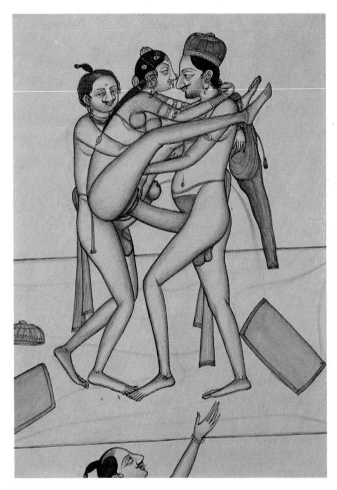

Erotic Scene
19th C Sikh School, India
COURTESY OF LAWRENCE E.
GICHNER

Konarak and Khajuraho where Tantric philosophy is reflected in sculpture. To the Western eye this erotic art may seem strange, perhaps even baffling at times. Some of the earliest temple sculptures show male and female figures standing on their heads in certain configurations meant to represent sexual intercourse. To achieve Vatsyayana's eighty-four positions – certainly to reach Yusodhra's 729 – such balancing acts would be required. A simpler explanation is that they represent specific yoga positions and religious experiences and are meant to be more symbolic than representational.

This is not to say that certain Tantric concepts are not found strange to other branches of Hinduism. Among the Saktas, for example, it was believed that the individual could rise above both good and evil, that sexual union with the goddess could be best achieved by congress in the flesh with beings below godhead. Following this logic, the ideal union was the perilous intimacy with a woman with whom one could never unite. The practitioner's objective was to reach increasingly higher levels of experience. The Sakta devotee progressed from adultery, virgin-taking and union with different castes and prostitutes, to incest, then to copulation with a demoness, and ultimately to the seventh and highest grade, union with the goddess herself. Because there is no good, there is no evil; hence, no act can be prohibited. Some Tantric sects believed that a man could attain the highest state by concentrating his mind on the soul resident in the female sex organs. The most famous temple reflecting this vision is at Gauhati in Assam and is dedicated to the goddess of love, Kamakhya.

It is not surprising, then, that when Marco Polo visited Malabar in the thirteenth century he found certain Indian customs somewhat peculiar but at the same time comfortable to his Venetian mind:

> They have certain abbeys in which are gods and goddesses to whom many young girls are consecrated; their fathers and mothers presenting them to that idol for which they entertain the greatest devotion. And when the [monks] of a convent desire to make a feast to their god, they send for all these consecrated damsels and make them sing and dance before the idol with great festivity. They also bring meats to feed their idol withal.

Later, another Western observer visiting the city of Bijangar described:

> A great bazaar of women that was six hundred yards in length, both sides of the thoroughfare lined with figures of lions, panthers, tigers and other animals that are so well painted as to seem alive. After bathing, an oil massage and a careful setting of the hair with flowers, the women appear on their verandas with a jewel and some paste of sandalwood affixing it to the forehead, a caste mark, antimony added to the eyes, pendants for the earlobes, a pearl or ring of gold for the nose, a necklace or garland around the neck, red henna for palms of the hands, a belt around the hips, preferably decorated with small bells, jewellery for the feet, and betel leaves for chewing.

Now there is a picture to catch any traveller's eye, a setting that many a subsequent madam has tried to capture but never quite did despite all the money spent on decorations and decorators. Reportedly, Bijangar's 12,000-man police force was paid entirely from bordello revenues. And, fittingly perhaps, the Avenue of Women was located directly behind the royal treasury. This convenient juxtaposition of court and cash and courtesan does not appear too different from London's or Rome's.

By the middle of the sixteenth century, Indian rajas, Arab caliphs and Turkish sultans had been replaced by Mongol emperors, descendants of Ghengis Khan and Timur the Lame. During the reign of Akbar the Great, 1556–1605, courtesans occupied a separate city adjacent to Delhi known as Shaitanpura. According to palace records the Emperor kept a large number of concubines in every city of his empire, with 800 in residence at Agra alone. In keeping with tradition, when the Mogul army was on the march, the best singers and dancers went along to entertain the military captains and generals. Great patrons of the arts, the Mogul emperors were not above playfulness. On occasion they were known to play giant games of chess, with the opponents using as pieces the most attractive women in their retinues. With the fall of the Mogul Empire, hordes of these *purdah*-ed women were driven into the streets. With no other job experience behind them, the displaced courtesans had to descend to the level of the common *kalutas*.

When the adventurous and acquisitive gentlemen of the English East India Company established their beachhead in India in 1610–11, long after the Portuguese and Dutch had dug in, all the public women they met claimed to be descendants of the unfortunate fine ladies who had been ousted from the Emperor's court. Tall tales about royal ancestry told by harlots were not unknown before, or since.

It took the British to add a fourth class of house to the traditional Indian trio of temple, court and bazaar, the *biebie-khana*. In the early years of occupation, the military men and civilians of the Honourable East India Company found their pleasures in the ordinary places where for a few annas they could be entertained. During the next two centuries, however, the tradition of the great regimental bordello developed wherein each military unit maintained its own stock of women. At times, in effect, the days of the invading Aryans were re-created, with the women following the camps on military campaigns. By the start of the nineteenth century, with more and more disapproving European women on the scene, the *biebie-khana* facility fell into disfavour. After the Mutiny of 1857, when wives and daughters fled, the *biebie-khana* had a brief resurgence. But when the British Crown took over the powers of the India Company a year later, the institution of 'the women's quarter' again went into decline.

Nevertheless, many of the Indian courtesans became number-two wives. For guidance, such a woman had only to turn to Vatsayayana's chapter in the *Kama Sutra* which would tell her everything she would need to know 'Of Living Like a Wife'. Alas, the great pedant had nothing to say on how to survive in the British caste system which was undeniably every bit as rigid as her own.

CHAPTER SIX

BLUE HOUSES, RED LANTERNS

WITH THE PASSING of the Mogul Dynasty in fourteenth-century China, as in India, the influence of European travellers like Marco Polo and his fellow Venetians wanes. However, Portuguese explorers and Christian missionaries reopen the commercial channels in the following centuries. By the middle of the eighteenth century British trade is more important than that of any other occidental people and is the monopoly of the English East India Company. Chinese teas, silk and cotton are in great demand in Europe and in the early years are paid for in gold. However, the importation of opium, chiefly from India and on British ships, continues to grow.

The trade had long been prohibited by the Manchus since the drug had been introduced by Arab traders from India in the thirteenth century. Now British merchants are insisting on more privileges than the Chinese are willing to concede and the first Opium War follows. Under the Treaty of Nanking in 1844 Hong Kong is handed over to Great Britain and the ports of Canton, Foochow, Ningpo, Amoy are opened for commerce with the White Devils.

At these harbours along the south China coast foreign merchantmen and naval vessels encountered China's unique contribution to the world's bordello tradition. Floating 'Flower Boats', some the size of contemporary excursion liners, filled the seaports as do the great floating restaurants of today. In the nineteenth century the seaborne bordels not only had sumptuous banquet facilities but dance-halls, theatres, gambling casinos and opium-smoking quarters as well. By the turn of the century twenty-seven per cent of all adult Chinese males were opium users and the narcotic had become a popular painkiller among the inhabitants of the houses catering to foreigners.

Visits to the Flower Boats were made usually on a group basis, great gangs of merchants or military men boarding together, rather as today's conventioneers gather for exhibitions and reunions. The menu, the type of entertainment and the quality and number of girls were all decided upon and ordered in advance. What with the exotic foods, the strange wines, the hard drugs, wild gaming and wicked women, many of the visitors from Victorian England literally lost their minds. Opium, of course, was not a stranger at home, as Coleridge and De Quincey attested, but the combination of wicked practices, so openly displayed, must have been unsettling indeed to the less sophisticated.

With the coming of Jack Tar and the British Tommy and tens of thousands of commercial travellers, the always flourishing business of sex reached unprecedented heights, never to be equalled again. A census of that day taken in Amoy, 300 miles northeast of Hong Kong, revealed that the busy seaport had a population of 300,000 with some 50,000 girls working in the city's 3650 bordellos, approximately one-half of the adult female population. It is doubtful that any other city in the world before or since matched that record for sinfulness.

Behind this remarkable statistic is the fact that during the years of the Manchu – or Ch'ing – administration (1644–1912), the number of Chinese people had more than tripled. For all their faults, the Manchus had provided long periods of relative peace and by the time of the first Opium War in 1839 the land could not support the vast surplus of womanpower. They were forced into the cities to survive and there the bordellos welcoming foreigners were the likeliest places to absorb their labour.

With the trade attracting worldwide celebrity, it was not long before enterprising foreigners were vying for a piece of the action. In 1851 one Madam Randall arrived in Hong Kong with a theatrical troupe from Australia. Soon, theatrical productions were forgotten and Madam Randall was advertising in the English-language newspapers that in addition to gin, brandy, sherry, port, champagne, claret, bottled beer and porter, her homey establishment was also ready to supply customers with 'A good quality of Special HONEY in small jars'. The address of the Randall house in Lyndhurst Terrace soon became famous throughout the Crown Colony and ultimately throughout the Empire. As frequently happens, after he has become accustomed to the native girls the foreign bordello patron likes a touch of home and is willing to pay the extra fee to obtain it. As a result the sales agent from Clerkenwell found himself spending a hundred times more at the Randall residence than he would have done at the Golden Lotus off Haiphong Road.

By the time of Madam Randall's arrival on the scene, between the Opium Wars, the bordello business was already well established in China. It was known on the official records at least as early as the time of K'ung Fu-tze (Confucius, 551–479 BC). Through one of those odd twists of time that pacific gentleman's name became synonymous with the martial arts and its accompanying grunts and kicks and movie mayhem. In this time, as in other early civilizations, the bordel business had its roots in slavery, with the victims of war pressed into service.

While in the process of developing their own distinctive types of bordello, the Chinese were simultaneously having a profound effect on sex practices in the other half of the known world. In the second century BC the emperor Wu-Ti

19th C Chinese painting on silk
COURTESY OF LAWRENCE E.
   GICHNER

19th C Chinese painting on silk
COURTESY OF LAWRENCE E.
   GICHNER

defeated the Hung-nu tribes and sent them packing westwards. When the Huns under Attila swept across central Europe 200 years later they put an end to the Roman military brothel system which was replaced by the local little board house, the bordel.

During the sixth century AD the Chinese in the north repulsed the Tu-Kiu who also took the advice to go west and eventually founded Turkey and the Ottoman Empire and introduced the harem to the lands of the Middle East. Still later, in the thirteenth century, Ghengis Khan and his Golden Horde of Tatars, with Chinese persuasion, headed west and then south to India where 300 years later was established the grandiose court life with courtesans galore under the greatest of Mogul emperors, Akbar the Magnificent.

With all these barbarian hordes banging incessantly at their northern gates century after century it was only reasonable that the Chinese erect the Great Wall, first built between 246–209 BC, and substantially rebuilt under the Ming Dynasty (1368–1644). It was here that the bordel first became an official military-political institution. The Great Wall might have looked formidable to the pony-riding shamanists on the northern side, but it would have been useless without a contented soldiery to man its ramparts. Women were recruited by the rulers of the Ch'ing Dynasty, who succeeded those of the Ming, to serve in the 'barracks brothels' sited strategically along its 1400-mile length. The *ying chi*, barracks harlots, not only performed their primary duties; they also trained as auxiliary soldiers and helped to defend the wall against the barbarians from Mongolia.

Almost a thousand years later, in AD 700, China experienced its first population explosion and large urban centres began to develop. Coincidentally, the owners of the bordellos, as well as other classes of businessmen, were required to restrict their pleasure-houses to certain limited areas of the new cities, the counterparts to the redlight districts established in Europe some 700 years later. Yanchow, a nexus for river transportation, became one of the wealthiest cities in the new Empire. Brothel-keepers, as always, followed the money trail here. A giant bordello area mushroomed much on the lines of Japan's later Yoshiwara. One of the main streets was lined on both sides with two-storey houses, all brightly painted, and stretched in an unbroken line for more than four miles.

During the later and more liberal T'ang period (618–906) elaborate taverns called *wa-tzu* opened in non-redlight districts. Here entertainment was offered as well as women, song and dance shows and rudimentary opera. The bordello owners favoured locations near the houses of the wine merchants so that men with their wits softened by rice wine might easily be enticed inside their premises. From all accounts, reluctant visitors might literally be hooked inside, relieved of their valuables, then tossed into the street, poorer and perhaps wiser when they sobered up. Reports of the street life at the start of the great period of Chinese literature suggest that it was no better nor worse than in London's infamous Bankside. Even during the rare intervals of peace, the administration of justice

Chinese Brothel
19th C Chinese painting
MARY EVANS PICTURE LIBRARY

was swift for evil-doers who could not come up with the necessary *kumshaw* to buy freedom or life. The Chinese have always favoured the sword and immediate decapitation was the accepted form of punishment for malefactors caught redhanded.

At night the houses lining the grand avenues in the larger cities were lit by lacy lanterns and, because most of them were painted in a celestial blue, the bordellos became known as Blue Chambers or Blue Houses and ultimately gave us the term Blue Movie. The working women themselves were euphemistically called 'Jade Girls' or 'Fairies of the Night'.

The Emperor's capital at Ch'and An was nearly as large as present-day Paris and was governed not by nobles or hereditary gentry but by a professional civil service which the British were to imitate a millennium later under Queen Victoria. Just as the invention of the plough led to village life in Europe, the development of irrigation in China led to the institution of the Civil Service. In order to oversee the distribution of water among the millions of individual rice paddies and to prevent squabbles and even bloodshed between neighbours, a hierarchy of countless thousands of administrators was established. From China came the world's first bureaucrat.

The following Sung Dynasty, 960–1279, produced an age of sophisticated luxury and dalliance. Hangchow became a city of pleasure gardens and graceful pagodas, of taverns where travellers drank spiced wines from silver cups and restaurants where the visiting Marco Polo enjoyed the flavoured ices he would later introduce into Italy. Paper was the money of exchange, backed by the royal treasury. A free dispensary, financed by the state, supplied medicines to the poor. And with her receipts of the night before, the singsong girl could buy ingenious toys, printed books and fans and a wide variety of cosmetics and even toilet paper.

When Marco Polo visited the royal court during the Yuan period, 1279–1368, he reported, '. . . the Emperor has four wives of the first rank, who are esteemed as legitimate. They bear equally the title of Empress and have their separate courts. None of them has fewer than three hundred young female attendants of great beauty, together with a multitude of youths as pages and other eunuchs, as well as ladies of the bedchamber, so that the number of persons belonging to each of their courts amounts to ten thousand.' The Emperor's courtesans, Marco found, 'were attired with great magnificence, heavily perfumed and attended by many handmaids and lodged in richly ornamented apartments'. Just below the courtesans, in and out of court, the Venetian merchant rated 'the singsong girls' who kept the cups full at the taverns and teahouses and sold their favours in adjoining rooms; the flower girls in the ornately painted and lantern-lit boats on the lakes; and, finally, their sisters in the brothels who advertised their business with a bamboo-shaded lamp over the entrance. All these the adventurous Polo summed up as 'a multitude of sinful women'.

19th C Chinese painting on silk
COURTESY OF LAWRENCE E.
   GICHNER

19th C Chinese painting on silk
COURTESY OF LAWRENCE E.
   GICHNER

The vast majority of courtesans in the royal household came from the north because it was the custom of the Emperor each year to send his commissioners to the province of Ungut where the women were known for their beauty and fair complexions. From all the girls in the province between twelve and sixteen years, the contest judges selected between 400 and 500 and sent them to court. Here they were re-examined and evaluated on a point basis for beauty of hair, eyes, eyebrows, mouth and the rest and for the symmetry of these in combination. The thirty or forty girls who received twenty-one or more points were sent to the Emperor's quarters while the remaining 400-odd were parcelled out to the lesser dignitaries of the court.

Needless to say, life was not always serene within the royal compound. One Imperial princess reportedly cut off the nose, ears and breasts of one of her competitors in a fit of pique and threw them into the Emperor's lap. The crime went unpunished. The court rivalries among the courtesans more than once brought China to the brink of ruin.

During the Ming period, 1368–1644, the fattest, the most extravagant and the most obnoxious of the Emperor's women, Yang Kuei-fei, was responsible for a multitude of disasters. From 1000 miles to the south relays of horsemen were employed to bring her fresh lychees to be enjoyed at breakfast each day. Like Jezebel she brought hundreds of her clansmen under the aegis of Imperial favour and had her feeble-minded brother appointed to the office of prime minister. She was both extravagant and unfaithful. Her private summer palace contained sixteen marble baths; her lover was a gross Tatar general who from his position of advantage led an insurrection which forced the Emperor to flee his royal palace. When the general's troops mutinied in their turn, they murdered Yang's sister, fed her brother's head to the pariah dogs and with the unrepentant Yang's sanction, strangled her with a silk cord, a practice reserved for upper-class royal favourites. A little mutilation might be winked at but not outright mutiny.

Naturally, only a very small portion of the female Chinese population ever got close to the Emperor's bedchamber. Confucius had put them in their place centuries earlier: 'Only women and small men are hard to keep. If you allow them close, they show no respect. If you keep them at a distance, they bear a grudge.' On the other hand, the boy baby was adored and when he grew to manhood he was expected to play around with courtesans and singsong girls even after marriage. A wife could be divorced summarily for either being too talkative or for committing adultery.

Against this background a time of great artistic and literary activity unfolded under the Mings. The poets of the courts and bordellos sang of 'Fallen Flowers', 'Flowers on the Wall', or 'Women of the Wind'. The pleasure-houses themselves were termed 'Hostels of the Singsong Girls', *ch'ang-chi*, or 'The Green Bowers of the Ladies', *ch'ing lou*. These damp-eyed poets and painters of the bedroom would have their counterparts in the brothels of Paris in the nineteenth century.

Chinese scholars prepared handbooks on how to behave in the Blue Houses akin to those by Vatsyayana and Nefzawi. The instructions and warnings are generally very courtly but tend at times to be somewhat cynical: 'Do not always believe her flattery or loving words!' In counterpoint, Sung K'ang's *Sisters of the Green Bower* contains the advice of a madam to her charges: 'Do not comment on the smallness of his Jade Stem. Make him feel that he is a Dragon-Lover'; and, 'If he returns several times in a single week, raise your prices!' The advisor to the girls in the bower also listed a variety of aphrodisiacs with which to ply their clients. Birds'-nest soup was much favoured. On the whole, the more expensive the love-food, the greater its anticipated potency. And the larger the customer's bill whatever the effect. Only untutored Westerners were foolish enough to try mixing powdered rhino-horn with opium in the dens of iniquity.

In fiction the Chinese approach to sex was even-tempered and almost matter of fact. The long comic-adventure novel *Chin P'ing Mei*, translated as *The Golden Lotus*, was considered so pornographic when first published in English that many sections were printed in Latin. The Chinese author, however, was not trying to be salacious. He merely reported his hero's sexual antics with the same

Courtesans Waiting on a Nobleman
Japanese woodcut by Utamaro
1753–1806
BRITISH MUSEUM

Flowerboat
19th C Japanese woodblock
COURTESY OF LAWRENCE E.
GICHNER

fond detail he gave to his other high-spirited adventures.

On another level the male and female elements which the Indians called *lingam* and *yoni*, symbolized by pestle and mortar, the more metaphysical Chinese called *yang* and *yin*, both physical and spiritual essences. When using metaphors for sexual congress the Hindu spoke in terms of deer, hares, horses, bulls and elephants; his Chinese counterpart wrote of 'The Butterfly Exploring the Flower', 'The Bee Stirring the Honey', 'The Erring Bird Returning to the Forest', 'The Hungry Steed Rushing to the Trough', and, the eighth position, 'The Posture of the Gobbling Fishes'.

Chinese paintings portraying bordello types and activities are generally light and airy with none of the smoky, murky qualities associated with similar premises in the West. The performers are delicate and almost whimsical in their embraces. Compared with contemporary Japanese figures they appear at times even ethereal. Outside the wood and paper bordels the ubiquitous, cloud-enshrouded mountains rise, while inside the house similar scenes appear painted on silk screens. For support the participants use chairs and lacquered tables, padded stools and reeds on the floor. Clearly, anything as cumbrous and awkward as a four-poster would be out of place in a Blue House or a Green Bower.

During the Ming period marvellous new amenities appeared to revitalize the hoary institution. As an offshoot of the military brothels established along the Great Wall, new houses were built for the exclusive use of the various grades of civil servants who administered the different provinces of the vast empire. The women who worked in these innovative establishments were given official status, receiving their salaries directly from government coffers instead of from the patrons. What the girls lost in incentive bonuses they more than made up for in security and peace of mind. Many ended up as the wives of powerful provincial governors. Soon the bureaucrats who held high government service posts enjoyed pleasure-houses which in winter were heated by coal-fed copper stoves and in summer were air-conditioned by ice stored in deep pits beneath the buildings. Such luxury in the other bordellos of the world would not be known until the middle of the twentieth century.

By the time the Westerners arrived in their great numbers in the middle of the nineteenth century, the Manchus had shaken up the complacent and frequently corrupt civil service. Its members were forbidden to visit bordellos under the threat of death. In the cities and towns registers were kept of all the prostitutes, but licensing was no longer required and the singsong and flower girls found themselves off the government payroll.

By the tens of thousands the displaced women flocked to the coastal cities which had been turned over to the foreigners for every kind of commerce under the terms of the Nanking Treaty. Here gin replaced rice wine in the taverns to loosen purse-strings. Under the Treaty of Tientsin in 1858 which terminated the Second Opium War, a price was set for the narcotic, in effect legalizing it for the first time. The British traders had achieved their goal. Not just the bordellos but the entire nation went into a long period of decline.

In neighbouring Japan the very opposite was true. There the Western world got its first comprehensive look at Japanese customs through the Americans, rather than through the British as was the case in India and China. Although the Jesuits had been in the islands since the sixteenth century spreading their brand of Christianity, it remained for Commodore Perry and his squadron of warships to negotiate a treaty of peace and friendship with the Japanese shogun in 1854. In India the bordello had its roots in religion; in China in Confucian philosophy and ethics. In Japan both traditions would be carried to their logical extremes.

With what equanimity the Japanese took this nineteenth-century invasion of barbarian sailors from the Americas is illustrated by two prints of the period. The first shows a big, long-haired and black-bearded American seaman with wine cup in hand. He is grinning salaciously at a courtesan who is offering him a giant bottle of *saké*. In the second print, the hostess has just given birth to a bouncing baby boy, the product, it would appear, of international relations. The infant is the size of a four-year-old and is blessed with long hair and a full beard and moustache. Dad is grinning, Mom is smiling and the midwife is utterly appalled.

Institutionalized sexual relations were approved by the freewheeling Japanese, but only by, for and between Japanese. When the Americans arrived, Tokyo's Yoshiwara – the name originated from the reedy swamp of the original site – the bordello district, had been in existence for 237 years. At its peak in the nineteenth century the Yoshiwara was accommodating more than two million customers a year.

The tradition of public prostitution in Japan was far older. As in India, and even earlier in the Middle East, temple-brothels were intimately connected with the various aspects of phallic worship. The Japanese should not have been surprised by the hirsute appearance of the Americans. Their ancestors, arriving from China through Korea, had done away for the most part with the original settlers of the archipelago, the dark-bearded, long-haired Ainu, who themselves had come from the steppes of northern Asia through the Sakhalin Islands.

Eventually, the phallic deities of the Shintoists, the *Sahe No Kami*, were worshipped throughout the islands of Japan. The giant symbols in common use in the temples were thought to possess powerful healing properties in themselves. *Konsei Myojin* was deified with images and replicas in temples. This was hardly an all-male self-admiration cult, however. The Venus of Japan, the *Kwan-Non*, symbolizing the female principle, received similar veneration. The shrines connected with such worship carried a wide range of sexual devices on their walls and the girls lived on the grounds, dedicated to the service of the sex goddess.

This service was commonly expressed through sacred prostitution, and in some orders the women were obviously selected for their youthful attractiveness. One order of particularly beautiful girls called *kikuni* lived in houses resembling the nunneries of Europe. Significantly, they were recruited on the basis of their good looks and their pliability. One of their common recruiting grounds was the secular, commercial bordello. In part, this practice of bordel-raiding for talent prompted one brothel-master of Yedo – early Tokyo – to call for a Japanese counterpart of the Bankside. Under the leadership of Shoji Junyemon, the construction of the first Yoshiwara district started in 1612, a year when James I was on the throne in England and the Puritans were calling for an end to dancing, sports and other public entertainments. The hundred square miles of the Yoshiwara, called 'The Floating World' and given over to all the pleasures of sex, was completed in 1617, a year after the death of Shakespeare. The regulations laid down by the central government were much simpler than Henry II's ordinances governing the Bankside and accomplished easily what many popes and kings had failed to do previously:

1 The profession of brothel-keeping shall not be carried out in any place other than the regular prostitution quarter and in future no request for the attendance of a courtesan at a place outside the limits of the enclosure shall be complied with.

2 No guest shall remain in a brothel for more than twenty-four hours.

3 Prostitutes are forbidden to wear clothes with gold and silver embroidery on them; they are to wear ordinary dyed stuffs.

4 Brothels are not to be built of imposing appearance and the inhabitants of prostitute quarters shall discharge the same duties as ordinary residents (firemen etc.) in other parts of Yedo city.

5 Proper enquiries shall be instituted into the person of any visitor to a brothel, no matter whether he be gentleman or commoner, and in case any suspicious individual appears, information shall be given to the *Boggo sho* (office of the city Governor). The above instructions are to be strictly observed.

(signed) The Boggo

Woman Kissing a Baby
Japanese woodcut by Utamaro
1753–1806
BRITISH MUSEUM

If little else was accomplished, the Boggo's orders defined the bordello district. It is interesting that at least half the edict concerned the character of the patrons. Concern with ostentatious dress by the women always appears when the self-declared upper classes feel threatened as the lower classes cannot distinguish between them and the ladies of the evening. And, as usual, rules for a redlight district look good on paper; how the Yoshiwara grew and blossomed in reality is quite another matter. One major factor in its formation was the order of Buddhism called Zen, widespread in Japan since the twelfth century. A second contribution of equal importance was made by the samurai, those knights of the Orient. When not doing battle for their shoguns, or testing their swords on the necks of the peasants, they found themselves with a good deal of idle time. How better to spend it than by meditating on the principles of Zen, making rock and sand gardens, dwarfing trees and creating rituals for everything from dressing to tea drinking? Just as the layabouts in the castles of medieval Europe busied themselves developing the intricate codes of chivalry, so the bored Japanese swordsmen set the tone for an entire civilization by making the very least of human endeavours follow a ritualistic form.

The women of Japan were no different from those in many other parts of the world where ladies of the court dressed as nuns or milkmaids and the courtesans dressed like nobility. The courtesies and disciplines of Zen found their way into the bordellos quite early. The ideals of Zen were reflected in the music and dance of the courtesans, in their clothing and in the way they set their hair, in the way they walked and talked, in the table settings, even in the pouring of rice wine and tea. Except in the basest of the low houses, everything was ritual and ceremony. While the Hindu harlot concerned herself with a profusion of flowers, her Japanese counterpart busied herself making sure the flowers in the delicate vase were arranged just so.

Some of the women in the Yoshiwara came from the ruling classes of the society. If a member of a samurai's family transgressed one of the clan's laws deemed that she could be sent away by her family for a period of five to seven years. Some may have welcomed the release from family pressures, but for most it was lasting disgrace. These *yakho*, however, made up a very small part of the bordello population. Bad crops, fires, floods, earthquakes and the inevitable wars between the shoguns were the natural allies of the brothel-masters. After every natural or man-made disaster the brothel-owners found a new supply of refugees eager to enter their houses as a way to survive.

In a society just as class-conscious as the English or the Hindu, the Japanese quite naturally defined many levels for the courtesans. In descending order they were *Tayu, Koshi-joro, Tsu-bone, Sancha-joro, Umecca-joro* and *Kirimise-joro*. The houses themselves were similarly graded. The prices were comparable to those existing in the United States today when all the gratuities were added to the basic bill.

Courtesan
Japanese woodcut by Utamaro
1753–1806
BRITISH MUSEUM

Just as the stove that heated the bathwater made the English stew synonymous with bordello, so the Japanese word for the brothel, *kutsuwa*, came to
identify the owner of the house. One theory holds that *kutsuwa* comes from the
Chinese character which stands for 'forget eight', implying that when one entered
the houses of The Floating World one immediately forgot the eight virtues: filial
piety, brotherly kindness, loyalty, faithfulness, politeness, righteousness,
integrity and the sense of shame. Those the customer could forget, but he must
not forget to take with him a large bag of money because there were many palms
to cross.

First, the customer had to contend with the *yarite* whose job it was to manage
the establishment while the owner occupied himself with other affairs. She
combined the roles of a French *concierge*, and English housemother and an Italian
ruffina. No one could fill this important post without a thorough knowledge of
the ins and outs of the Yoshiwara so that for the most part the *yarite* – later 'auntie'
– was picked from the ranks of the courtesans who had served their time on the
mats and had retired from active duty. In the upper-class houses she would have a
shinzo who acted as assistant manager.

On hand, too, was the *wakaimono*, 'the young man', no matter what his age
or physical condition. He was watchman, guard, bouncer, bathroom and bedroom attendant and handled all the room-service business of a modern hotel.
Every courtesan worthy of the name had at least one or two personal maids,
kamuro, who entered the house when still children. They were taught how to
play musical instruments, to arrange flowers, to perform the tea ceremony and to
assist the courtesan with her elaborate makeup and costuming. If they made
good, they would one day become courtesans themselves.

Before running this gauntlet of outstretched hands anticipating 'tea money',
the customer had to go through certain other formalities. Upon presenting
himself at the house he was greeted by delighted cries of '*Irrasshai! Irrasshai!*'
from the brothel manager and her assistant, a greeting that announced that the
entire household had anxiously been awaiting his arrival and his alone. If he were
a stranger to the house and had no particular *oiran* in mind, he would be
questioned about his tastes: tall girl, short girl, slim girl, fat girl. (In later years
photograph albums would be produced for his inspection.) Once the selection
had been made, the courtesan's maid appeared and conducted him to the proper
quarters. Here the child performed *mawasa*, bustling about to make sure that
everything was in order for the guest's comfort and the entrance of the courtesan.
If the gentleman desired the entertainment of a *geisha*, the tiny maid would
arrange for this, too.

Just as the first European visitors to the Middle East were confused by the
harem, so later Western travellers to Japan were puzzled by the *geishas* and never
did quite figure out the place of these women in the bordello scheme. *Gei*
translates as 'art' and *sha* as 'person'. These 'art persons' were trained as

entertainers of men, singers and dancers, and were educated in the hundreds of ceremonies that defined Japanese culture. They were not prostitutes and in the early days were forbidden to compete with the courtesans. Later, they might be kept by wealthy men as a separate class of super-courtesan. But for the average bordello-goer they were strictly entertainers and their price was high. In effect, they served as a warm-up act for the real business which was to follow.

To complicate matters further for the Western observer the customer might opt for a *san-san ku-do* ceremony, a custom not unknown to Teutones and Arabs, by which he took a 'temporary wife', with customer and courtesan going through the ceremony of a legitimate nuptial agreement. This perhaps eased the consciences of some patrons, married or not themselves. The practice is no stranger, perhaps, than the Western taboo which forbids a client from kissing the mouth of a prostitute because it would be too intimate an act.

The Japanese regulations under which a woman could join the ranks of professional courtesans smacked more of Imperial Rome than of the Royal Bankside. First, the Japanese maiden had to submit a written petition to her local police station which declared that she was over sixteen. She had then to present a document of consent, signed and sealed by her parents or legal guardian. The other seven requirements for information sounded much like those demanded when one applies for a passport today: proof of birthplace, reason for travel request, intended length of stay and the like, very formal, very reasonable.

A certificate of health was also demanded of her, but nothing was said about other physical qualities. Some degree of attractiveness, except in the lowest houses, would obviously be required. Writing of the ideal beauty in the seventeenth century Ihara Saikaku reported:

> Her face holds the glaze of poise, is smoothly rounded, her colour is pale pearl-pink cherry blossoms. Her features contain no single flaw. The eyes are not narrow, the brows are thick but do not grow together. The nose is so straight, the mouth so small, all the teeth white and regular. As for the ears, charmingly long with the most delicate rims and stand away from the hair so that one can see where they join the head.

If Saikaku had mentioned the colour of the hair as being blonde we might well confuse him with Agnolo Firenzuola describing the ideal beauty of the Renaissance. In Japan, however, this concern with the beauty of the face hardly seems justified because the entire countenance would be masked. Making up the head and hair was a ritual as stylized as the most formal tea ceremony. After scrubbing the face clean, the courtesan first put on a base of camellia oil, then added a thick half-mask undercoating. Over this a layer of white was applied and the pink and white were then blended to achieve an ivory look. Next, red eyebrows were painted on, then overlayed with black so that only a thin line of red was revealed. A bright rosebud mouth was painted on above the white-coated throat and shoulders. The neck, that great erogenous zone for the Japanese male, was similarly painted and powdered.

If making up was a chore, dressing the body was a labour. A manual on proper robing advised:

> First put on a white undershirt and white underskirt and an undersash. Then don the white socks. The undergarments are tied at the waist with a waist-tie and an undersash. The robe is slipped on, putting the right side under the left side. This is closed tightly with a waist-tie, just below the waist. Now tie another waist-tie about the waist and wind an undersash around the waist. . .

These directions go on and on, seemingly for ever, with more waist-ties and sashes and *obis* added and twisted and rolled into tubes until the poor girl sounds more like an upholstered mummy than a sex-object. When it is considered that all this would have to be undone before the customer could possibly fulfil his primary intent, it becomes clear that the disrobing was as much a part of the titillating ceremony as the rest of the rigmarole.

For all the wrapping and tying the work was still not complete. The courtesan's bound-up hair – later a wig – was pierced with a variety of pins and bones and bedecked with jewels and a variety of shell combs and coronets. On her feet she wore wooden platforms called *geta* which made the high-heeled *choppines* of the Venetian ladies seem comfortable in comparison. Some *geta* were twelve inches high and a pair of maids were required to support the ambulatory courtesan. None the less, her special walk induced by the extravagant platforms was called *nukiashi chu-binera*, 'grace-footed sway-hips in voluptuous movings'.

The paying visitor would be greeted by this work of art in the first of her three rooms, the *zashiki*, which was furnished with eight mats and decorated with screens, scrolls and artistic calligraphy. Here the courtesan also kept her musical instruments and books of love poetry. From this parlour the client moved eventually into the reception-room where *saké* was served for a price which would appear later on his bill. Here a few verbal intimacies might be exchanged before he moved on to the third plateau in this ritual of stylized fornication.

Except for a brief period following the American incursion in the middle of the nineteenth century, beds were unknown in the Japanese bordello. Once the customer had moved from reception-room to the sleeping chamber proper, a *futon*, or mattress, was rolled out on the floor. A second was laid atop this and in first-class houses three *futons* were used. These were covered with red crêpe in the better houses and were bordered with black velvet to give the impression of *kagami-buton*, 'a mirror in its frame'.

When the beauty of a bordello's women or its excellent cuisine failed to attract enough customers in the years following the arrival of the American and European traders, the bordel-owners decided that it would pay to advertise, chiefly with handbills. One such proudly announced:

> .I have engaged a large number of *filles de joie* who are guaranteed to afford satisfaction to guests in every respect, and I propose to pay scrupulous attention to the

Leading Courtesan in Her
  Household
From the film *The Scent of Incense*
NEW YORK PUBLIC LIBRARY

quality of *saké*, food and bedding. I shall be greatly obliged if you will kindly inform your friends of these improvements introduced by me and earnestly beg that you will favour me with a visit, either in the day time or the night time. . .

The advertiser goes on to say that he supplies the Masamune brand of *saké* exclusively and swears that his menu is equal to that of the finest restaurants in the city.

On-site advertising was done by the girls themselves, at least in the cheapest bordels. After nightfall, when the lamps were lighted, the girls were exhibited in long, narrow cages along the sides of the brothel facing the street where they sat with rouged lips and powdered faces looking like an array of wax dolls. With the coming of photography, the more progressive houses placed framed portraits of the cocottes on the outer walls. After 1882 the larger establishments provided prospective clients with albums containing pictures of the residents. While the gentleman caller perused the *shashin mitate-cho*, the auntie of the house extolled the physical and spiritual virtues of each girl as well as her qualities as an entertainer. A pretty voice was often as valuable an enticement as a pretty face and a girl familiar with the poetry of old was highly prized. A recitation of a piece by the ninth-century poet Ono No Yoshiki never failed to catch at a visitor's heart:

My love
Is like the grasses
Hidden in the deep mountain:
Though its abundance increases,
There is none that knows.

The food was frequently as important to the total environment as the poetry
and the brand of *saké* available. A typical menu was sure to include such listings as
chopped burdock root fried in *goma* oil, dried young sardines roasted and boiled
in sugar and soy, seaweed, river mushrooms, salted fern roots, conch flavoured
with the young leaves of the *sansho* plant, lotus roots and a dozen other different
kinds of fish, raw or cooked.

For the client whose sexual appetite needed stimulating, powdered horn of
rhinoceros and the ever-popular Chinese ginseng root were available. Another
favourite aphrodisiac was *fugu*, the Japanese blowfish. This was not only an
expensive item but a dangerous one as well. Unless properly gutted, minute
quantities of tetroxin, contained in the liver of the male and the ovaries of the
female, could find their way into the stomach of the customer and his ardour
would be cooled for ever. An ounce of the toxin is sufficient to kill 30,000 people.
Few other nations had a love potion comparable to this.

When it came to charms and superstitions, the courtesans of Japan were on a
par with those of Europe. A knot tied in a courtesan's petticoat would send an
unwanted client away. Warm ashes under the bedclothes near his feet would
rouse him from the deepest sleep and send him packing. Curly-haired men were
thought to be lecherous beyond all reason. A sneeze was full of omens. Sneeze
once, someone was saying good things about you. Sneeze twice, someone was
saying bad things about you. Three times, someone is in love with you. Four
times, you've caught a cold.

One could, of course, catch a cold simply by plucking lint from the navel. On
the other hand, if one put a mushroom in the navel, one would become seasick.
Shaking one's legs brought on a severe case of poverty. Cutting toenails after
nightfall brought bewitchment. And as every Italian *strega* well knew, placing
human hair or nail clippings in a fire brought madness.

For the *geishas* and courtesans alike another sort of madness was induced by
kabuki actors and *sumo* wrestlers. The tales of the women who lost their heads
and hearts over these professional performers were legion. The fact that a goodly
share of the actors were homosexuals and most of the wrestlers impotent did little
to diminish the passion of the night-ladies for these types, no more than today's
young music-lovers are turned off by reports that their idols may be as gay as
springtime or impotent as mules through drug abuse.

The suicide rate among the residents of the Yoshiwara was always high, but
then so is the rate for all Japanese because it is not considered sinful, and more
likely honourable. The double suicide of courtesan and favoured client was

commonplace and called *shinju* or *aitai-jinji*, death by mutual consent. During the seventeenth and eighteenth centuries *shinju* was so popular that for self-protection the brothel-keepers were forced to expose the bodies of the girl and her customer to the public to dispel any rumours that their houses were unsafe to the health of the customers.

The Japanese bordellos may not have harboured many murderers, but certainly they did not bring long life to their women in residence. All the Japanese counterparts of the great Renaissance courtesans like Imperia, Beatrice, and Nana died young. Tamakoto, at one time the most celebrated resident of the Yoshiwara, succumbed at twenty-five. Usugumo (Pretty Cloud) and Kaoru (Sweet Smell), two other courtesans with national reputations, were not much older when they died. Whatever today's sexologists have to say about it, a very active sex life need not be conducive to long life. Too much *saké* night after night with the clients was little help either.

Whereas the Arabs were inclined to be quite literal in their use of metaphors when it came to the activities of sex, and the Indians to turn to the animal kingdom for comparisons, the Japanese, like their Chinese antecedents, showed a penchant for botany. The images include 'splitting the melon', 'the tree of flesh', 'black moss mingling with dew', 'fruit seeking the seed' and 'twirling the flower stem'. All this seems more appropriate for the garden party than the bedchamber, although it does fall more pleasantly on the ear than the Anglo-Saxon equivalents for the same business.

The great seventeenth-century fires of Tokyo and London fell within a few years of one another. On 2 March 1657, when the cherry blossoms were in bloom, a fire broke out in a temple which raged throughout the city for three days and three nights and burned to death 108,000 people. Arson was attributed to a mad temple priest. The Yoshiwara perished in the flames, but like the Phoenix another nightless city rose from the ashes, twice as big as its predecessor. A century later, this Yoshiwara also burned to the ground. The Japanese rebuilt it. Every five years thereafter serious fires broke out and each time the indefatigable Japanese rebuilt their 'City of Intemperance and Wantonness'. By the end of the nineteenth century there had been at least twenty more great conflagrations which laid waste the Yoshiwara. The Great Earthquake of 1923 was followed by a fire that levelled twenty-five square miles of the city, including the Yoshiwara. Undaunted, the resourceful Japanese rebuilt their pleasure-city once again with an almost manic determination to see it live for ever.

Despite all this dedication, the elaborate ceremonies, the poetry readings and the talk of fitting birds to their nests, the reality was not much different from that in the houses of London, Rome and Istanbul, of Baghdad, Delhi and Peking. In the 1920s the writer Fujimoto described the attitude prevailing in most of the bordellos thus:

The visitor must always be very attentive, otherwise his purse would be squeezed out by the clerks and maid-servants of the place. Those in these houses, as well as the girls themselves, cannot be said to be honest and kind, and if they see a guest to be a provincial or unaccustomed to this quarter, their endeavours to lure him into temptations are so dreadful that he would be at last compelled to spend all the money in his pockets.

East or West, the message is the same, even when couched in decorous Japanese phrases: protect your back and your purse at all times because the name of the game is money. But it was not to last too much longer in the Yoshiwara. A disaster far greater than the Great Earthquake lay ahead for the city of a million red lanterns. Almost exactly a century after Commodore Perry arrived with his warships, the Americans would return and through their influence the seemingly immortal Yoshiwara would be wiped out, apparently for ever.

CHAPTER SEVEN

OF BROTHEL HOUSE
AND KINGS

WHILE VARIOUS Companies of Honourable Gentlemen and their American counterparts are revolutionizing life throughout Asia, another revolution is taking place on the homefronts. In the first half of the eighteenth century pig-iron production triples in England and the flying shuttle is invented by John Kay. The Industrial Revolution gets under way. Less noticeable at first is the revolution in the bordello industry as the population shifts from bucolic farm to boisterous city. Not since the days of the Crusaders has there been such a superabundance of womanpower in the industrializing urban centres. As a result, a whole new cottage industry springs up in the shadows of the factories and workshops.

Before long, the moralists are shaking their sticks furiously. The Black Lists of the Society for the Reformation of Manners in 1719 contains copious references to the fast-growing number of prostitutes in the streets and lanes of London where country girls are soliciting gentlemen to visit their lodgings. The Lists call particular attention to one Fanny Hussey who has six convictions for prostitution in one year and to the incorrigible Many Sanford who garners ten. Apparently, revolving-door justice was as common in that time as it is in our own.

For the poor there were alehouses. The middle and upper classes had their clubs. And there were taverns for all. Women as well as men came to the taverns and many of the women were for sale. Almost as popular were the theatres with their nearby brothels. Watchful preachers complained that 'to the said plays and interludes great numbers of men, idle and disorderly people do commonly resort and after the performance is over from thence they go to the bawdy houses'. But it was not just the indolent who enjoyed the trade. Nearly all classes who could afford it patronized prostitutes and it was tacitly agreed to condone the habit as unavoidable, given the contemporary stage of male development. The scene was coloured with a sprinkling of black doxies who drew customers from the nobility. Boswell describes Lord Pembroke as exhausted after a night 'in a black bawdy house'. Dr Johnson himself was moved to observe that not since ancient Rome or medieval Istanbul had history known so vast and rich and complex a city as London.

The Haymarket at Midnight
*London Labour and the London
Poor* by Henry Mayhew 1812–87
BBC HULTON PICTURE LIBRARY

Many of the women who gave the city its vibrancy were equally enthralling. Kitty Fisher was one, a girl of humble origins who rose to great prominence in British society. Born Catherine Maria Fisher of German parents in Soho in 1738, she was apprenticed to a milliner while in her teens. Like the theatre, milliners' shops were great showcases for girls with ambitions in the courtesan trade. Soon she was set up in her own digs by Army Ensign Anthony Martin. When Martin was posted overseas Kitty found a new supporter in Thomas Medlycott, heir to a great fortune, who taught her decent manners and instructed her in the grand fashions of the day. Medlycott was soon followed by Navy officer Augustus Koppel who introduced her to high society. Koppel, in turn, was succeeded by such admirers as Admiral Lord George Anson, General John Ligonier and Edward, Duke of York, the brother of the future George III. During her six-year reign as quean of London society she rubbed shoulders with King George II, prime minister William Pitt the Elder, the peripatetic Casanova and was much admired by the poet Oliver Goldsmith. At the peak of her success her price was 100 guineas a night. When the Duke of York unwisely gave her a £50 note she

Raid by the Law on Prostitutes, *c.*
1780
Engraving from *Moeurs et
Coutumes de L'Ancien Paris* by
H. Guttmann
BBC HULTON PICTURE LIBRARY

threw him out of bed. Reportedly, she then had the banknote baked in a pie which she ate for breakfast. In 1769 Kitty married John Norris, Member of Parliament, and died five months later at the age of twenty-nine.

Far from all of Kitty's sisters reached such eminence. By 1770 it was estimated that one of every ten women in London was into whoring. During the reign of George III (1738–1820) philanthropist Jonas Hanway reckoned that 3000 Londoners were dying of venereal disease each year. An even greater scourge loomed, however. Cheap gin replaced beer as the national drink. The frightful consequences of that change were captured by Hogarth when he compared the horrors of Gin Lane with prosperous Beer Street. One out of every eight deaths was attributed to gin-drinking, while total deaths outnumbered births in the London region by two to one.

Small wonder that so many city people used gin to deaden their senses: a large part of the population was packed into slums filthy with garbage and offal, breeding grounds for numberless diseases. In the Wapping and Limehouse sections of London every other inhabitant lived from hand to mouth, depending utterly on charity or prostitution. Here, too, the thieves, highwaymen and professional assassins made their homes. One gang, calling themselves the 'Mohocks' with wild redmen of the New World in mind, amused themselves by pricking gentlemen with their swords, making women stand on their heads in the street, and gouged out the eyes of victims who were reluctant to play their games. 'Thieves and robbers,' Tobias Smollett reported in 1730, 'were now become more desperate and savage than they had ever appeared since mankind were civilized.' Two decades later Horace Walpole observed that, 'One is forced to travel even at noon as if one were going to battle.'

It was against this background that the women plied their trade. They were found in the taverns of the city and in roadside inns, in city gardens and at public dances, at concerts and, as always, in the theatres in ever-growing numbers. In Exeter Street and the Strand they sat at their windows, like the whores of Hamburg today, to entice passers-by. Novelist Henry Fielding of *Tom Jones* fame took the time and trouble to conduct his own survey and found that there were thirty bordellos in St Mary-le-Bone alone, another thirty in Hedge Lane. The business of the Bankside had bounced across the Thames and was spreading throughout every level of society.

Despite the generally cavalier attitude of the population, the law at times had no mercy on the women of the street. If found soliciting, they were taken to be whipped and pilloried. The *Grub Street Journal* described the fate of one such wretch: 'Yesterday the noted Mother Needham stood in the pillory in Park Place near St James's Street and was severely handled by the population. She was so very ill that she lay along the pillory, notwithstanding which she was severely pelted, and it is thought that she will die in a day or two.'

For the most part, however, only the poorest of the poor reached the pillory. More often than not the street solicitors evaded the law by bribery or their pimps and landlords bailed them out. Occasionally there were popular outbursts against the brothels, but to little effect. Samuel Pepys in the seventeenth century quotes Charles II as saying, 'If the public don't like the brothels, they need not go to them.' By the reign of George III (1760–1820), bordello-hopping was an established feature of London life. Certainly there was no want for accommodation. If the figure of 2000 bawdy houses is correct for the time, there was one bordel for every fifty adult males in London.

The better-class houses were found in the Westminster district. One contemporary observer wrote: 'There are so many noted houses, situated in the neighbourhood of St James's, where a great number [of women] are kept for people of fashion. A little street called King's Place is inhabited by nuns of this

Reception Room of a Bordello,
  1830
Lithograph of *Bazard du beau sexe*
  by Carnavalet
PHOTO BY BULLOZ, PARIS

order alone, who live under the direction of several rich abbesses.' George III himself maintained a number of houses near St James's Palace for his private use. The occupants were not allowed to walk about the town, but had to confine their promenading to the royal parks. If George had devoted more time to affairs of state and less to the light-ladies the business of the American colonies might have turned out quite differently.

Le Serail Parisien, 1802
Alphonse Naudet
COURTAULD INSTITUTE OF ART,
LONDON

Much of the credit for the new diversity and sophistication that entered eighteenth-century English bordel life must be given to Mrs Goadby of Berwick Square, Soho, who opened her revolutionary house in 1750, the same year the English Jockey Club was founded in London and the Hambledon Cricket Club in Hampshire. The visionary Mrs Goadby had done her research in the famous houses of Justine and Montigny in Paris and designed her own bordello along their lines. Hers was the first house-of-all-nations in Britain, populated by a variety of beauties recruited from a number of different countries on the other side of the Channel. Contemporary observers reported that she was the first madam in England to employ a house physician to keep her charges in relatively good health. Her price card listed services from five to fifty guineas, with 'virgins' going for twenty guineas.

The success of the Goadby girl-house led to the establishment of a veritable clutch of similar establishments in the West End. Mrs Nelson of Wardour Street specialized in very young girls. It was her quaint custom to masquerade as a

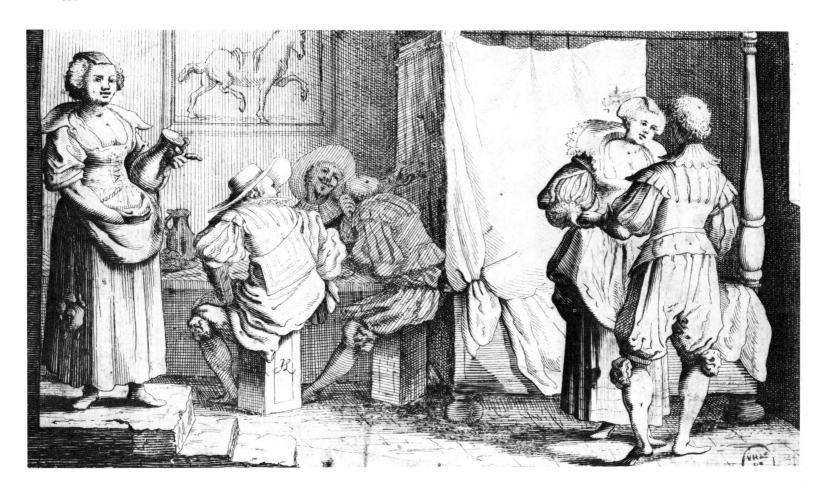

Interior of a Bordello
17th C French
PHOTO BY BULLOZ, PARIS

governess in order to have access to pre-pubescent girls whom she could turn to the trade. Charlotte Hayes of King's Place became an entrepreneur whose entertainments were almost as important as sex. Much impressed by the explorations of Captain Cook in the South Seas, at her 'Cloisters', Miss Hayes offered dramatic presentations based on the explorer's accounts of sex practices among the natives of the coral isles. These pageants lasted as long as two hours and it was not uncommon for the members of the audience to leave their seats to join in the ceremonies, so moved were they by the verisimilitude of the South Seas life portrayals. Nearby, the Jamaican Miss Herriott offered a taste of real West Indian island sexuality. Moll King's bordello in Covent Garden was immortalized by William Hogarth.

Another innovator like Mrs Goadby was Madam Falkland who founded the Temples of Aurora, Flora and Mystery. Each of these adjoining houses was occupied by twelve girls. The youngest of them served in Aurora for a time before graduating to Flora. The Temple of Mystery was reserved for gentlemen with peculiar if not downright perverse sexual appetites. Lord Hamilton, Lord Bolingbroke, Thomas Sheridan and Tobias Smollett were all reported as frequent celebrants at the Temple of Flora, while Lord Pembroke was familiar at the Mystery establishment. It is not surprising that even the richest and most successful courtesans like Kitty Fisher died before they reached thirty years of age. If gin and disease did not do them in, more often than not sheer physical labour did the trick once they passed their prime and were forced to forsake quality customers for quantity.

In contemporary France conditions were little different, certainly no better. Employers paid their female help less than they needed for the necessities of life and expected them to make up the difference by streetwalking. Estimates of the day set the number of prostitutes in Paris at 40–60,000. The business was popular among rich and poor alike. Everyone with eyes in his head was aware that many nobles, clerics and wealthy businessmen helped to create the demand that generated the supply. If a woman got into too much trouble with the law, or gave offence to a man of influence, she could be shipped off to Louisiana without a moment's notice. The New World was fast becoming a convenient dumping ground for all of Europe's monarchies. And the effects of such transportations from France were felt up to World War I in New Orleans, and in San Francisco played a large part in setting the moral tone a century later.

The same ostentation that offended the sensibilities of Renaissance Italians annoyed many Frenchmen as insolent courtesans displayed their fancy carriages and flashy jewels on the Cours-la-Reine in Paris and on the promenade at Longchamps. Many of these flamboyant women secured immunity from the law for selling their bedroom services by joining the Comédie Française or the Opéra, since their members were exempt from punishment for conduct forbidden to ordinary citizens. Many of these upper-class harlots captured husbands and fortunes, even titles. One such girl of the streets made it through the performing arts to become the Baroness de Saint-Chamond.

Like whoring, crime was widespread at all levels of society. It sprang from the greed of the rich, the need of the poor and the uncontrollable passions of all classes with murder as popular as it is in the United States today. Many highborn ladies enjoyed the skills of Catherine Montvoison or the Marquise de Brinvilliers, both of whom specialized in preparing poisons of great subtlety. Poisoning was so popular that special courts were set up to deal with it and no proper dining-room was without its credenza, or credence table, where all the food was tested for poison before serving. Among La Voison's clients was Olympe Mancini, the King's mistress. In 1679 a commission investigating her activities found evidence involving so many members of the court that Louis ordered that the entire record be suppressed. La Voison was burned alive the following year.

Though poisoning love rivals was considered bad form, in general the French condoned concubinage. Nearly every man who could afford to pay the freight kept a mistress or two and the men prided themselves as much on their liaisons as they did on their swordsmanship and a woman felt desolate if only her husband evinced any interest in her charms. None the less, the agreeableness of French-women lagged behind that of men and as a result the number of prostitutes labouring to meet the swelling demand continued to rise. In Paris three main

Le Souper fin
Engraving from *Monument du Costume* by Jean-Michel Moreau le jeune 1741–1814
BETTMENN ARCHIVE INC., NEW YORK
BBC HULTON PICTURE LIBRARY

types were recognized: the *chèvre coiffée*, she-goat with hair-do, for the court; the *petrel*, chattering bird, for the bourgeoisie; and the *pierreuse*, who served the poor and lived in some dismal basement or squalid rookery.

By the time the French had introduced the table napkin as an adjunct to fine dining, prostitution was flourishing to a point where, aside from moral considerations, it had become a threat to the state. A large standing army had come into vogue with Louis XIV, King from 1643–1713, and harlots were not only needless distractions from the commander's point of view, they also spread debilitating diseases. Louis XIII, in his reign, 1610–43, had been content to whip and shave the head of any camp-follower who could not bribe her way out of punishment. With a much larger army to maintain, the usually tolerant Louis XIV declared that any woman caught with a soldier within five miles of Versailles would have her nose and ears cut off, a punishment designed to discourage all but the most determined customers.

Within the court itself the champion adulterer and model of fashion was Louis François Armand de Vignerot du Plessis, Duc de Richelieu, great-nephew of the mighty Cardinal. Titled ladies by the score toppled into his bed, drawn there by his position, his money, and possibly because of his reputation as a great lover. His popularity declined, however, when he began pimping for the King. Neither his hobby nor his avocation seem to have done him much harm; he died at the age of ninety-two. His great-uncle, renowned churchman, once paid 50,000 crowns for a night in the arms of the equally renowned courtesan Ninon de Lenclos, who craftily accepted the money but sent her maid to take her place in his bed.

The fabulous Ninon was the daughter of a nobleman, a freethinker and something of a cavalier, according to some sources. On the other hand, Voltaire claimed that her father was a poorly paid musician who supplemented his income by pimping. Her real name was Anne de Lenclos. In any event the girl who became Ninon ranks with Theodora and Nell Gwyn in the annals of whores who made good. Although she had little formal schooling, Ninon learned to speak Italian and French which aided her greatly in her commercial sex ventures which commenced at the age of fifteen. Her first affair of note was with young Comte Gaspard de Coligny. The count was followed simultaneously by the Abbé Dessiat and the Maréchal d'Estrées who settled a small matter of paternity by a roll of the dice. Later clients included Sainte-Evrémond, La Rochefoucauld, the Duc d'Enghien and the Marquis de Sévigné, his son and, eventually, his grandson. Her longest relationship, with the Marquis de Villarceux, lasted all of three years.

When her sexual extravagance became more than she could bear, the King's mother, Anne of Austria, had Ninon shipped off to a convent where she charmed the nuns until she was pardoned in 1657 by Louis, who was himself enchanted by her. That same year she opened her School of Gallantry, a euphemism for School

Ladenbordelhaus or Milliner's
  Brothel
John Erdmann Hummel 1769–1852
MARY EVANS PICTURE LIBRARY

of Lovemaking. Her students were young aristocrats enrolled by their under-
standing mothers. The curriculum included the care and handling of wife and
mistress, the correct approach to courting and seduction, and the physical aspects
of artful lovemaking. What the venerable Vatsyayana and Shaykh Nefzawi
preached Ninon practised.

Men came from all over Europe to court her and to study her methods, but
her lovers never quarrelled over her, she reported, 'because they had confidence
in my inconsistency; each awaited his turn'. In her will she left 1000 francs to the
son of her lawyer so that he might buy books and advance himself in the world.

That little boy took his inheritance, bought the volumes as directed, read them assiduously, and grew up to be Voltaire.

From the time of the fabled Ninon onwards, France became internationally famous for the three most important Fs: Food, Fashion and Fornication. There, *naturellement*, matters sexual became inseparable from the dining-table. In his *Almanac des Gourmands* Grinod de la Réynière assured his readers that ladies are more amiable at suppertime than at any other hour of the day. This profound observation gave rise to the *petite-souper*, little supper, held in the pleasure-houses of the wealthy. Soon the madams who ran these elegant bordellos were forced to recognize the aphrodisiacal qualities of the *petite-souper* and were soon vying with one another in drawing up strange and wonderful menus that would catch the attention of the semi-impotent clients who seemed to abound in the upper classes. The faddist Duc de Richelieu carried the idea to its logical conclusion. At his private sitdowns, he and his friends and their lady friends dined in the nude.

Nude but for wigs, of course. At the centre of European civilization the French took particular pride in their sophisticated dress. Wigs were the rage for all classes and one felt totally stripped without one. The towering hair-do usually associated with the court of the Sun King did not come into vogue until 1763. As a contemporary chronicler put it, among the aristocracy 'men were slaves to women, women were slaves to fashion, and fashion was determined by couturiers', a notion not alien to the women of today who wear gunnysacks if a designer's label is attached.

The labels attached to the *mignons* of France changed over the years. Just as in every earlier society they were graded into different classes. At the bottom of the pack were the common streetwalkers who were not registered with the police and were called *insoumises*, the unruly ones. *Grisettes* or *midinettes* were the seamstresses, laundresses and shopgirls who were only part-time whores. *Gigolettes* operated in and around the public parks where their pimps often waited in the shrubbery to waylay unwary customers. *Lorettes* worked in the vicinity of Notre Dame de Lorette and were noted as jolly drinking and gambling companions. The *demimonde* was a term coined in the nineteenth century by Alexandre Dumas and was applied to married women who strayed. Eventually, the word came to signify a *poule de luxe*, a high-class whore. Among the élite in this group were *les liones*, *les grandes cocottes* and *les horizontales*, the top-crust courtesans who were kept only by one or two wealthy lovers. In keeping with tradition, these last had their own apartments and villas in the country, paraded about town in ornate horsedrawn carriages and enjoyed the attention of many servants. Occasionally they were given to presiding over salons in the mode of Ninon de Lenclos. The notorious eighteenth-century actress who called herself Mlle DuBois suffered from no such pretensions. 'Her greed for gold,' a chronicler of the day reported, 'was equal to her greed for pleasure.' This stage lady once made

Madame Juliette Récamier, 1800
Jacques-Louis David 1748–1825
LOUVRE MUSEUM, PARIS

a catalogue of her lovers over a twenty-one-year period; the final tally came to 16,527 individuals, or an average of three lovers a day. Her exploits were much admired by the great French novelists of the following century and her contemporary, the Marquis de Sade, was much impressed with her reckoning. The picture offered by the career of Mlle DuBois is probably closer to that of the typical courtesan than that of Dumas in *La Dame aux Camélias.*

During the reign of the divinely appointed Louis XV (1715–74) there was not in all of France a brothel to equal that maintained for the King himself. Located on the grounds of his palace at Versailles it was called *le parc aux cerfs,* 'the deer park', and cost over a million dollars a year to run. Two hundred years later sometime novelist Norman Mailer would use the term for his fictional account of life among the movie moguls of Hollywood, among whom was another Louis of stature. As for the original *parc,* it was supervised by no less a light than Madame du Barry whose chief of staff was Mère Bompard, whose task it was to keep it stocked with nymphets between the ages nine to eighteen for the thirty-four years Louis XV kept an interest in it. Ostensibly, until the girls were fifteen they merely

studied the arts of lovemaking, then went about giving pleasure to the monarch. After their eighteenth year the worldly-wise girls were married off to gentlemen of the court.

Just how seriously Louis took his sex-life may be seen by taking a look at Madame du Barry's bedroom, in reality a shrine and sanctuary dedicated to pleasure. The altar itself – in this case the bed – was set aside in a sort of alcove and was a marvellous construction of precious woods carved and modelled by the greatest sculptors in France, gilded by the hands of the great Clagny himself. Four grand columns supported the canopy and these were entwined with garlands of myrtle and ivy, surmounted by a cascade of roses. A rug of white silk covered the flight of steps by which one reached the voluptuous edifice. The sides were hung with curtains of rich silk embroidered in a design of rose clusters which were repeated in the draperies which covered the windows and in the upholstery of the thirteen chairs, reserved for a congregation, clustered at the foot of the bed. Everywhere doves and cupids disported themselves among the gold, marble and crystal furnishings. On the face of the room's clock it was the golden arrow of Eros that pointed the hour. All in all, it was not a bad boudoir for a girl born plain Becu who started her working life as a hairdresser's assistant and made her way to Louis' court through a millinery shop.

Despite the lengthy efforts of many malicious court personages, it was never established that Jeanne Becu Rancon du Barry had ever been enlisted on the rolls of the notorious Madame de Gourand, whose house was just off what is now boulevard Sebastopol. In Louis' Paris the most famous of the bordels had two entrances, one in the rue des Deux Portes for devil-may-care visitors, the other through an antique store in the rue Saint Sauveur for more circumspect clients, a device to be used by Sally Stanford in San Francisco many years later. Even in these pre-Revolutionary days the Gourand place was democratic. One of the main salons was stocked with common girls of the street who sold for a *sou*. In another chamber girls fresh from the country were bathed and tidied for presentation, a toilette which could be observed by voyeurs for a price. In the main salon the leading performers were prepared to costume themselves as milkmaids, nuns or woodland fairies as the customers desired. In the Infirmary, under-par visitors could buy aphrodisiacs or rent mechanical devices to raise their spirits. The Vulcan Room was furnished with an entrapment chair where compliant tarts seemingly placed themselves at the mercy of playful sadists. In *La Salle des Voyeurs* idle aristocrats and agents of the Sûreté rubbed shoulders while observing the antics of their confrères, later to report at Versailles or the police courts. In the final analysis, the Gourand enterprise probably represents the first full-service bordello in the Western hemisphere and much credit should be given to this innovative Frenchwoman by the thousands of imitators who followed her lead both in the Old World and the New.

Even before the Revolution of 1789 the bordellos of Paris were equal-

'Les voyeurs voyeured', Parisian
brothel of 1768
Engraving from *Nuits de Paris* by
Restif de la Bretonne
MARY EVANS PICTURE LIBRARY

opportunity employers, but after Napoleon's expedition to Egypt in 1798–9, black women in large numbers came to the City of Light to work in established brothels or to walk the streets on a freelance basis. In one edition of *Les Bordels de Paris* a black establishment is listed as 'the house of Mademoiselle Isabeau, formerly at rue Neufe de Montmorency, but now at the house of M Marchand, pawnbroker, in the rue Xaintoge', keeping alive the centuries-old tradition of linking whores with penury. The guidebook also points out that some establishments had no fixed prices for the services of 'negroes, mustees and mullatos'. The women reportedly offered themselves on a bidding basis, 'as women are sold from an oriental caravan'.

With the Revolution, of course, towering wigs and little suppers, among other things, were lost to the aristocracy, and the oystermen of Brittany fell on hard times. And by the end of the Napoleonic régime in 1815 the Paris police had established bordel regulations which would last a hundred years and more. *Les poules* of all grades were confined to licensed bordellos or restricted to houses of accommodation and were obliged to submit themselves to frequent medical examinations. Those found to be afflicted were packed off to the hospital of St Lazare prison and were kept there until they were supposedly cured of their contagions.

Public Coupling in Bordello
19th C French
COURTESY OF LAWRENCE E. GICHNER

None the less, French whoremasters were still operating a number of bordels that had been functioning successfully since the Middle Ages. In *The Pretty Women of Paris*, a nineteenth-century guide to the brothels with brief descriptions of the character of each house, one establishment at 12, rue de Charbanais claimed to be 'the oldest, the biggest, the finest bagnio in the world'. Ranging downward, others were reported as being 'a good, old-fashioned bordel', 'a very curious old mansion', 'a comfortable little house' or, simply, 'a stew'.

The English physician William Acton in 1869 gave a fair description of what one might expect to encounter in a first-class Paris house of the time:

> The visitor discovers, on entering, scenes of sensual extravagance to which his eyes are unaccustomed in England. Here vice finds a treat of voluptuous splendour, to which in soberer climes she is a stranger. The visitor is received by the mistress of the house, and ushered into a sumptuous ante-room; on a curtain being drawn aside, a door is revealed to him, containing a circular piece of glass about the size of a crown piece, through which he can reconnoitre at his ease a small, but well-lighted and elegantly furnished drawing-room, occupied by the women of the establishment. They are usually to be seen seated on sofa chairs, elegantly attired in different-coloured silks, with low bodices and having their hair dressed in the extreme of fashion; the whole group being arranged artistically, as in a tableau vivant, and the individuals who comprise it representing the poses of different celebrated statues, selected apparently with the object of showing off to the best advantage the peculiar attractions of the different women.

That was Paris. There was neither such sensual extravagance nor voluptuous splendour in the provinces. Although his is a fictional portrait, Guy de

Flagellation Scene in Bordello
19th C French
COURTESY OF LAWRENCE E. GICHNER

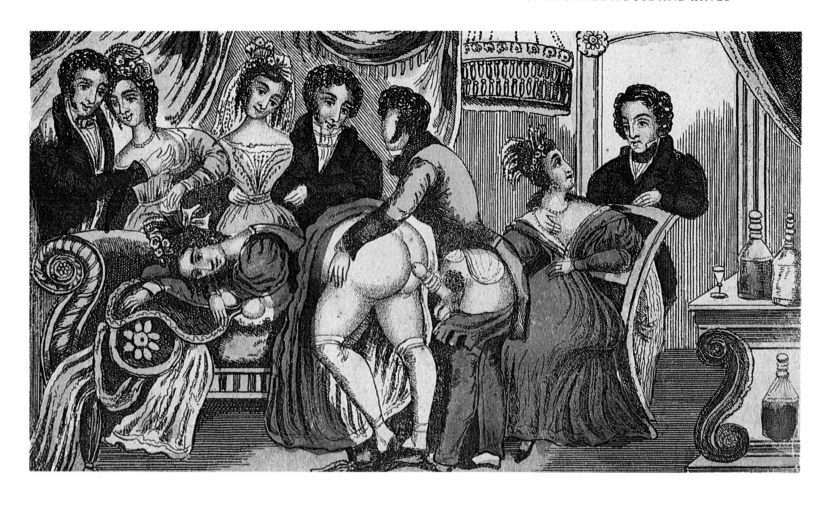

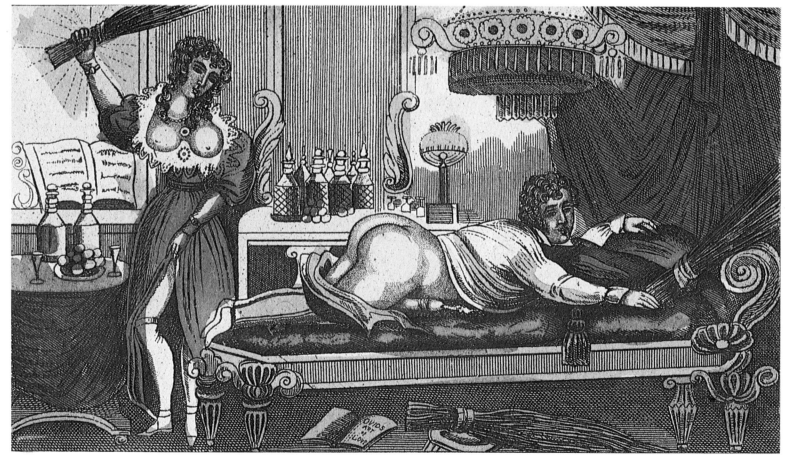

Maupassant's nineteenth-century description of *La Maison Tellier* in the town of Fécamp gives a felicitous glimpse of what bordello life was like in the outer departments:

> The house had two entrances. At the corner, a sort of low café opened in the evening for common folk and sailors. Two of those who performed the duties of the house were assigned to the needs of this section of the clientele. The three others (for there were only five of them altogether) formed a sort of aristocracy, and were reserved for the upstairs company, unless they were needed downstairs and there were no visitors above. The Jupiter Room, where the bourgeois of the neighbourhood gathered, was papered in blue and decorated with a large picture depicting Leda stretched out beneath a swan. To reach this room, one came up a spiral staircase, leading from a narrow door, modest in appearance, giving on to the street, and over which there shone, all night long, behind a griddle, a little lamp like those that in some towns are lit at the feet of a madonna.

There was nothing to stand in the way of a girl from the provinces with strong ambitions from making her way to Paris there to find fame and sometimes fortune, frequently through Les Folies Bergère. Every aspiring streetwalker knew of Liane de Pougy who met the Prince of Wales at the Folies and later travelled to Russia with her own jeweller in tow, sure in the knowledge that some Romanoff prince would be offering her diamonds and pearls. Or Marguerite Bellanger who just happened to meet the Emperor Napoleon III while chancing through the Bois de Boulogne and thereafter won his heart and his bed. In late nineteenth-century France anything was possible. The fabled Cora Pearl, born Emma Crouch in England in 1842, rose charmingly to the couch of Prince Jerome Bonaparte and a position where she could demand thousands of pounds for a single night's entertainment. La Belle Otéro, a simple gypsy girl from Spain, survived rape and the Folies stage to steal the hearts of Commodore Vanderbilt and Prince Peter of the Russians and to have her portrait painted by Renoir. In later nineteenth-century Paris half the painters of note seemed to find the city's bordellos their chief source of inspiration.

Among the great bordellos of the period the most famous is associated with Toulouse-Lautrec and was located at 24, rue des Moulins in the neighbourhood of the Bibliothèque Nationale. This house offered its clients every convenience and facility and was even opened periodically to tour groups. The beds were designed in various Louis-styles. The great bed at Versailles was duplicated with its crimson velvet curtains on which 'The Triumph of Venus' was embroidered. Ornate candelabra, paintings, tapestries and statuary abounded. In some of the rooms the ceilings as well as the walls were mirrored.

There were Ducal Rooms and Chinese Rooms and African Rooms and even a grand salon decorated in the style of a Moorish castle. These bordellos became the prototype for hundreds of theme-houses which were to proliferate around the world in the century ahead. For some reason or other, the Moorish Castle idea captured the fancy of many of the leading madams in the United States. From

Wood Engraving by René Lelon, 1903
From *La Maison Tellier* by Guy de Maupassant
MARY EVANS PICTURE LIBRARY

New York to Miami, Chicago and Los Angeles, captains of American industry would be able to take their sexual pleasures in surroundings in which only a Moor should have found himself comfortable. The madams of America somehow managed to confuse the architecture of northwest Africa with the harem-settings of fabled Baghdad, Damascus and Istanbul.

While the French may have been the great innovators in whorehouse styling, the English were not slow to imitate a good thing. Hand in hand with improving the accommodations, the English followed the French example in the nineteenth century by trying to regulate the business of sex. The tarts, quite naturally, objected to any interference with their own exercise of free enterprise. In London, as in Paris, every conceivable subterfuge was employed in an effort to carry on the trade outside the laws on residence, registration and physical examination. In the newspapers odd-sounding furnished rooms were advertised extensively, foreign-language courses were offered to an extent that the impression was abroad that half the British public had eyes for the diplomatic corps, exotic fruits and sweets were tendered and satisfying massages promised by versatile practitioners who claimed to have learned their skills both east and west of Suez. What has been passed off as the chaste, prim and righteous Victorian Age was in reality quite a different kettle of fish. The respected medical journal, *The Lancet*, reported in 1857 that there were 6000 brothels in London alone, occupied

Grande Odalisque, 1814
Jean-August-Dominique Ingres
1780–1867
LOUVRE MUSEUM, PARIS

Madame de Pompadour, 1755
Maurice Quentin de La Tour
1704–88
LOUVRE MUSEUM, PARIS

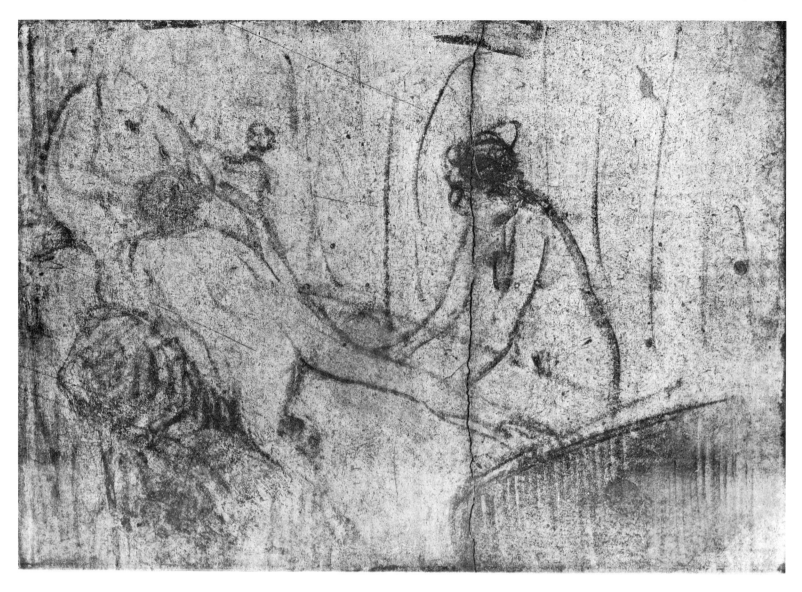

Massage Scene in a Brothel
Zinc by Degas 1834–1917
BIBLIOTHÈQUE NATIONALE, PARIS

Oriental Salon in rue des Moulins,
  Paris
NEW YORK PUBLIC LIBRARY

by 60,000 strumpets; one house in every sixty a bordello, one women in every sixteen a whore. Even the visiting Dostoyevsky, no stranger to vice and corruption, was flabbergasted by the scene in the West End where it seemed to him 'a female army of occupation' was in power.

There were mothers, as well as bawds, offering young children for the entertainment of the bewhiskered, frock-coated gentlemen of the town. Notorious madams held nightly revels in their spacious drawing-rooms packed with harlots and bottles of imported wine. The popular courtesans arrived in their carriages from the villas in St John's Wood for oysters and champagne with the nobility and the *nouveaux riches* lords of industry and commerce. The taverns and supper clubs stayed wide open until three or four in the morning, mixing a menu of fish and chips or grilled chops and baked potatoes with sex circuses of the most obscene order. Chroniclers of the age wrote of 'wild young noblemen' and 'drunken workmen, soldiers and sailors' as the main body of customers, but this assessment of the scene is patently absurd. There just weren't enough young

Scene in a Brothel, Rue Blondel,
  Paris
Lithograph by Reginald Marsh
NEW YORK PUBLIC LIBRARY

noblemen with enough money to occupy all the fancy houses night after night, and as far as the 'lower classes' were concerned, all those drunken blue-collar workers spent shillings rather than guineas. So, this wanton nightlife must have depended chiefly on the patronage of the great middle class, those stern husbands and strict fathers who trumpeted about purity and chastity and honour at home and in their private clubs.

Of course, what drove most girls and women into the ranks of prostitution was poverty, the hard conditions of female labour, and starvation wages. Women earned so little that they couldn't live without a second source of income. In the factories an attractive woman who accepted the advances of a foreman could in a single night earn many times her normal weekly wage. Domestics and governesses were little better off. If they refused the master's advances they could be let go, with no letter of recommendation.

Next stop for these unfortunate women was all too frequently the gin-serving 'blue ruin' shop where 'white satin' could be downed until their plight was

Girls of the Seine Banks
Gustave Courbet 1819–77
NATIONAL GALLERY, LONDON

forgotten. There were more than 4000 of these licensed public houses in London, one for every 200 citizens. For all their fancy gaslights and mirrors, the taverns, clubs and dance-halls presented conditions little better than those prevailing in the Middle Ages. In the middle of the nineteenth century – after the invention of the telegraph and the development of anaesthetics – 270,000 homes and public buildings had cesspools to accommodate waste, sometimes three or four foul-smelling pools per house.

The lowest bordels were located on the south side of the Thames, just as they

Previous page (left):

Filles publiques faisant le quart,
Avril 1921
La Villette
THE ABOTT LEVY COLLECTION
PARTIAL GIFT OF SHIRLEY C.
BURDEN MUSEUM OF MODERN ART,
NEW YORK

Previous page (right):

Rue Asselin, 1924–25
Eugene Atget
THE ABOTT LEVY COLLECTION
PARTIAL GIFT OF SHIRLEY C.
BURDEN MUSEUM OF MODERN ART,
NEW YORK

were 300 years earlier, in the Lambeth district and in the narrow streets off the Waterloo Road below the Bankside in Southwark. The poshest places could be found in the area north of Oxford Circus, between Hyde Park and Regent's Park. Like Paris, London too had its park-women, shilling performers who specialized in fellatio.

Just as in previous centuries, the most popular of London spectacles for all classes was a hanging. More than two hundred capital offences were still on the books. Not until 1829 did London get an organized police force, but even thereafter crime was popular because it was the essence of all economic activity in England that it was uncontrolled. Everything from purse-snatching to foreign trade was left to individual enterprise. When enterprising quadruple-murderer John Gleeson was hanged in 1849 more than 100,000 cheering spectators were on hand for the occasion. In a letter to *The Times* Charles Dickens penned a description of another high jump which took place in front of the Horsemonger Lane gaol:

> When the day dawned, thieves, low prostitutes, ruffians and vagabonds of every kind, flocked to the ground, with every variety of offensive and foul behaviour. Fightings, faintings and whistlings, imitations of Punch, brutal jokes, tumultuous demonstrations of indecent delight when swooning women were dragged out of the crowd by the police with their dresses disordered gave a new zest to the general entertainment.

Among the 'low prostitutes' described by social critic Bracebridge Hemyng were married women who 'in the custom of Messalina', frequented the brothel-rooms usually occupied by streetwalkers and dollymops turning tricks on their days off from domestic work. In Hemyng's middle class were the women who 'usually congregated in the houses in which each had her own private apartment', while his upper class was comprised of women with independent means, which is to say a wealthy benefactor.

'The Queen of London Whoredom', in William Hardman's phrase, was Laura Bell who reigned during the 1850s. Born in Antrim, Ireland, in 1829, she was the daughter of a bailiff on the estates of the Marquis of Hereford. Starting as a shopgirl in Belfast, she moved on to Dublin to become a lady of pleasure before moving her business to London at about the time of the Great Exhibition. When she appeared in one of the London parks in her open phaeton she attracted as many fans as would a film star today. Among her clients she counted Jungh Badahur, wealthy prime minister to the Maharajah of Nepal. For one night with her she demanded £250,000; he paid. In 1852 she married Captain Augustus Frederick Thistlewayte who set her up in Grosvenor Square, where she continued her spendthrift ways to an extent that made it necessary for the Captain to advertise in *The Times* that he would no longer be responsible for her debts.

Thistlewayte himself was not without his faults; it was his custom to summon his servants by firing a pistol through the ceiling of their bedroom. In her later

Woman Pulling up Her Stocking,
1894
Henri de Toulouse-Lautrec
1864–1901
MUSÉE TOULOUSE-LAUTREC, ALBI

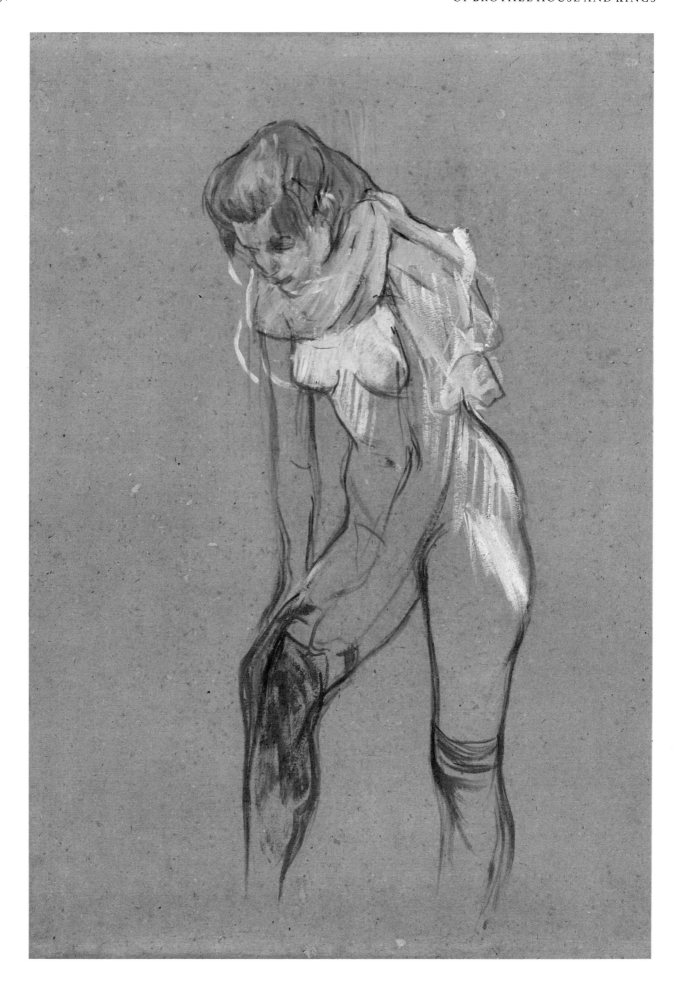

years Laura became a close friend of Gladstone, Prime Minister, in the 1880s and 1890s. He, too, recent research has shown, was not without his own peculiarities. When affairs of state were done for the day, he was given to roaming the backstreets of London where he confronted streetwalkers and tried to talk them out of their wanton ways; thereafter, he repaired to 10 Downing Street where he set about flagellating himself, a diversion he may have learned at Eton.

Laura Bell's place at centre stage was taken by Skittles, born Catherine Walters, in Liverpool in 1839. Her appearances in Hyde Park were known to cause traffic jams. After eloping to America with Aubrey de vere Beauclerk, a married man and kin to the Duke of St Albans, Skittles next appeared in Paris under the protection of the Marquess of Hartington. When she returned to London her Sunday-evening parties in Chesterfield Street were attended by many of the fashionable world, not the least of whom was the Prince of Wales who enjoyed the reputation of one of the Kingdom's greatest womanizers.

The Italian connection, established after the Great Fire of 1666, was not forgotten by the Countess Nicchia de Castiglione, mistress of Napoleon III of France and Prince Jerome Bonaparte and one of the most beautiful women of her day. Like Laura Bell the Italian contessa was wildly extravagant. When the Earl of Yarmouth, one of England's wealthiest men, offered her a million francs, nearly half a million dollars in today's currency, she condescended to accept. In his desire to get his money's worth, the Earl occupied her so vigorously that she was forced to spend a week in bed recuperating.

Lesser prima donnas than Laura, Skittles and Nicchia tended to make their more modest appearances at the Argyll, the Holborn and the Portland, three of London's leading dance-halls. Often after making their assignations, the night-ladies would make their way with their escorts to Mrs Kate Hamilton's supper club in the neighbourhood of the Haymarket. Among other things, food was served here. One remarkable menu included 'capons, turkeys, fatted pullets, fowls, grouse, pheasant, partridges, plovers, snipes, quail, woodcocks, pigeons and stuffed larks'.

Second only to the dance-halls as favourite meeting-places were the theatres where solicitations were made in the lounges and saloons. For this reason many respectable Victorian ladies shied away from the theatre. The playhouse-harlot tradition was kept alive by one Louisa Turner who first appeared on stage in the opera houses of the day and then went to work in a bordello in Little Titchfield Street near Oxford Circus where she apparently found the work easier and more rewarding than flying through the air as a Victorian nymph or sylph.

In a nation of small shopkeepers it was not surprising that many of the Victorian bordellos were essentially family business concerns. No outside girls were employed; the clients were catered to by the members of a single family, often by more than one generation of tarts. The popular Mrs Leah Davis was known to have introduced thirteen of her daughters to the trade, a practice commonplace in India and Renaissance Italy. Eventually, however, the market became so glutted that a night with a purported virgin brought only £5 instead of the earlier price of fifty guineas.

Child brothels were another favourite facility with Victorian rake-hells and debauchees. Folklore had it that intercourse with a virgin was a cure for venereal disease. When practice proved the falsity of the belief, the prices fell along with the expectations of the clients. One such establishment of prominence was found in Seymour Place off Branston Square. It was run by a Frenchwoman, Marie Aubrey, and her lover, John Williams. For a time the Aubrey house enjoyed an international reputation with clients flocking to it from all parts of the Continent. This business suffered a crippling blow when W.T. Stead published a series of articles in the *Pall Mall Gazette* called 'The Maiden Tribute of Modern Babylon' in July of 1885. Stead wrote of padded rooms in the West End where unwilling girls as young as thirteen were stripped and offered to callous customers for as little as £5. Stead also revealed that prominent Harley Street physicians were writing the certificates attesting to the girls' virginity as a highly lucrative sideline. In another series of articles the indefatigable Stead attacked the 'White Slave Trade' which existed on a reciprocal basis between Liverpool and Hamburg through the port of Hull. His attacks were intermittently successful.

While the *Pall Mall Gazette* was giving its attention to child brothels another kind of speciality house was flourishing under the reign of the staid Victoria and proper Albert. As early as 1704 whipping services were known to have been available at the standard, run-of-the-mill bordello. By the middle of the nineteenth century, establishments had sprung up which were devoted exclusively to this form of activity. Many observers have commented on what seems to be a peculiarly English custom and attribute it to the public school, which entails whippings. One of the flagellant houses was said to have enjoyed the patronage of royalty. George IV was known to have occasionally called at the house of a Mrs Collett in Tavistock Court, Covent Garden, where sado-masochistic sex was featured. In this case the business also appears to have been a family affair because Mrs Collett's niece, Mrs Mitchell, ran a similar pleasure-house in the Waterloo Road. Other establishments popular with the whip-and-jackboot set were run by Mrs James in Soho and Mrs Philipps in Upper Belgrave Place.

The grandest pain palace of all was operated by Mrs Theresa Berkley at 28 Charlotte Street whose contribution to the curious entertainments was immortalized in a work entitled *The Venus School Mistress*. Mistress Theresa's greatest claim to fame was the invention of the Berkley Horse, an ingenious machine designed for flogging on which the happy customer could be stretched out and tortured in a variety of Procrustean positions. A print in Mrs Berkley's memoirs portrays a naked gentleman strapped to this device while Mrs Berkley applies the whip to his bare buttocks and a young girl, as it is delicately put, 'manualizes his embolon'. After her passing, this wickedly delightful machine was presented to

the Royal Society of the Arts by the executor of the Berkley estate.

When the future King of England himself visits a speciality house it is clear evidence that the status of the bordello in English society has risen mightily since the days of the poor Roman slave girls and the later rough and ribald era of the Bankside. Certainly the country which gave the world the spinning jenny and the Berkley Horse could be expected to make eminent contributions to the bordello culture in other parts of the world in the decades ahead.

The Salon in the Rue des Moulins, 1894
Henri de Toulouse-Lautrec
1864–1901
MUSÉE TOULOUSE-LAUTREC, ALBI

CHAPTER EIGHT

NEW SHORES, OLD WHORES

ENGLAND'S CONTRIBUTION to the continuation of the European bordello tradition in the New World has its start with the first shiploads of colonists sent to the Americas. In the ensuing years as new territories are added every settlement boasts a flourishing bordel before it has a state flag. By the middle of the nineteenth century brothel-life is being dubbed the 'social evil of the century' by most civic leaders. Comparatively speaking, the institution is only in its adolescence by this time. With an estimated 50,000 prostitutes in London, 30,000 in Paris, New York City is able to muster only 20,000 in 1860. However, this imbalance will be adjusted shortly. The Civil War (1861–5) will help the development of the sex industry as much as does westward expansion. And industrialization, as elsewhere in the world, will be the greatest contributing factor. How could a country that is to give the world mass-production technology fail to claim first place in any business enterprise? Certainly all the raw materials needed are on hand in the young nation.

As early as 1619 the Great Charter of Virginia provided that the ministers and church wardens should search out 'scandalous offenses and suspicions of whore-doms, dishonest keeping of women and such like'. The author of *The Narrative of the Indian and Civil War in Virginia* in the years 1675–6 wrote of one Lawrence of Jamestown and his concubine and of 'soldiers' wenches' who accompanied the troops as servants. These women fashioned small tents or hovels near the military camps to satisfy the men's sexual needs as well. The forces of Christendom were off on another Crusade, but now the enemy was another sort of heathen.

During the seventeenth century Virginia became the dumping ground for 'the wretched refuse of England'. Narcissus Lutreel described, in November 1692, how a ship lay at Leith, bound for Virginia, on board which the local magistrate had ordered 'fifty lewd women out of the city's pleasure-houses' and thirty other unfortunates who had been picked up while walking the streets of the seaport.

Leith was the town where Defoe's *Moll Flanders* and her highwayman lover ended up. In real life their ilk were dealt with in a far less sympathetic way than Defoe depicted. Shanghaiing was one of the hazards of the seaman's trade and so it became also for the women who bartered themselves for the sailors' gold, what little they had of it. One night they were bedded in some waterfront rookery, the next at sea in a hammock en route to a primitive land.

In the first seventy-seven years of the seventeenth century somewhere between 9000 and 12,000 officially undesirable women were transported to the American mainland colonies. Given the projected number of descendants of the English slatterns a century later, it is surprising that the Daughters of the American Revolution are so mightily proud of their ancestry. Nevertheless, hunt-the-whore was not the test for the English at home that it was for the colonists intent on lecherous adventure in Puritan New England. Indeed, the hunt in Boston in the early days found few maidens in the haystacks. Still, there is some evidence that one Alice Thomas in 1672 was operating a bordello in Boston. This early New England mistress was found guilty of 'giving frequent secret and unseasonable Entertainment in her house to Lewd, Lascivious and Notorious persons of both Sexes, giving them opportunity to commit carnal Wickedness, and that by common fame she is a common Baud'.

Two other pieces of evidence of harlotry come from church records. The Boston Church in 1653 dealt with one James Everill for, among other scandalous pursuits, frequenting 'a house of ill-repute'. And in 1694 a woman was excommunicated from the Roxbury Church for 'Bawdry'. An idea of colonial demographics can be gained from the knowledge that aboard one ship bound for America in 1686, one-fifth of the passengers, twelve of sixty, were 'notorious prostitutes'. When the average Londoner in the next century referred to the rebellious colonists as 'whoresons' he wasn't far from the mark.

The English were not alone, however, in their contribution to the lively profession in the New World. When former Amsterdam barmaid Griet Reyniers arrived in Manhattan in 1633 the streets were muddy lanes where hogs and goats roamed freely. The houses, scattered about haphazardly, were built entirely of timber, including the chimneys which gave even the best of them a transitory quality. Although Griet had dispensed her favours freely during her Atlantic passage among the Dutch gentlemen officials who were her companions, once ashore she decided that being 'a gentleman's whore' was not to her taste. Instead, she took up with a Dutch-Moroccan, Jansen van Salee, mistakenly nicknamed 'the Turk' after his birthplace at the port of Fez. Griet and Turk opened a tavern and with his help she became New Amsterdam's first and most famous whore. Her reputation was such that twenty-five years later mothers in the homeland lowlands were writing to warn their emigrant sons 'to shun the company of light women of whom Nieuw Amsterdam is full'. Unfortunately, nowhere in present-day New York is Griet Reyniers honoured by plaque or park memorial.

'La triste embarquement des filles
    de joie'
18th C French
NEW YORK PUBLIC LIBRARY

A century later, in 1744, Alexander Hamilton was reporting that the New York Battery was a rendezvous for the expanding city's harlots and that prospective patrons had 'a good choice of pretty lasses among them, both Dutch and English'. A decade later eleven women were publicly whipped in the Wall Street area for taking men into their homes for 'lewd purposes'. Moreau de St Méry, a French emigré who arrived in America in 1790, wrote in his journal that prostitution was 'shockingly rife' in New York, a shocking commentary by a Frenchman, certainly. De Méry's observation was supported by Philip Hone, merchant, man-about-town and later mayor of the city. Hone recalled in his memoirs an incident in 1793 in which a young man named Henry Bedlow was accused of raping the stepdaughter of his ship's pilot in a bordello run by 'Mother Carey of Beekman Street'. When Bedlow was acquitted, friends of the offended father tore Mother Carey's brothel apart and drove the inhabitants of that and other nearby bordels naked into the street, a raid reminiscent of the action taken against *The Holland's Leaguer* in London 100 years earlier.

The first great hullabaloo about New World whoredom came with the Reverend McDowall's publications concerning vice in New York City. *McDowall's Journal* carried the names and addresses of so many hundreds of bawdy houses that it came to be known among the rakes of the early 1800s as 'The Whorehouse Directory' and was highly prized by visitors to the city. Using the Magdalen Society's figure for the number of strumpets in the city at the time, Robert Dale Owen estimated that if each working woman received three visitors a day, collectively they were used ten million times in a single year. And thus, through creative accounting, Owen reckoned that half of all the adult males in New York were visiting bordellos three times a week. On what the other half were up to he did not speculate.

The character and career of the New World trollop in the first half of the nineteenth century were epitomized by Helen Jewett whom the New York tabloids dubbed 'The Girl in Green'. Born of English parents in Augusta, Maine, in 1813, her real name was Dorcas Doyen. Her mother died when she was nine and when she was eleven she was seduced by a local boy. Fleeing from her alcoholic father, she entered a Portland bordello when she was sixteen and made her way to New York through houses in Boston and Albany before she was twenty. While working in an off-Broadway bordello run by Rosina Townsend she fell in love with a young jewellery clerk called Richard Robinson. In her idle hours Helen and young Robinson read to one another from Byron's works or visited the Park Theater where she invariably wore a green evening gown. At about 9 p.m. on Sunday, 10 April 1838, her body was found by Madam Townsend in the bed where she worked. She had been hacked to death with a hatchet. Many of her regular customers were questioned, but it was Robinson who went on trial at City Hall. 'The evidence in this trial,' said the *New York Herald*, the newest paper in town, 'and the remarkable disclosure of the manners and morals of New York is one of those events that must make philosophy pause, religion stand aghast, morals weep in the dust, the female virtue droop her head in sorrow.' The crowds in the courtroom were deeply divided. On one side were the moral reformers, jeering Robinson. On the other side was the sporting element, cheering him. Robinson was acquitted and he disappeared from the city. Subsequent evidence, in particular a letter to him from the young victim, pointed to his guilt. One story had it that Robinson had become a Mississippi riverboat gambler, while another maintained that he had fled to California where Sutter's Fort was already paining the Mexican government.

There, on the young nation's opposite coast, a whoredom had sprung up overnight, producing in a matter of months what it had taken New York more than a century to achieve. With the coming of the California Gold Rush, San Francisco found itself with 10,000 ladies of the blue chamber even before the sidewalks were laid. The infamous *Bella Union*, in operation from 1849 to 1906, featured such quaintly named girls as Rotary Rose and Always Ready Rita.

Mrs Irene McReady, called 'The Countess' and not to be confused with Nicchia de Castiglione, was the first madam of note to establish herself in San Francisco. She arrived from New Orleans in the summer of 1849 with a bevy of

Interior of a Bordello
Jacob Duck 17th C
COURTESY OF HOOGSTEDER-
NAUMAN, LTD, NEW YORK

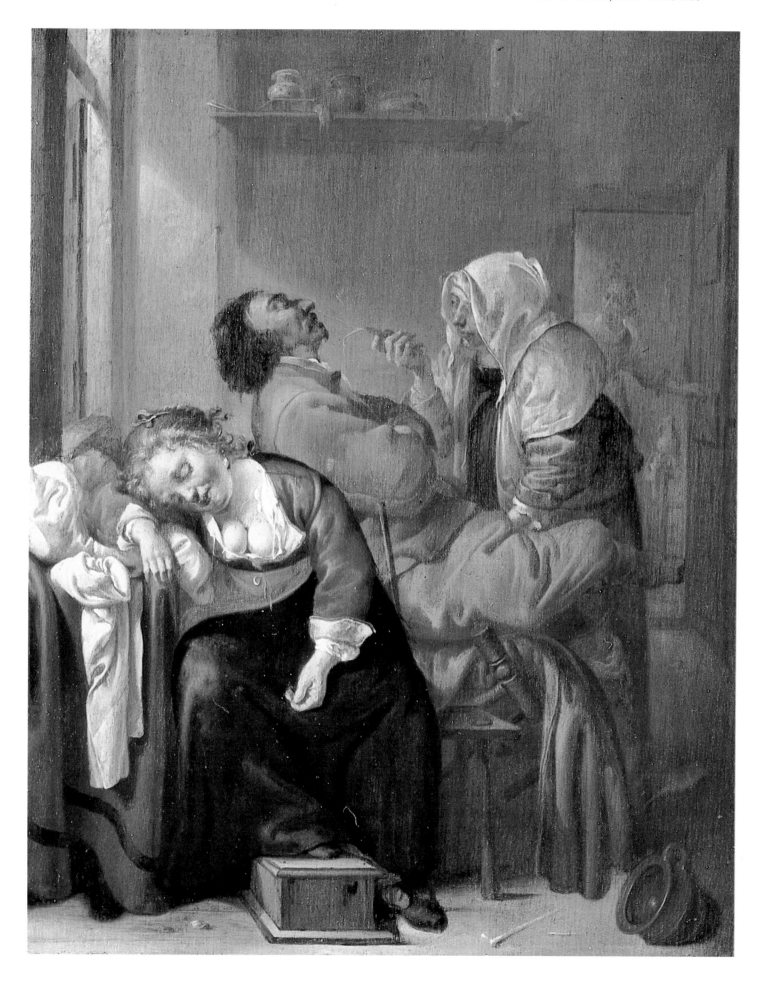

girls tried and true to open a house on Washington Street across from the Plaza. A successful prospector in town for a good time could be expected to pay off in gold for his night's entertainment, frequently as much as six ounces of the stuff. This was an even grander pay scale than Kate Fisher enjoyed for her 100-guinea nights of bedroom sport.

That same year a twenty-two-year-old Chinese girl named Ah Toy arrived and opened her first house, a shanty in an alley off Clay Street just above Kearny. A year later two girls fresh off the boat went to work for her. The lines outside Ah Toy's tiny sex shop stretched for blocks each day, from dawn to dawn. This was hardly surprising because in 1850 there was only one Chinese woman in San Francisco for every 1700 Chinese males. For the most part, white whores looked upon Orientals as an inferior race and would have nothing to do with them until they were in their last years at the trade; by that time even the most desperate of Chinese men preferred to stand in line for hours to enjoy his pleasure with a girl from home rather than a toothless Anglo. As for Ah Toy herself, despite her labours as a young woman, she lived to be 100 years old and spent her later years in comfortable retirement at San José until 1929. She and Louis du Plessis would have made a charming pair.

Of all the great Gold Rush parlourhouse madams probably the most famous was Belle Cora. The daughter of a Baltimore minister, she, too, found her way to San Francisco by way of New Orleans. It is interesting that the euphemistic 'parlour-house' replaced whorehouse, brothel and even bordello in nineteenth-century American parlance, 'parlour' coming from the medieval latin *parlatorium*, the room in a monastery or nunnery where visitors were received.

Although most of the Forty-niners appear to have wanted no-nonsense sexual experiences, there were still enough roguish types about to support *The Lively Flea* run by Madam Gabrielle who may have been familiar with the wiles of Madam du Gourand. This establishment contained a much-publicized 'Virgin Room' wherein gullible yokels were introduced to the young professional virgin and performed beyond the peepholes for the delectation of other customers who had undergone the indignity only minutes earlier.

At the start of the Gold Rush things were neither so sophisticated nor so fancy. As in Biblical times, the first flesh trade was carried on in tents set up on the edges of the gold fields. These soon gave way to wooden structures which became the centre of small-town life, the combination bar-room and gambling hall with accommodations for the sporting girls overhead. The first bar, or serving counter, consisted of a couple of rough planks supported by empty beer or wine barrels. When the establishment began to acquire class, a piano would be added, whence the 'barrelhouse syle' of musical accompaniment. Uniformly, such places were decorated with paintings of naked ladies from mythology or the artist's conception of life in the ubiquitous 'harem'.

The inmates of these primitive bordellos were of many nationalities and

Cora Pearl

192

represented different classes, or as many as the country was able to offer at the time, with the best-looking and most fashionable, of course, occupying the most expensive houses. Among the first of the professional women on the scene in California were representatives of the French *demimonde*, 300 undesirables shipped over by the government of France in one of its less advertised contributions to American culture, thereby maintaining the tradition set before the Louisiana Purchase in 1803. Latin America was represented by hundreds of women who arrived by ship from Chile. They were imported partly for their reputation as dancers, particularly of the popular 'fandango'. More fandango-ing was done upstairs than on the dance floor. For pay and status, of course, the Chinese women in the cribs were at the bottom of the scale.

Some of the adventurous visitors mixed sociology with their other activities. Visiting Canadian William Perkins wrote of the women of different nationalities: the Spanish girls were 'warm, generous and unartificial'. The French women were 'fascinating in conversation, but avaricious, vain and shameless'. Of the English women who came by way of Australia and the eastern United States he reported they were 'vulgar, degraded and brutish as they are in their own countries, and a trip to California has not, of course, improved them'. So much for Anglo superiority.

By 1853 San Francisco had, according to *The Christian Advocate*, forty-eight first-class parlour-houses, more than 150 second-class bordellos and countless dens and cribs like Ah Toy's. The Chinese slave-whores were hardly a passing phase of the Gold Rush days. In the 1870s there were approximately 2000 such women working in San Francisco and even after the Oriental Exclusion Acts of the 1880s when they had to be smuggled in, the Yellow Slave Trade thrived. Since their first arrival in 1849 they became so much a part of the scene that they were still working in the cribs and neighbouring opium dens even after the earthquake of 1906.

Nevertheless, as early as the mid-1850s the public authorities were being urged to close the fandango houses by the blue-noses and the first prosecution of a streetwalker in San Francisco took place in 1858. A sure sign that hard times were coming came two years later when Madam Mary Miller was charged and convicted of keeping a disreputable house. A decade earlier she would have been honoured for opening one. When the whoring population of San Francisco began to stabilize, the scene of greatest bordello activity in the West switched to other mining towns like Cripple Creek, Colorado, and Butte, Montana. The latter, with a population of 10,000, enjoyed the presence of 1000 light-ladies in the saloons, hotels and storefront bordellos. A visit to these shops was as essential for the visiting miners as a stop at the hardware store. In one such establishment worked Mabel Ford, wife of Robert Ford, 'the dirty little coward who shot Thomas Howard', then the alias of Jesse James. Not until the present decade have Hollywood film-makers recognized the fact of the symbiotic relationship

Amorous Couple
Jacob Van Loo 1614–70
COURTESY OF HOOGSTEDER-
NAUMAN, LTD, NEW YORK

between cowboys and the cheapest whores.

The legendary Calamity Jane, for example, was the daughter of a prostitute. This very good friend of Wild Bill Hickock not only worked in a whorehouse herself, she also patronized them while disguised as a man. Eventually she became a madam with a house in Blackfoot, Montana. The name Calamity came from what her unlucky customers suffered after contact with her in the bedroom. In reality she bore a greater resemblance to Wallace Beery in drag than to Jean Arthur; nor did Wild Bill look much like Gary Gooper, whatever he was wearing.

Many other legendary names have bordello links: Butch Cassidy and the Sundance Kid (Harry Longbaugh) operated out of Fannie Porter's brothel in Fort Worth, Texas. Cole Younger and Myra Belle Shirley were part of the bawdy cast. Myra became Belle Starr after marrying an Indian of that name. She was a notorious horse thief, cattle rustler, stagecoach robber, prostitute and finally a madam who gave sanctuary to countless murdering bandits when she settled down in her own parlour-house. Dodge City, Kansas, also produced many legendary Western characters. Doc Holliday, the gun-toting dentist, was a close friend of Madam 'Big Nose Kate' Fisher and a favoured customer of one of her prettier girls, 'Squirrel Tooth Alice'. It was in Dodge City that the murder of Dora Hand, a member of the footloose band of light-ladies calling themselves 'The Fairy Belles', called forth a posse which had among its members Wyatt Earp, Bat Masterson and Charlie Bassett. In point of historical fact, there are few Wild West figures glamorized by Hollywood who were not born or bred in or who lived in whorehouses during those romanticized days. The cathouses of the frontier were today's short-stay motels where now drug deals are made and hijackings planned instead of bank robberies and stage holdups.

Thanks to Mae West's many performances, perhaps the most famous trollop turned bordello-keeper was Idaho's 'Diamond Tooth Lil' who ran her place well into Prohibition days. Among her illustrious clientele from the world of pugilism were Kid McCoy, Spider Kelly, Tom Sharkey and a legend in his own right, Tex Richard.

Not all of the ladies who gained fame in the West were as 'vulgar, degraded and brutish' as Mr Perkins would have us believe. In her own day the grandest courtesan of them all was Lola Montez. Like the 'Queen of London Whoredom', Laura Bell, Mistress Lola came out of Ireland. By the time she was thirteen she knew that there was more money to be made from selling her body than from dancing. After taking three husbands and countless lovers, including Franz Liszt and Alexander Dumas *père*, she became the mistress of King Louis I of Bavaria who, according to one source, 'gave her his kingdoms' when she 'caused him to achieve ten orgasms in a twenty-four-hour period'. Her carryings-on with Louis brought about a crisis of state which ended with his abdication. Lola returned to the British Isles and eventually found her way to America where she lectured and

Calamity Jane, *c.* 1850
DENVER PUBLIC LIBRARY, WESTERN
HISTORY DEPARTMENT

Calamity Jane,
Gen. Crook's Scout.

danced her interpretation of the jig; when not touring the dance-halls, she found time to take on innumerable wealthy American patrons who had made their fortunes plundering the West. Like so many of her predecessors, in her autumnal years the fabulous Lola devoted much of her wealth and more of her energy to assisting fallen women.

While the cities of the Wild West were making the headlines for lawlessness and profligacy, the delta city of New Orleans had already established its pre-eminence for vice in the New World. San Francisco could scarcely have achieved its overnight success as a fleshpot without the amount of talent supplied by New

Interior of a Bordello
Dutch school 17th C
COURTESY OF HOOGSTEDER-
NAUMAN, LTD, NEW YORK

Hole in the Wall Gang: L.R. Harry
Longabaugh, Bill Carver, Ben
Kilpatrick, Harvey Logan alias
Kid Curry, Robert Parker alias
Butch Cassidy
DENVER PUBLIC LIBRARY, WESTERN
HISTORY DEPARTMENT

Orleans. In the finest British tradition, the French early on sent hordes of
convicted felons and harlots to its possession at the mouth of the Mississippi. In a
sense, these women came to New Orleans under royal auspices because it was the
French Kings, Louis XIV and Louis XV, who had thousands of troublesome
wenches shipped to the Louisiana colony. By the middle of the eighteenth
century New Orleans was revelling in its reputation for iniquity. For all that,
bordello life did not accelerate rapidly until the American acquisition of power in
1803 and the imposition of Puritan morality. Nothing succeeds in fanning the
flames of vice like attempts at suppression. Another boost to the sex business
came when Andrew Jackson brought in his scrounging bands during the War in
1812. The accompanying band of camp-followers decided to stay on because the

'Moral Conditions', Leadville
   Colorado
DENVER PUBLIC LIBRARY, WESTERN
   HISTORY DEPARTMENT

'Diamond Tooth Lil'
DENVER PUBLIC LIBRARY, WESTERN
   HISTORY DEPARTMENT

regular trade provided by the Mississippi river boatmen was far more reliable than that of the catch-as-catch-can soldiery.

For all its frogs' legs and French frippery, New Orleans had another claim on international fame. Only here could be found an entire class of women bred, raised and trained for life in the bordello, the great caste of Creole quadroons and octaroons. Just as black males were bred for work on the plantations, the mixed-blood females were raised like cotton to fill the brothel-houses. Those with the fairer complexions and better features were able to set themselves up as private entrepreneurs. To meet an available mulatto girl a New Orleans swell had only to attend one of the periodic Quadroon Balls and then negotiate with the girl's mother or 'auntie' for the services of a full-time mistress. The young women would then be set up in a private house in the Ramparts Street district which is memorialized today by the jazz classic *South Rampart Street Blues*. During the area's heyday fire-and-brimstone New Orleans preacher Philo Tower asserted that three out of every five houses in the heart of the city were operating as bordellos or were occupied by various grades of courtesan. Neither New York nor London could boast such popular urban planning.

After the Civil War the popularity of black and mulatto harlots declined and various types of white women moved in to replace them. Many women who tired of the great trek from the east coast to California and the Pacific northwest simply gave up the trip and floated down the Mississippi to what might have appeared as a more leisurely life in the great Sin City on the Gulf. What the migrants out in San Francisco called a 'fandango palace' the residents of New Orleans called a 'dance-house'. Here the near or totally naked women, unpaid by the management, danced with the customers to provide samples of what was available upstairs or off-premises for a modest price. Among the leading dance-houses of the day was one operated by the notoriously hot-tempered Daniel O'Neil from 1860 to 1869. On one occasion when one of his strumpets offended him, Mr O'Neil drugged the object of his displeasure, stripped her of the few garments she was wearing and threw her into the alley behind his dance-hall. There she was gang-raped by a collection of layabouts and hooligans. Although the odious O'Neil was acquitted of complicity in the sordid business, his Amsterdam Dance House was eventually closed by the authorities. In a letter to the *Daily Picayune* he had the temerity to complain that he was put out of business because he had not kept up his regular payments to the New Orleans police department.

Gradually the primitive dance-houses gave way to the more comfortable parlour-houses of South Basin Street. These swank establishments were run by such pioneering ladies as Minni Ha Ha, Kate Townsend and Hattie Hamilton. Hattie was the Crescent City's first madam with real political clout. She was the mistress of Senator James Beares and it was with his financial assistance that she built her bordello on South Basin Street called *Twenty-One*, not to be confused with New York's *21* which was simply a prohibition speakeasy. A reporter for the *Picayune* covered the opening of Hattie's house in February 1869 with these words: 'The entrance was through a passageway adorned with a couple of statues representing some obscure divinities of light, and in whose hands were held lighted flambeaux. Beyond this lay the drawing-room, peopled with a few figures in glittering attire, and who, from their costumes and manners, might have been visitants from the Mountains of the Moon.' Clearly, high fashion had come to the new New Orleans to save it from the degradations sponsored by the likes of O'Neil.

None the less, some of the original brutishness survived behind the scenes. Big Kate Townsend was murdered in her $100,000 parlour-house by her Creole paramour, Troissant Sykes. This imaginative citizen claimed to have slain Madam Townsend with a Bowie knife in self-defence, and then sued in probate court to be declared her sole heir. The Dickensian-like Sykes received only a nominal sum

Dance Hall, New York 1868
Wood engraving by Frank Leslie
NEW YORK IN THE 19th C. BY JOHN
CRAFTON, DOVER PUBLICATIONS
1980 DOVER PICTORIAL ARCHIVE
SERIES

from the normally corrupt court which proved perhaps that even New Orleans had a shred of conscience. Before her untimely demise Kate ran what was probably the fanciest whorehouse in North America. Champagne went for $50 a bottle and the girls' prices ran from $100 up. Kate Townsend was also the first madam in American history to deal in credit, a forerunner of the credit-card prostitution to be instituted a century later.

Luckier than Kate Townsend was Fanny Sweet, New Orleans' answer to Montana's Calamity Jane. Procuress, thief, lesbian, sometime Confederate spy and skilled poisoner, Fanny's business affairs were guided in part by the contemporary queen of voodoo, Marie Laveau who sold her advice and magic much as Fanny sold flesh. Miss Sweet's speciality was providing older men with time-honoured 'virgins', then blackmailing the gullible gentlemen for their weakness. Fanny's voodoo beliefs and practices seem to have stood her in good stead, because although she was accused of poisoning her lover and doing away with several other persons by the same means, she never spent a day in gaol and died in pleasant retirement in Pensacola, Florida, near the end of the century. Thanks to the recent influx of illegal aliens from the Caribbean, voodoo is still alive and well in metropolises like New Orleans and New York today, with St Dambulla statuettes almost as prevalent in some neighbourhoods as brownstone cathouses.

Badjicans and *mambos* aside, Fanny Sweet was far from alone in her specialized trade. Just as in Victorian London, the procurement of virgins in New Orleans was big business. As early as 1845, when James K. Polk was in the White House, one Mary Thompson was using a cigar store as a front for her traffic in under-aged girls. Queen Mary, as she was sometimes called, charged between $200 and $500 for the merchandise available through her corner store on Royal Street. Fifteen years later the price for supposedly unsullied girls had gone up to $800. Schoolteacher Louisa Murphy, who used her position to special advantage, put that price on the little students she provided to the wealthy old men she serviced. A few years later, because of the hot competition between the procuresses, the girls were discounted at a price as low as $100.

Probably the most successful among these harridans was Agnes Herrick. Also known as 'Spanish Agnes' to the police and to her friends in the underworld, her cover was an employment agency on Burgundy Street which she operated with impunity for more than forty years. Although she was brought up on charges innumerable times with blatant evidence against her, Spanish Agnes spent not a single night in gaol, clear evidence that it paid to have friends or conspirators in City Hall.

In 1867, the year before President Andrew Johnson was impeached, a law was enacted requiring the madams of New Orleans to purchase licences to operate for $250. Soon both sides of Canal Street for thirty blocks were lined with licensed bordellos. For the rest of the country a trip to New Orleans was equated with a voyage to Sodom and Gomorrah. Advertising directories published during this era proclaimed the cultural and sexual accomplishments of the ladies, a practice clearly borrowed from the earlier houses of Paris. Opium, morphine and cocaine were very much a part of the scene, much used by the inmates of the houses and available to the customers on request. In the semi-official publications, on the order of the Guide Michelin, the establishments themselves were graded in ascending order: Clip Joints, Cribs, Whorehouses, Bordellos, Houses of Assignation, Sporting-Houses and Mansions. In the clip joint the customer found himself being masturbated under the table by one hand while the other removed his wallet. Cribs were generally tiny lattice-fronted shops occupied by other races, refugees from the plantations and the Orient. Whorehouses lined the waterfront where seamen were usually too inebriated to realize what they were getting into. In the better bordellos it was promised that bedsheets were changed every day, while a house of assignation was a place where you would not be ashamed to take a fellow club-member's wife. Sporting-houses, of course, were favoured by the free-spending gambling types when they had had their fill of horseflesh and fighting cocks. In the mansion/parlour-houses the real gentlemen

A Crib Girl at Home
Storyville by Lee Friedlander
COURTESY OF LEE FRIEDLANDER

were entertained by the city's finest ladies amid feather boas and gold spittoons.

The Arlington at 225 Basin Street, named after its proprietor Josie, was a major house four storeys high topped by a neo-Byzantine cupola. Josie's advertisement in the New Orleans *Blue Book* presented the premises as 'absolutely and unquestionably the most decorative and costly fitted-out sporting-palace ever placed before the American public'. The Arlington featured a Turkish Parlor, a Hall of Mirrors, a Japanese Parlor, a Viennese Parlor and an American Parlor for any old-fashioned chauvinists who might turn up. In a day when the *sine qua non* of luxury was measured by the number of lifelike and lifesized statues and paintings on hand, Josie's place was unparalleled save for Lillian (Lulu) White's

THIS BOOK MUST NOT BE MAILED

TO KNOW the right from the wrong, to be sure of yourself, go through this little book and read it carefully, and then when you visit Storyville you will know the best places to spend your money and time, as all the BEST houses are advertised. Read all the "ads."

This book contains nothing but Facts, and is of the greatest value to strangers when in this part of the city. The names of the residents will be found in this Directory, alphabetically arranged, under the headings "White" and "Colored," from alpha to omega. The names in capitals are landladies only.

You will find the boundary of the Tenderloin District, or Storyville: North side Iberville Street to south side St. Louis, and east side North Basin to west side North Robertson Street.

This is the boundary in which the women are compelled to live, according to law.

The Arlington

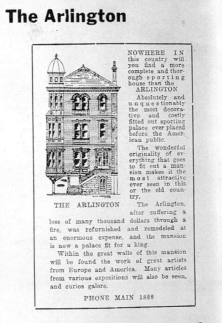

NOWHERE IN this country will you find a more complete and thorough-sporting house than the ARLINGTON

Absolutely and unquestionably the most decorative and costly fitted out sporting palace ever placed before the American public.

The wonderful originality of everything that goes to fit out a mansion makes it the most attractive ever seen in this or the old country.

THE ARLINGTON   The Arlington, after suffering a loss of many thousand dollars through a fire, was refurnished and remodeled at an enormous expense, and the mansion is now a palace fit for a king.

Within the great walls of this mansion will be found the work of great artists from Europe and America. Many articles from various expositions will also be seen, and curios galore.

PHONE MAIN 1888

225 N. Basin

PREFACE

"Honi Soit Qui Mal y Pense"

THIS Directory and Guide of the Sporting District has been before the people on many occasions, and has proven its authority as to what is doing in the "Queer Zone."

Anyone who knows to-day from yesterday will say that the Blue Book is the right book for the right people.

WHY NEW ORLEANS SHOULD HAVE THIS DIRECTORY

Because it is the only district of its kind in the States set aside for the fast women by law.

Because it puts the stranger on a proper and safe path as to where he may go and be free from "Hold-ups," and other games usually practiced upon the stranger.

It regulates the women so that they may live in one district to themselves instead of being scattered over the city and filling our thoroughfares with street walkers.

It also gives the names of women entertainers employed in the Dance Halls and Cabarets in the District.

---

emporium at neighbouring 235 Basin Street. A rather dumpy woman of questioned ancestry, Miss Lillian nevertheless managed to capture the fancy and the pocketbooks of a number of leading New Orleans businessmen, including a prosperous oilman, a railroad baron and a department store owner. With their financial aid she was able to build Mahogany Hall, the most celebrated bordello in the country. The *Mahogany Hall Souvenir Booklet* reported:

> The house is built of marble and is four story; containing five parlors, all handsomely furnished, and fifteen bedrooms. Each room has a bath with hot and cold water and extension closets. The elevator, which was built for two, is of the latest style; the entire house is steam heated and is the handsomest house of its kind. It is the only one where you can get three shots for your money –
> The shot upstairs,
> The shot downstairs,
> And the shot in the room. . .

Nothing is said about a shot in the back, not an infrequent occurrence in freewheeling New Orleans where murder ran far ahead of death from natural causes in the mortality tables. Lulu White achieved immortality with the jazz piece, *Mahogany Hall Stomp*, recorded by such artists as Louis Armstrong.

New Orleans' world-famous redlight district, Storyville, named after Alderman Sidney Story, moralist and jazzophobe, came into existence in 1898, the year of the first modern Olympic games. It lasted until federal military authorities deemed it a hazard to the troops preparing to fight in World War I. The War Department was determined that the youth of America training in

Louisiana should not be corrupted as had been Caesar's legions or the yeomen following the banner of Richard Coeur de Lion. Fabled Storyville was unique among the young nation's legalized bordello areas. It was a zone, carefully delineated by statute, outside of which loose women and common prostitutes were forbidden to reside or to practise their trade. Of all the great houses in the designated working zone, the most enduring was run by Nell Kimball who opened her first house in New Orleans in 1880. She had started in the whoring business in St Louis at the age of fifteen and like so many others had drifted down the Mississippi to find her fortune on the delta. There she remained active as a madam until her forced retirement in 1917. Her memoirs, published after her death, give the best picture available about bordello life in nineteenth-century America.

Nell paid her girls one-third of what they earned. The rest went for the upkeep of the house, the mandatory payoffs and her own small profit. She allowed the pimps or boyfriends of the girls only one visit a month and believed there was nothing lower in life than a pimp, except some politicians she had known. She never met a whore with a heart of gold. They were, as a rule, mean but sentimental, giving to crying over dogs, kittens, kids and sad songs. They never opened a newspaper until the comics were added to its pages.

A typical day at Nell's mansion started with a supper at four o'clock. The girls were served a soup, meat, potatoes and other vegetables, then pie and stewed fruit for dessert because constipation was one of the major ailments common to all her workers. Until nine in the evening the girls sat around smoking, doing their hair, exchanging small talk about their lurid experiences and thumbing through picture magazines. All of them knew of John L. Sullivan but none had heard of Huckleberry Finn. Electric lights were adding a marvellous new ambience to their residence, but many of the older girls hated it and would work only by candlelight.

At nine o'clock a black jazzband started to play in the front parlour and a piano player went to work in the back parlour which was reserved for the big-spenders. Ragtime was the rage.

By midnight on an average evening there would be fifteen to twenty customers in both parlours where maids circulated with trays of drinks. Most of the girls wore evening gowns decorated with lots of feathers and frou-frou. Others wore jockey uniforms complete with boots and riding crop. Some dressed as little girls with ribbons and bows and patent leather shoes. Like so many madams before and after her, Nell knew she was selling the realization of suppressed dreams as much as she was common sexual expression. Among her favourite clients were prize-fighters and actors, and despite her claims to the contrary, so were senators and judges. Early in her career Nell recognized that there was an actor inside every politician. While she admired the former for their largesse, she catered to the latter unashamedly because she knew that without their support,

Crib Girl
Storyville by Ernest Bellocq
COURTESY OF LEE FRIEDLANDER

clandestine or open, she would not be long in the business.

By two in the morning all the bedrooms were occupied, either by short tricks or all-night johns. By three o'clock the last customers would have arrived. On the third floor some sort of sex circus or bogus voodoo show would be under way, and, on special occasions, a group orgy. Unless there was an all-night ball in town or a boatload of tourists making the rounds, the house on Basin Street closed its shutters at five o'clock. The night's take would not be counted until the following morning when Nell got up at ten or eleven o'clock. The hard-working madam felt that running her business was as complex a job as that of any small corporation executive. After counting the revenue of the previous night, the cut for the police and city hall had to be placed in appropriate envelopes. The laundry was inspected with the housekeeper, cleaning bills were paid, broken chairs, lamps and soiled linens replaced. Food had to be ordered after consultation with the cook, the liquor supply replenished. And so it went until supper at four when the drill started all over again. Nell Kimball never went in for fancy gold cuspidors and chamberpots as Kate Townsend had done. Hers was a $25 sporting-house which she believed gave the johns good value for their money. It must have done to stay open successfully for thirty-seven years.

Now, like jazz, a slang word for sex, harlotry also travelled well up the Mississippi from New Orleans. Along the way famous houses opened in places like Memphis and St Louis, but none to match the greatest palace of all in Chicago, an incomparable bordello established by the Everleigh sisters. Ada and Minna Everleigh were a pair of Kentucky belles, daughters of a successful lawyer, who were born shortly after the Civil War ended. They married a pair of local brothers and separated from them promptly to go on the stage, one of the few respectable occupations open to women at the time other than schoolteaching. In 1898 they inherited $35,000 from their father's estate and went to Omaha, Nebraska, which was the site of the Trans-Mississippi Exposition. There they discovered that the biggest money in town was being made in the better bordellos. Wisely, they invested in one of these houses and by the time the Exposition was over and they were ready to leave, they had more than doubled their investment. On the advice of a visiting madam from Washington, DC, Cleo Maitland, who knew her politicians, too, the Everleigh girls selected Chicago for the location of their first solely-owned pleasure-palace, keeping alive the tradition of Theodora and Hong Kong's Madam Kimball, two earlier troupers who made good in the bawdy trade. They invested more than two-thirds of their capital furnishing the Everleigh Club on Chicago's South Dearborn Street which opened 1 February, 1900, the same year Theodore Dreiser's *Sister Carrie* was published. The Everleigh house was to be the fanciest bordello in the western hemisphere, what has been described by the cognoscenti as 'the most luxurious and profitable bordel ever operated in the United States, or the world for that matter'.

The mansion consisted of adjoining three-storey brownstones. In addition to a library and an art gallery, there were fourteen separate parlours and private bedrooms for thirty girls. These entertainment suites were furnished with mirrored ceilings and giant brass beds and each bedroom contained some peculiar attraction designed to amaze or tickle the fancy of the patron. One had a wall-to-wall mattressed Persian rug on the floor, while another offered an automatic perfume sprayer over the bed which could be filled with an aroma of the visitor's choice. Ada and Minna had their own separate boudoirs where they never entertained; the servants had their own quarters in the basement. In every corner of the house there were always fresh roses, and on nights when the mood possessed her, Minna would release live butterflies to flutter about the premises.

Crib Girl
Storyville by Ernest Bellocq
COURTESY OF LEE FRIEDLANDER

During their adolescent years the sisters had been greatly affected by the pre-Raphaelite poets, but this did not distort their business sense or weaken their dramatic flair.

The Gold, Silver and Copper Parlours were reserved for mining magnates who made their fortunes in those popular metals, the counterparts of today's oil sheikhs. The club also contained a Music Room and a Ballroom, complete with Oriental fountain. And another spectrum of parlours: a Red Room, Rose, Green, Blue and Green Room. There were Asian, Japanese, Egyptian, and Chinese Rooms, and the inevitable Moorish Room. All of these were designed to meet the most outlandish tastes of the *nouveaux riches* customers which at best could be described as Victorian baroque. They were furnished with cushions and divans and incense burners and knick-knacks gathered from the four corners of the world. Two curving staircases at opposite sides of the house were lined with potted palms and marble statues purporting to be Grecian goddesses and led to even greater wonders on the upper floors. In the Gold Room the spittoons were of eighteen-carat gold, the fishbowls were gold-rimmed, the $15,000 grand piano gold-plated, and golden draperies hung behind chairs covered with gold cloth.

Word of the fashionable Everleigh Club spread like wildfire, claimed its boosters. As evidence, they cited the fact that when Prince Henry of Prussia, Kaiser Wilhelm's brother, visited the United States in 1902 and was asked what he most wanted to see, he promptly named the classy bordello on South Dearborn Street. Such was its luxury that prominent Chicago lawyer 'Colonel' MacDuff made it his habit to spend his annual two-week vacation on the premises. Among the gentlemen from the world of sports who frequented this sporting-house were 'Gentleman Jim' Corbett, world heavyweight champion, Stanley 'The Michigan Assassin' Ketchel, world middleweight champ, and 'Bet-a-Million' Gates who was equally well known around the nation's prize rings and racecourses. No actor worth a billing failed to spend at least a night strutting his stuff among the girls. At the height of its fame, a Congressional investigating committee from Washington showed up to conduct most of its explorations of sin in the upstairs bedrooms.

So much for glamour. The working day started earlier here than at Nell Kimball's, at two in the afternoon when the girls were served breakfast consisting of cold clam juice and aspirin as an appetizer, followed by a choice of eggs, sautéed kidneys, clam cakes with bacon, planked whitefish, shad roe, or breast of chicken, accompanied by toast and Turkish coffee. The late supper menu for the clients and the wholesome girls they selected for the night listed fried oysters, naturally, guinea fowl, Welsh-rabbit, pheasant, capon, devilled crabs, broiled squab, lobster, roast turkey, caviar, duck and goose. Baked, stuffed swan was occasionally available. Many of the visitors to the club, according to their reports, showed up for the food alone.

Like the lupanars of ancient Rome, this grand house was staffed by cooks,

Oriental Music Room at the
Everleigh Club
CHICAGO HISTORICAL SOCIETY

waiters, dressmakers, hairdressers, barbers and masseurs. It advertised steam heat in winter, fans in summer, and on busy nights the club had three four-piece bands to enliven the scene. This creation of the girls from Kentucky was a $50 house; their competitors generally charged from $5 to as little as $1. This was only the basic fee; food, drink, tips and general largesse could bring a single night's bill up to $500 or $1000, this in the days when there was still a glass of beer for a nickle and a good 5c cigar. On an average night the Everleigh sisters took in thousands of dollars and at the end of the month, after deducting the usual political payoffs and operating expenses, they showed a $10,000 profit. When Ada and Minna retired and moved to New York they were millionaires. Though it was in operation for less than a dozen years, the Everleigh Club set the standard for American bordels for decades to come. When it was closed in October 1911, the police officer in charge was, fittingly, Chief John McWeeny.

The Everleigh Club was scarcely the first popular American bawdy house to go down under the cold breath of the blue-noses. The distinction for trying to regulate brothels for the first time in the United States goes to the city of St Louis, Missouri, but its history has a twist to it. The regulatory experiment between 1872 and 1874 failed miserably for the ages-old reason: the corrupt relationship between government and property interests. Borrowing from the Paris regulations, the Missouri legislature required that all prostitutes be registered in one of three classes: Inmate Houses, Occupants of Rooms outside such houses, and those known as Kept Women. All such women were forbidden to change their places of business without notifying the authorities. Solicitation on the streets or from a window or doorway was prohibited. Nor could a red light be used outside the premises to attract customers. For a time, the statistics on whore-control looked good.

The doughty city fathers had failed, however, to look ahead. As the unfortunate women tried their best to conform to the new laws, it turned out that the regulations threatened to endanger the incomes of the local political figures and the real-estate operators who had learned to depend upon protection money and exorbitant rents over the years. Ultimately, these two special-interest groups joined forces with the concerned clergy and proponents of purity and demanded an end to this compromise with sin. Obviously, Americans preferred the abolition of prostitution to its regulation; but it was the type of abolition that could soothe the strict conscience while simultaneously filling the pockets of politicians and avaricious landlords. In St Louis, as elsewhere and always, it was back to business as usual.

The same society which boasted of Comstockery, strict continence and Horatio Alger's priggish heroics, looked with less pride on the statistics concerning prostitution at the end of the nineteenth century. A poor third in mid-century, New York found itself with the world's largest bordello population by 1893. As is always the case, the procurers preyed on the weak, the poor and the newly arrived immigrants, the exploited shopgirls and domestic servants. New York could now share a reputation for whoredom earlier enjoyed by London, Paris and Rome. Americans were determinedly unwilling to take a back seat on any level of cultural achievement.

The nationalities of the girls lured into the trade followed the patterns of immigration. In the 1850s the colleens and fräuleins stocked the bordels. By the 1880s, Jewish, Polish and Russian girls made up the bulk of the inhabitants. Then, after the turn of the century, Italian women provided most of the bedroom workers. As usual, the bordello population and the ethnic groups found dominating the prize-fight racket ran parallel.

Mary's Dance-Hall
COURTESY OF LAWRENCE E.
    GICHNER

Because the average working life of a girl in the trade was five years, a new supply had constantly to be found. It was estimated at the turn of the century that three-quarters of the women occupying the bordellos in the United States started out in New York and were taken by their pimps to other cities throughout the country. At the time, Bishop Simpson of the Methodist Episcopal Church of New York stated authoritatively that there were more women in the whore-houses of New York than there were Methodists in the entire city. Police Superintendent John A. Kennedy called this statement something of an exaggeration, but the knowledgeable police official did admit that there were 621 known bordels, ninety-six houses of assignation and seventy-five dance-halls of 'ill-repute'. Clearly, San Francisco and New Orleans had dropped out of the running as the Capitals of Sin, while Las Vegas had yet to exist. Then, as now, New York was anything but a classless society and its different grades of brothel-house reflected the marked distinctions.

In the shabbiest tenement cribs, the older and least attractive women charged 50c for a few seconds of dubious pleasure. Middle-class clientele in middle-class houses were charged a dollar or two a trick. The upper-class houses catering to politicians and wealthy gentlemen charged $10 and up. Among the last was an establishment called *The Seven Sisters* which pre-dated the oil cartel by several years. This was a parlour-house occupying no less than seven sturdy brownstones in a row on West 25th Street. With great ceremony the madam running the conglomerate left engraved invitations for men registered at the best hotels in the immediate area. Formal wear was obligatory at the *Sisters* of an evening. Not so large but even more exclusive was Josephine Wood's girl-house on Clinton Place, west of Broadway. There only visiting aristocrats, men of great wealth and politicians of stature were admitted. Unless he was a regular customer, each visitor had to have his credentials approved by a burly butler, something akin to the admission policy of today's discotheques.

The parlours where these robber baron patrons and their friends waited for their entertainment were furnished with crystal chandeliers, velvet carpets, pornographic paintings, gilt-framed mirrors and sofas upholstered in satin and brocade. Only champagne was served while the men made their selections from the barely literate girls on hand. Later, brandy and cigars were served on the house. The girls were reported to earn $200 each on an average night.

With extramarital sex so popular in nineteenth-century America, it is small wonder that, real or imaginary, permanent or temporary, impotence was a source of grave anxiety among the upper-class male population. All the quack remedies and superstitions of the Bankside, the Renaissance courtesans and medicine-men of the Orient, may not appear so odd when compared with some of the remedies concocted by the American quacks. Although the victims of this curious condition have been noted throughout history – from Egyptian King Amasis and Roman Emperors Nero and Honorius to the Frankish monarch Charlemagne and even the robust Henry VIII – the disorder was particularly disturbing to the nineteenth-century hypochondriacs of the United States. Perhaps it had something to do with the already emerging myth of the American Frontier and its underpinnings of extravagant virility. Whatever the case, the fears were real and some of the prescriptions fearsome. One popular remedy consisted of a combination of opium, musk and ambergris. Some highly respected doctors were advising the sexually bankrupt to drink a small glass of warm blood before breakfast; whose blood was not advised. Oysters, as always, were popular as supposed aphrodisiacs, as were arsenic and gold chloride. The list of chemicals a patient might be advised to take reads like an alchemist's handbook. If the gentleman was lucky enough to avoid contracting a disease from one of the parlour-house girls, he stood a fair chance of poisoning himself while beefing up his masculinity in preparation for his next visit.

With or without the aid of myriad patent medicines guaranteed to keep the

American male fit for the saddle, the brothel customers multiplied at an alarming rate. The last decade of the nineteenth century and the first of the twentieth mark the Golden Age of the Bordello in the United States. Then, in 1911, in an effort to stop the infamous 'white slave trade', the Mann Act was passed which made it illegal to transport under-age women across state lines. Simultaneously, the 'age of consent' was raised from a low of seven in Delaware to a uniform eighteen throughout the country. Like the fandango palaces and the saloons with their hot entertainment rooms upstairs, the tenderloin districts began to disappear from the American scene. In the first decade of this century there were 141 recognized redlight districts in the major cities of the United States. In the ten years that followed all met their end.

The Everleigh Club in Chicago was shuttered in 1911. St Louis, Minneapolis, Portland and Los Angeles shut down during the next two years. Denver and Baltimore closed their parlour-houses in 1915. Finally, in 1917, San Francisco's Barbary Coast, Seattle's Skid Row and New Orleans's Storyville closed their world-famous sporting-houses. This looked to be a sad ending indeed for the ancient and venerable profession.

CHAPTER NINE

QUEENS OF THE QUEANS

IF THE REDLIGHT districts are doomed to extinction, it means only that the way is open for more clandestine and higher-class bordellos. The lower and middle classes might have a more difficult time finding their sexual entertainments but certainly not the upper-income high-rollers. More important, politicians and real-estate operators find that there is more money to be made from one garish illegal house than from a dozen quasi-legal supervised brothels. The $2 and $20 ladies of the evening give way to the girls who perform at $100 a shot and on their passports bill themselves as 'model' or 'actress'. Robber barons are on the decline. Prohibition and bathrub gin are in. And so is the Mafia, a fraternal organization formed in Sicily during the Middle Ages to protect the peasants from marauding Norsemen. The brotherhood now extends its beneficent arms to embrace the sisters in the American sex industry.

After serving her apprenticeship in the cathouses of foggy San Francisco, Beverly Davis moved to sunny southern California the year after the Everleigh sisters closed up shop in Chicago. In 1913 Beverly opened her own sporting-house in the Belmore district of Los Angeles, then an exclusive residential area, and called it a private club. In her first effort as an entrepreneur she grossed between $1500 and $2500 a night. And this was in the days before Hollywood was *Hollywood!* True, five million Americans were going to the movies every week, but only a few of the silent moving pictures were being made in California. When pioneering Cecil B. DeMille arrived the following year to make *The Squaw Man*, he found Los Angeles to be 'a compact little inland city, thriving in its modest way'. Making his way 'out through the open country to Hollywood' he compared to making 'a safari'. To DeMille's mind the future world film capital was an 'all but unknown quiet village of orange groves and pepper trees, out there to the northwest of Los Angeles'. In the beginning Beverly Davis was about as prescient as Cecil. Nevertheless, she was in the right place at the right time with the right product. In her biography, *Call House Madam*, Miss Davis reports that Hollywood was raw, both professionally and emotionally:

Households can't last unless they're artificially stimulated. A kick a minute. Nothing's nutty enough. Give them a new slant, the jolt, something cuckoo. If you cater, with houses, to sex, you'll have all kinds of appetites to feed. They know they can ask for anything, and copy each other. Nobody eats a square meal of healthy food. It's got to be tainted, overdone too long like game, for the putrid pleasure of lust. When the game smells, it's good. That's what's abnormal, queer or perverse about these people. As a madam, I've seen it all.

Beverly certainly must have seen a great deal because, after the opening in Belmore, she later ran houses on Sedgemont Street, De Lambert Avenue, North Fairmont, Redfern Drive, Franklin Avenue, North Estabrook, Princess Road, on La Reina Drive in Santa Monica and in the Mainbocher Hotel. In all she pandered to the tastes of Hollywood for more than a quarter of a century during the tinsel town's most important period of growth. Beverly's favourite establishment was the one on North Estabrook, 'the handsomest call house' she ever ran. When it had its gala opening in the late 1920s, movie attendance in the United States had grown to 115 million patrons a week. In the movie colony itself she had become nown as 'The Madam of the Stars', while she preferred to call herself more modestly a simple 'nookie-bookie'.

When Miss Davis moved in, the Estabrook house was a brand new apartment building on a corner lot surrounded by gardens, a triplex in 'Moorish style' with white stucco walls and a red tile roof. Beverly had the entire building remodelled to contain a variety of parlours, bedroom suites, dining areas and cocktail lounges. This wholly owned investment, she claimed, was paid for with the proceeds from the houses she had run earlier, the profits left her after regular payoffs to 'the underworld side', a subject she was reluctant to talk about even in her last years. The initial cost of the Estabrook was $100,000, with another $85,000 for the renovations.

The front for the operation was a French restaurant on the ground floor called *The Beehive*, a name showing that she and Hong Kong Kimball shared the same kind of wit. On the floor above the restaurant with its 'New York-cut steaks' were the bedroom suites to which dinner trays could be sent directly from the kitchen. The building's third floor contained the reception parlours, two bars and a private dining-room where movie stars and movie investors could celebrate their productions with the beauties in residence. From its hillside location the Estabrook hive overlooked the sprawling blanket of lights of Los Angeles and those on the Hollywood hills beyond. The gardens immediately below the grand house were planted with magnolia, bougainvillaea, wisteria and great beds of pansies.

In support of the eighteen resident hostesses were musicians, waiters, waitresses, housekeepers, maids, porters, laundry hands, garagemen and a security force. Opening night for this tasteful bordel ws considered a 'première', lacking only floodlights to sweep the sky. According to Miss Davis, 'Every screen personality seemed to be on hand. It was a turnout in evening clothes second to no feature film.' It was the year after the first talkie, when Chaplin and Garbo were on top and people were singing *Button up Your Overcoat.*

Once the Davis Hive became firmly established as an 'in' place for the movie folks, Beverly started to take outside orders. She described the Hollywood couple's typical evening request:

> When the two want diversion from the eternal feuding, the actor-husband calls up and will ask me to send one or two of my girls to their house in the hills above Brentwood to entertain them both. The house is a palace. Their servants think they're crazy. It has to be a triple-act or a quartet for any satisfaction to both. And the actress is very sadistic and likes to scratch and claw. If they were the only ones, I'd have to go out of business.

Never one to overlook a source of revenue, during the afternoon Beverly's houses catered to women who were charged one-third more than men because they took up more of the girls' time. Sex circuses could be arranged for the evening's programme and for those tired from a day performing on the set there were comfortable voyeur accommodations.

While the sex philosophers of the East occupied themselves by grading men according to their physical characteristics, Beverly, quite naturally, ranked her customers according to the amount of money they were willing to spend. Stars, she found, did not pay as much as featured players, while character actors generally paid more than featured players. Bit players and extras were the freest with their money, but, for obvious reasons, did not appear too often. Bankers were 'filthy pay' and Wall Street types 'hard to strip'. Gamblers, Jews and politicians tended to spend big money. The oil and railroad tycoons, great practical jokers all, tended on the whole to have little interest in sex. Putting all their energy into squeezing dollars out of the public, Beverly surmised, left them little spirit for anything else.

While Beverly Davis was busy with her sociological research in California, at the same time on America's opposite coast, New York's favourite madam, Polly Adler, was grading a different class of client. In her biography, published in 1954, *A House is not a Home*, which made her the country's most famous housekeeper, Miss Adler drops such names as Al Capone, Frank Costello, Arnie Rothstein, Dutch (Arthur Flegenheimer) Shultz, Bo Weinstein and Vincent ('Mad Dog') Coll. Gangsters and gamblers made up only a small part of Polly's trade, however. Of crusading Judge Seabury's investigation into vice in New York in 1929, Polly wrote:

> Personally, I had nothing to fear from Judge Seabury. This time the heat was on the law givers and the law enforcers. Investigators knew I had entertained many members of the magistrates court and vice squad and numerous other city officials and because I had paid thousands of dollars in bribes to keep my house running smoothly and my girls and me out of jail.

Polly Adler with a Friend, 1935
COPYRIGHT *THE NEWS*

Polly never had the temerity to open one of her bordellos with a fanfare such as Beverly Davis did, but she knew very well that the city's axis of power ran from Centre Street to Chambers with the real power brokers only a few blocks south.

Born in 1900 in Yanow, a Russian village near the Polish border, Polly Adler came to the United States as a child and was enrolled in the public school system through the first two years of high school before trying her luck in the sex business. With a good head for commerce, she realized by the time that she was twenty that there was a lot more money to be made by managing a stable of girls than by working as a freelance herself. She served her apprenticeship years as a madam near the upstate Saratoga racetrack where she enlarged her acquaintance-ship with most of New York city's leading gamblers, professional thieves and sports-minded politicians. In later years, Polly's 'House' of bestseller fame was not a single bordel but a series of apartments in mid-Manhattan on both the East and West sides.

By the time she was twenty-nine Polly was overseeing an establishment at Madison Avenue and 59th Street in what has been called the Silk Stocking District. That the area has a greater population density than Calcutta seems to be overlooked by the reporters. Two years later her house was on West 83rd Street, just off Central Park West, which today is near *The Erotic Bakery* and in an area sprinkled with an assortment of Hispanic bordellos. Her next move was to West 54th Street, then, in 1934, to a twelve-room apartment on Madison Avenue and 55th Street. While Mayor LaGuardia was in office and was busily cleaning up New York by shutting the burlesque houses, Polly was occupying the entire second floor at her new address. In addition to the girls, her in-house payroll included two maids and two cooks. Her immediate out-of-house payroll in-cluded the elevator operators, the building superintendent and, of course, the building's management; and beyond them the precinct house and the specialists of the vice squad. The FBI terminated John Dillinger's career that year, but there were still enough public enemies shooting up New York to occupy the attention of the local constabulary; there was little call to bear down on a small, open-handed madam.

A year later the political climate changed. In 1935 all the payoffs failed and Miss Adler was arrested and spent time in the clink. Thereafter, she reports, she never had girls living on her premises but became what would be correct to call a call-house madam who occasionally gave 'private parties'. After her humiliating experience with the law she set about re-establishing herself in modest quarters on 65th Street and by the following year was back on fashionable Central Park West where it was reported she was 'the proprietor of New York's most opulent bordello'. By 1939 she had reached such prominence in the sex trade that she was profiled in *Fortune Magazine*, which usually concerns itself with the nation's 500 leading corporations.

Although Polly's girls never at one time reached the number of those

Polly Always Covers Up
UNITED PRESS INTERNATIONAL
PHOTO

employed by the Everleigh sisters, she did manage and procure for enough of New York's leading whores to form a good picture of the kind of girl attracted to the profession. Most were of at least average intelligence and few of them ever thought to make a lifetime career of it. Generally, the goal proclaimed at least was to make enough money to retire, to learn another business, or to ensnare a wealthy husband. Some had genuine talent, actresses who had not had the big break, singers and dancers between gigs, or showgirls waiting for a new club to open. On the whole, confirming popular opinion and that of Nell Kimball, they were a sentimental lot whose favourite songs included *Heartaches Inside*, *Melancholy Baby* and *Broadway Rose*. Their interest in world affairs extended no further than Broadway gossip and their favourite reading matter ran to *True Confessions* and *Modern Romances*. They liked going to the movies and loved visiting nightclubs with their business dates. In places like the Stork Club and El Morocco they could powder their noses in the company of real debutantes like Brenda Frazier. As a rule her girls were compulsive buyers who never planned a wardrobe and instead bought anything that caught their fancy.

When they tired of New York's grey and grim winters they headed for the Florida sun in Miami and West Palm Beach. Once there, more often than not, they checked into a convenient brothel like Madam Sherry's and rarely thereafter saw the light of day. Other more adventurous girls travelled as far as California to become one of Beverly Davis's busy little bedroom bees. Some, according to legend, actually made it to the Silver Screen. Still, only the smart few saved money against the day when their youthful good looks would no longer appeal, a fact which gave Polly much concern:

> It worried me to see so many of them making no preparations for the future, and I used to nag and prod the girls to read good books and make something of themselves. Marching into the living-room, I would inquire of one of the lazy ladies lolling on the sofa what she expected to do for a living when she was thirty-five, and all too often the only answer was a bored sigh. Or perhaps one of them might say, 'Oh, don't worry about me, Polly. I won't wind up in the poorhouse. Just as soon as I lay my hands on enough money, I'm going to open a shop. I'm quite creative, you know; I took a correspondence course in designing.'

When it comes to the entire business of the sex business, Polly Adler echoes the words of most twentieth-century madams: 'What it comes down to is this: the grocer, the butcher, the baker, the merchant, the landlord, the druggist, the liquor dealer, the policeman, the doctor, the city father and the politician – these are the people who make money out of prostitution, these are the real reapers of the wages of sin.'

Miami's Madam Sherry voices many of the same complaints as did Polly Adler. If gambling money was Polly's main connection, booze was the lifeblood for Dade County's première madam during the first fifty years of this century. Sherry's real name was Ruth Barnes and she was bankrolled by Prohibition

Polly Adler

rum-runners operating between Cuba and Key West. With an $80,000 advance from bootlegging fiends she marched into a builder's office in the late 1920s and ordered him 'to build me a Moorish castle'. Two months after the stockmarket crashed in 1929 the Moorish castle dubbed *Chez Cheri* opened on Biscayne Boulevard at 54th Street.

In her life story, *Pleasure was My Business*, Miss Barnes shows a remarkable respect for tradition and class. She reports that into her fiefdom came the loveliest girls in the world, cultivated ladies who had worked previously with Polly Adler in New York and Billy Schibel in Pittsburg. Others had had experience in the *International* in Paris, the *Cushion House* in London and the *Coconut Club* in Panama City. Some came from the most famous houses in New Orleans and at one point she even employed a maid who had worked for the legendary Everleigh sisters in Chicago. Taking a clue from Polly Adler's book, Madam Sherry had her *filles de joie* parade themselves at Miami's racetracks. From the start, *Chez Cheri* was a great success and the eager patrons marched in, 'awed by the Byzantine architecture of Islam'. The décor can best be described by Madam Sherry herself:

> Multicolored light that filtered through imported stained glass windows illuminated an enormous vestibule from which a spiral staircase wound its way to the second-floor bedrooms. The walls of the anteroom were decorated with interlocking vari-colored squares into which were woven intricate floral designs. Jade incense burners gave off an exotic aroma and a faint light glinted off each of the gold leaf designs on the floor.
>
> To the right off the foyer was the main parlor, tastefully furnished in a formal regency mode with green and gold, all of which were set off with Italian travertine marble tables and Capri de Monte lamps and figurines. In the center of the room, set off by a mantel to ceiling fireplace mirror was an enormous Czechoslovakian chandelier.
>
> Off the vestibule to the left was the Victorian Room, reserved throughout the history of the establishment for the $100 trade. Done in lavish Louis XIV antique white with deep hues of red and gold with purple carpets and matching draperies and accessories, this room was worthy of royalty. It was unlocked only for special guests.

A bit stunned, perhaps, by this smörgåsbord of architecture and interior design, royalty of a kind did visit this sunshine bordel. Next to the venerable Victorian Room was the castle's most famous parlour, 'The Jockey Room'. Here the burnished copper walls were hung with famous racing prints under which the country's noted sports gentry paraded during the winter season after a day at Hialeah when Man O'War was king of the racing world. Across the hall were three additional reception rooms where the customers made their selections for the night before leaving for the upper levels of the castle.

There all the bedroom walls and ceilings were hung with mirrors. Deep pile carpets matched the silk and brocade draperies in colours of royal purple, golden rod and burnt sienna. Giant bed-divans were strewn with plush pillows and cushions. Each of the private bathrooms was equipped with a porcelain bidet, a great novelty at the time. In these pre-television days each room was equipped with a radio and phonograph player to enhance the aura of exotic romance.

A few favoured guests were allowed to enter a secret corridor which ended with see-through mirrors giving a view of two of the bedrooms. Here the voyeurs watched the bedroom activities from the comfort of club chairs with cool drinks in hand. Among Sherry's more notable customers were Tommy Manville, the commuting Dutch Shultz, Prince Alfonso, heir apparent to the throne of Spain's Alfonso XIII, and John Jacob Astor III, whose great bulk was found oppressive by the girls. Listed on Madam Sherry's outside payroll were the Miami bail-bondsmen, members of the police department, officials of the court, local mobsters, and, of course, the 'syndicate', the euphemism for the emerging Mafia. Initially sponsored by rum-runners who ran the Cuba–Key West–Miami route, the *Chez Cheri* was a safe-house frequented by 'the boys' from New York when they were checking on the southern end of operations.

The popular *Chez Cheri* castle remained in operation until the attack on Pearl Harbor in 1941. Ruth Barnes supported the war effort first by operating the 'Denice Massage Parlor' at 20th Street and Northwest 3rd Avenue, then in the management of a small business in the LaRue Hotel on Northwest 1st Avenue. Following the war it was back to the big-time when she opened the Rancho Lido on two and a half acres at 3120 Northwest 41st Street outside the Miami city limits in Dade County. One of her celebrated guests here was Egypt's King Farouk who on four different occasions reserved the entire house for himself. Foukie, as he was called, preferred three girls in bed at one time. When he denied this report and sued, the obese pornography collector lost the case. Madam Sherry, in turn, lost her ranch when she was sentenced to six months' imprisonment in 1950 during one of the periodic crackdowns on vice. This was a bad-time sentence for a lady whose favourite author, purportedly, was Rabelais.

The social history of California was more to the reading taste of San Francisco's grandest madam of the same period, Sally Stanford. Sally was born Mabel Janice Busby in Baker City, Oregon, in 1903, and made her way down the Pacific coast as a working girl who was determined to bring upper-class values to the bawdy houses of the Golden Gateway city. Her first step was to borrow the Stanford name from Leland, the railroad baron who gave his name to the university. Next, she opened an orderly disorderly house of her own at 793 O'Farrell Street during the last year of the Hoover administration.

Writing of San Francisco's rowdy district fifty years earlier B.E. Lloyd reported that 'licentiousness, debauchery, pollution, loathsome disease, insanity from dissipation, misery, profanity, blasphemy and death are here. And Hell, yawning to receive the putrid mass, is there also.' But what marvellous changes Sally wrought! At the peak of her career newspaper columnist Herb Caen dubbed her residence 'The Sally Stanford School of Advanced Social Studies'. Only licentiousness now remained, and that of the finest calibre. Before attaining this eminence there was a series of houses, each a bit grander than the last, at 1526 Franklin, 271 Austin, 1001 Vellejo and 929 Bush before her crowning achievement at 114 Pine Street, known to the citizens and police of San Francisco as *The Fortress*.

This Golden Gate landmark was built five years after the great earthquake and fire of 1906 by millionaire Robert G. Hanford for chocolate heiress Gabrielle Guittard who became his third wife after their long and much-publicized affair. Mr Hanford referred to his love nest as 'The Garden of Allah'. Nob Hill fortress or Islamic garden, the Stanford riding academy was something of both. The mansion was fronted with large blocks of dark granite and access was gained through a large and ornately latticed iron gate behind which the doorman lurked in a shadowed alcove. Once he was inside, the gate was locked behind the visitor. If his credentials were in order, the patron was allowed to pass through a second door which opened on to a landing from which a winding staircase led upward to a short hallway opening on the Pompeiian Court, an ornate chamber measuring 50 by 138 feet; in the centre a great fountain spouted jets of multi-coloured water illuminated by spotlights from above, the entire court ceilinged with double panels of transparent and translucent glass. A fireplace large enough to accommodate a spitted ox dominated the west wall.

It was in this setting that Mabel – Sally Stanford – Busby greeted the well-heeled gentlemen of all ages who were desirous of improving their knowledge of the social graces. Once the awestruck initiate passed muster with the Pine Street impresario he would be introduced to some of the 'debutantes' in residence. Corridors from the parlours led to a number of bedrooms, bathrooms and a capacious steamroom where lightheaded students could sweat out the champagne bubbles before or after their lessons in boudoir etiquette. This floor of *The Fortress* covered more than 6000 square feet. The floor above contained a variety of additional bed- and exercise-rooms and was connected to the street by a secret stairway used by visitors who might want to keep their presence unobserved by fellow students within or by the nightwatchers outside.

An ardent preservationist, Miss Stanford did little to change the décor of the Garden of Allah after she took it over from the Hanford heirs. As a result, it retained all of its turn-of-the-century charm, because, as she told the *San Francisco Examiner*'s Freddie Francisco, 'I like nice things and I am sure that my visitors appreciate them. After all, the élite of San Francisco have passed through my doors. This, of course, does not include Sgt John Dyer.'

Dyer, of the San Francisco vice squad, was Sally's nemesis and the two fought a long war of spying and concealment during the years before *The Fortress* surrendered in 1955. During her heyday the country girl from Baker City was undoubtedly San Francisco's leading businesswoman, numbering among her friends and customers many of the most prominent private citizens, politicians and business tycoons on the west coast. When she retired from the sex industry *Life Magazine* estimated that she probably was many times a millionaire. However, idleness never appealed to Miss Stanford. Taking up residence in Sausolito

The Accused Sally Stanford on Trial
SAN FRANCISCO EXAMINER

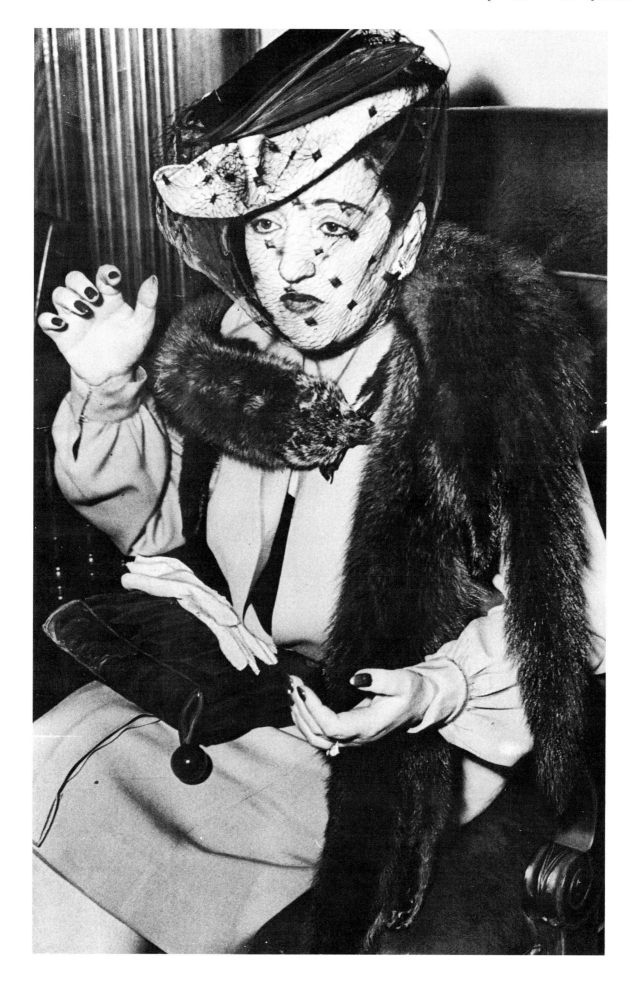

across the bay, she opened and ran a successful restaurant in much-celebrated Marin County for several years before running for councillor. Unsuccessful in politics at first, she was finally elected in 1976 to the office of mayor of Sausolito. Two years later she was immortalized in the eyes of the American viewing public when actress Dyan Cannon appeared in the Sally Stanford role in a television movie purporting to tell her life story. Thus Mabel Busby joined that select circle of American bawds which includes Belle Starr and Diamond Lil who have achieved international fame through the movies.

While many of her contemporaries were running bordellos on a hotel-like scale, Detroit's Helen ('Rocking Chair') McGowan did conduct most of her business in hotels. During one of its periodic investigations into the mercurial operations of organized crime the US Senate's probers found Miss McGowan keeping house at the Seneca Hotel on Third Street, one of a four-hotel chain licensed to one of the motor city's leading mobsters. Like Polly Adler, Helen McGowan claimed Al ('Scarface') Capone as a pal. She also reports to have been on very good terms with Public Enemy No. 1, John Dillinger. Again, like Polly, she was upset greatly by the division of income derived from the hard work of her girls. In her memoirs she reflects that 'my very old profession is still flourishing and profitable, but the chief money-makers are not the girls or the madam. Pimps, bondsmen, lawyers and the rackets take most of the love money.'

Born in 1911 in Malden, Missouri, Helen dropped out of school at the age of twelve and set out on the road as Mae Abshier shortly thereafter. She served her apprenticeship in small houses in places like Cicero and Peoria, Illinois, before arriving in Detroit in 1930. Here, with $50 and a short list of names borrowed from an underworld pimp she opened a two-girl establishment in an apartment house owned by a friend of her generous procurer friend. More than 1000 girls later she reports that she did not believe in paying off the cops. She saw no point in trying to bribe someone she did not expect to see again. In one year alone Helen moved her place of business thirty-five times, hardly consistent with her 'Rocking Chair' nickname.

In her biography, *Motor City Madam*, Miss McGowan reports just how profitable it was to be Detroit's top brothel-keeper:

> If the take was a thousand dollars for a particular night, five hundred went to the rackets boys, four hundred to the girls and one hundred to me. Out of my hundred I had to pay the rent for the apartments and all such incidentals, such as food and drink. I always had money, but not too much of it. The great bulk of our funds went to hoodlums and lawyers, thanks to our righteous laws that 'protect' the public against the oldest profession.

The 'thousand dollars a night' figure poses some interesting questions. According to McGowan she ran a $5 house, half the going rate in Detroit at the time, which caused her no end of problems with rival brothel-keepers like Brown Bessie and Mamie Moss. She also relates that most of the time hers was a

Sally Stanford on Her Seventy-
   eighth Birthday
SAN FRANCISCO EXAMINER

seven-girl stable. That shakes down to 200 tricks a night or twenty-eight-plus johns per girl during an average shift. Either the girls were extraordinarily hard-working or old Rocking Chair Helen was dispensing a lot of fake champagne and watered whisky to the Motor City lovers.

In contrast, one of the South's more notorious madams, Pauline Tabor of Bowling Green, Kentucky, reports that her six-girl stable rarely entertained more than thirty customers between them on any given night. An all-night stay cost $25 at Pauline's while the short-timers were entitled to twenty or thirty minutes' entertainment for their $5. Unlike most successful bordello entrepreneurs, Pauline claims never to have been a bedroom worker herself. A divorced mother of two young sons in the early years of the Depression, she found selling stockings and cosmetics from door to door not too lucrative a way of earning a living. Somewhere during her rounds she decided that what Bowling Green needed most was a good whorehouse, so she invested in a trip to Memphis,

Tennessee, where she took a crash course in bordello management. In the years following she ran establishments not only in Bowling Green but in Louisville, Kentucky, and Columbus, Indiana, as well. Her most famous house was at 627 Clay Street in Bowling Green.

As the successful operator of open bawdy houses for nearly four decades, Pauline gives five basic reasons why her business was permitted to exist with impunity. First, the illicit operator has influential friends in positions of power. Second, these powerful friends are frequently given a share of the business. Third, protection money is paid to the right people. Fourth, the men in power are convinced that the illicit operator has knowledge that if made public could be a cause of embarrassment to the authorities. And fifth, in towns the size of Bowling Green, it is better to deal with the devil you know than the devil you don't. Better to have a hometown girl running the sex business if it has to exist than some sinister stranger representing the Mob, the Syndicate, the Mafia, call it what you will. Tabor's Laws still apply. In the small towns the bordello functions when the madam and the local politicians work hand in hand. In the big cities it is a troika arrangement among the madams, the power brokers and the wise-guys. The quadrennial campaign rhetoric about housecleaning is so much poppycock.

Just as Helen McGowan saluted Detroit's police department as one of the finest in the land, so Pauline Tabor had no quarrel with the law enforcement officers in the towns where she ran her houses. Rather, it was with the politicians who were not crass enough to expect the weekly bagman with his satchel of cash, but who did expect 'campaign contributions' with relentless regularity. Second on her list were a dozen other charities which, though publicly deploring her activities, were nevertheless constantly knocking on the door, with hand open for a 'generous gift for a worthy cause'.

To Pauline's mind the most worthy causes were those of her employees, few of whom entered the life because they were lazy or sex-starved. By far the greatest number entered the business out of economic necessity, high school dropouts with no skills or deserted women with no other work experience. In addition to the town's men of influence, the staff also regularly took care of the needs of students from Western Kentucky University and servicemen from Fort Knox and nearby Camp Campbell.

With the onset of World War II, homey institutions like the house on Clay Street and the great pleasure-palaces of Miami and Los Angeles ran up against bold new competition. While the excesses of Storyville during World War I caused the closing of the great redlight district in New Orleans, World War II brought about the debasement of the four-star bordello. Popping up around every military camp in the country were trailer and pre-fab cities designed to service the sexual needs of America's armed forces in return for a share in the world's largest military budget.

Not yet a state, Hawaii offered a sterling example of how harlotry can work

Sally Stanford's Lavish Living-
room
PHOTO BY EDDY MURPHY, SAN
FRANCISCO EXAMINER

on a mass-production basis, too. Honolulu whoredom was immortalized in
James Jones's *From Here to Eternity* and William Bradford Huie's *The Revolt of
Mamie Stover*. Mamie allegedly made Helen McGowan's hard-working girls
look slothful as her customers' allotted time was measured in seconds instead of
minutes. The leisurely visit to the parlour-house clearly was a thing of the past. In
North Africa and Europe the artfully decorated bedroom gave way to the
business on a rug in the *suq*, in the hay of an Italian barn, the flatbed of a truck in
France, a doorway in the London blackout. In the Pacific, bumboats put out
from the palmy island shores to send the native girls up rope ladders dropped over
the sides of the troopships. A couple of boards and a poncho up in a tree created a
lofty but tiny bordello on the edge of the dripping jungle. Polly and Sherry and
Sally and their ilk would have been appalled.

When the post-war reaction set in, the opulent, worldwide network of
whorehouses withered and died. Centuries-old brothel areas in Europe, the

Middle East and MacArthur's Japan were eliminated by government edict or legislation. All the major cities of the world were hell-bent on cleaning up. A new Age of Morality was upon us. The prospects of the fashionable, upmarket bordello were dim indeed.

CHAPTER TEN

GOING PUBLIC

CONTRARY TO WHAT might be expected, the bordello enters a new era of unparalleled profitability and popularity in the second half of the twentieth century. By the 1980s thousands of buses operated by New York City's Metropolitan Transit Authority are sporting on their tops signs twenty-seven feet wide advising the area's citizens to 'Have Fun at the Whorehouse!' The house advertised is not one of Manhattan's four-star bordellos but the hit Broadway musical, *The Best Little Whorehouse in Texas*, in which, in the long and ripe tradition of the Folies Bergère, almost every form of sexual activity known to man is simulated. When the 'Whorehouse' movie opens, starring two of the decade's leading sex-symbols, full-page ads in the *New York Times* invite the whole family to enjoy the fun because of or despite the fact that there 'ain't nothin' dirty goin' on here!'.

Curiously, while both productions are enjoying great popularity in the Times Square area, the city administration is engaged in one of its regular crusades to clean up that torrid zone of illicit sex and pornography. And in Texas itself the real thing, *The Chicken Ranch*, has been closed for several years. Caught between the forces of the Moral Majority and the ACLU the nation is evidently in some confusion about its sex practices. In all of America there is only one state where bordello-life is blatantly legal – in the great State of Nevada.

Between California and Utah on Route 80 which bisects the Sagebrush State there are more than a score of houses which have been in operation since the gangsters of California, led by the far-sighted Bugsy Siegel, discovered Nevada in the 1940s. Some of the better-known bar-houses and parlour-houses bear names like *Fran's Star Ranch*, *Cotton Tail Ranch*, *Starlight and Moonlight*, *Sherri's Place*, *Betty's Coyote Springs Ranch*, *The Stardust*, *The Hacienda* and *The Green Lantern*. Madam Beverly Harrell, who runs an eight-girl trailer establishment, from time to time runs for the Nevada State Legislature, following a course pioneered by Sally Stanford.

Nevada's number-one pleasure-palace, the *Mustang Ranch*, until recently was run by one Joe Conforte. On an average day there were thirty-eight girls on duty, supported by a staff of maids, cooks, cashiers, security guards and the like. The working girls handled anywhere from 100 to 600 customers a day, depending on the time of year and the number of conventions being held in the area. Traditionally, the *Mustang Ranch* was a parlour-house, as opposed to a bar-house where drinks are served. As in the case portrayed in *The Best Little Whorehouse* this lack of booze is not designed to promote temperance. Rather, drinking wastes the house's time. When no drinks are served to the prospective customers, the turnover is quicker, and the girls can earn more in an hour or a night.

Conforte and his wife Sally have admitted to earning around $1 million a year; observers reckon that the figure is closer to $5 million. In September 1980 several of the brothel-keeper's prettiest workers helped to convince a federal judge in Washington that he should cut in half a £4.7 million tax claim against the *Mustang Ranch* when it was proved that on an average day each girl earned only $130.55, not twice that as the Internal Revenue Service had estimated. In 1981 Joe Conforte planned to sell his ranch for approximately $19.8 million to Gina Wilson, madam of the nearby Salt Wells Guest Ranch brothel, and Wayne Drizin, a south-Florida lawyer and real-estate developer. This plan fell through, however, thanks to continued interest on the part of the IRS, and Mr Conforte decided that he would be wise to let Mrs Conforte run the business while he sought seclusion in Rio de Janeiro.

Despite his own earlier success in the bordel business, Mr Conforte has estimated that along the Las Vegas Strip the girls 'do two hundred times' as much business as his employees at the *Mustang Ranch*. Even if this is taken as something of an exaggeration, there is little doubt that the whoring trade in Las Vegas is a billion-dollar-a-year activity. In March 1981 a crackdown on streetwalkers on The Strip resulted in the arrest of 300 hustlers in a single day. The jailed women, who usually started their working days at noon, came from every state in the Union.

Such freelancers are discouraged in Las Vegas, not on moral grounds, but because they compete with the city's better-connected fancy ladies. These well-paid escorts are supplied by the management of hotels and casinos to the high-rolling junketeers who arrive with the 'executive package', as one owner and developer, Del Webb, admitted to a Congressional investigating committee. Behind the floodlit façades and above the oriental splendour of their lobbies, gambling halls and entertainment lounges, the luxury hotels of Las Vegas offer a bordello-lifestyle with more comforts and entertainment possibilities than were enjoyed by the Emperors of Byzantium, the Popes of Rome or the Kings of England. And, on the whole, the quality of the women offered for sale here is better, too, thanks to compulsory education and modern medicine.

Although Nevada countenances open prostitution, the other forty-nine states are not deprived of illicit pleasures whatever their laws. The TAB Report, a newsletter catering to the United States sex industry, recently issued the results of its latest survey. The figure for the nation as a whole: 1.3 million full-time prostitutes, with 11,328 in Detroit, 11,605 in Houston, 16,160 in Philadelphia, 22,298 in Los Angeles and 25,836 in Chicago. New York, of course, is tops, with 62,360, even without the attractions of open gambling casinos or desert landscapes.

At last report, the best little whorehouse in New York was located at the corner of Park Avenue and 86th, Polly Adler's favourite neighbourhood. It was called by the New York Police Department 'probably the most exclusive and certainly the most expensive house of prostitution in the metropolitan area'. Here the going rate is $100 an hour for straight encounters, $200 and up for unconventional exercises. A dozen women are employed in two shifts, from noon to 8 p.m. and 8 p.m. to 4 a.m., with an average of thirty-six tricks per shift. A four-bedroom apartment with two baths, the house collects fifty per cent of whatever the customers pay, or $3600 a day, $1,314,000 a year. After $27,000 monthly expenses are deducted, the house still clears more than $1 million tax-free. Law enforcement officials estimate that there are forty-five other similar establishments in the city, that is fully developed bordellos which do not masquerade as massage parlours or Oriental spas and the like. Other well-known establishments at the time of the last survey were found at 807 Lexington Avenue, 411 Park Avenue South, 150 East 52nd Street, 96 Fifth Avenue, 141 East 55th, 208 East 39th, 211 East 51st, and 132 East 45th Street. These are all multiple-occupancy dwellings and most are on 'the fashionable upper East side'. Moreover, a good number of the new high-rise apartment buildings and condominiums in the well-termed Silk Stocking District are being occupied by the city's better-paid 'models' and call-girls who formerly lived and worked further downtown. The locations of the girls who are receiving rather than visiting may be identified by the waiting, double-parked limousines bearing Z-plates, which indicate a rented vehicle with chauffeur. These are usually hired by New York-based corporations for the entertainment of visiting customers and clients. On the other hand, the unattended businessman may avail himself of an 'Escort Service' which will send the limo and charge him $125 an hour.

The upper East side is much favoured by the outgoing types who advertise their services and specialities in periodicals like *Screw Magazine*. Lori, for example, is: 'A 5th Avenue girl. Very private, very discreet, very cooperative. $100 an hour.' Another has 'a very pretty East 40s apartment and some really cute girl friends'. If the customer dares to leave the East side precincts he may visit the Coed Dormitory, 'the most famous house in the US' or 'NY's famous Housewife House' featuring ladies who entertain while 'their husbands are at work'. For the art-minded, another offers 'full-figured Rubensesque women'. A somewhat enticing establishment calling itself *Dungeon of Torment* offers 'around-the-

The Best Little Whorehouse in
New York at the Corner of Park
Avenue and 86th Street
PHOTO BY MARILYN WARNICK

world, English, Swedish, French and Greek' amusements. One advertiser, who enjoys catachresis as much as any American sportscaster, reports: 'With unadorned modesty, I can only describe myself as too beautiful to be remembered in every aspect, albeit never to be forgotten in any way. Superlative in the proportions of my figure and in the perfection of my features. As for my cerebral charms, I am cultured in every grace, art and amenity. So if you're prone to one who is young, truly glamorous and at times brilliant, you now have the number of my private duplex apartment.' Such felicitous phrasing is clearly the work of her business manager.

Out in the open, Times Square is twenty square blocks of ambulatory and massage-parlour sex, while on the less fashionable West side off Central Park the action-minded tourist need only look for the brownstones fronted by pimp-mobiles and double-parked economy cars from New Jersey. In warm weather the visitor follows his ears to the salsa music blasting into the street from the rooming-houses which identify the bordello as readily as the red lamp of old.

The Roman legions sent thousands of slaves home to stock Rome's *lupanaria*. Today, Latin America exports its women to New York to populate its voyeur theatres and its hot-sheet hotels which proliferate throughout the city. Entire neighbourhoods like Washington Heights, once predominantly Jewish and Irish, have become Spanish-speaking enclaves where drug-dealing and prostitution are primary business concerns. The famous Lower East side ghetto of the nineteenth century has fanned out to embrace nearly two-thirds of the island of Manhattan and, as with previous generations of immigrants, the lowest income group provides the women to stock the bordellos, which operate under half a dozen guises.

In the mid-town area, with its more than 100,000 hotel rooms, twice the number available in Paris and London combined, the Big Apple makes Las Vegas pale in comparison when it comes to corporation-provided sex, as any public relations man worth his marguerita can testify. A spokesman for the New York Police Department's Office of Public Information explains the official position: 'The problem is a matter of priorities. We're concerned with what the people are concerned with. Street prostitution and massage parlors generate most citizen complaints. The volume of complaints about penthouses and that type of house is much less. So we direct our enforcement actions along the lines of citizen complaints.' Is the selective toleration of the business of sex in New York any better or worse than the other major cities of the world?

Certainly there is nothing out in the open in London today on the order of the private clubs of the Edwardian era. The Street Offences Act of 1959 drove the streetwalkers indoors for the most part and in effect created the same climate as New York's with thousands of single-occupancy rooms in boarding-houses which are in reality individual-enterprise bordellos. None the less, the literacy and imagination displayed in London's adverts are superior to those found in New York's sex periodicals. Under the illuminated doorbells in the girls' lodgings the small cards cleverly describe the erotic services to be found at the head of the stairs: 'Full wardrobe for hire. Wigs, boots, whips, chains, etc.'; 'Basket chairs recaned here'; 'Student-teacher seeks new position; no post too large or small'; 'Stocks and bonds for rent'; 'Young lady gives corrective discipline for even most difficult students'; 'Fly buttons sewn on or removed expertly'; 'Lessons in all exotic languages; including Tongue Lashings', 'Oxbridge grad can teach or learn anything'.

While the English ladies of the bedroom and the pillory enjoy their circumlocutions, across the Channel in Amsterdam's Walletjes district the goods are openly displayed in street-level windows. As early as the sixteenth century with its renowned *Holland's Leaguer* in London, the bordello ties between the English and the fastidious Dutch have been close. Taking advantage of this two-way street of commerce in the 1870s a Hollander called Klyberg and his wife were the principal exporters of girls from London for service in the bordellos of Belgium, France and the Netherlands. Some time later what was considered the world's most luxurious bordello offered the burghers of Amsterdam nightly entertainment at *The Fountain*, a multi-storeyed building which contained restaurant, dance-hall, private rooms and a billiard parlour where the hostesses could be admired while they played the game in the nude. Today, the city offers the *Massage Institut of Sex* and cheerful places like the *Maison Cent-Sept* with its dungeon, chains, whips and peculiar instruments of torture. The English, evidently, have no monopoly on the enjoyment of pain.

The Netherlands, which gave the world Xaviera Hollander (via South Africa), also produced the popular Monique van Cleef. When she came to New

York, Monique opened her first establishment on the East side, naturally, at 333 East 75th Street. When she found, in late 1964, those quarters too confining, Monique took over a large house at 850 Lake Street in Newark, New Jersey. With hundreds of prominent politicians, judges and lawmakers on her list of kinky clients, her conviction in 1967 for running a sado-masochistic sex business was overturned by the New Jersey Supreme Court two years later. A *scandale majeure* was successfully covered up, but Monique none the less abandoned her adopted country and re-established herself in the Netherlands where she is available for consultations in her arcane art.

In neighbouring Germany today the bordello scene changes from city to city. Privately operated brothels are illegal in Berlin, but there are at least a dozen clandestine first-class houses just as there are in London and New York. The pre-war decadence, as so graphically portrayed by George Grosz, has disappeared or gone underground. For proper Germanic wickedness, the visitor has to turn to Hamburg, founded in AD 811, appropriately, by the lusty Emperor Charlemagne, no stranger to bordellos himself. Each year thousands of girls who leave the provinces of West Germany eventually find themselves in Hamburg's St Pauli district where two or three thousand harlots work in the Herbertstrasse alone. As in Holland's Walletjes area the women of Hamburg occupy their places behind street-level picture windows, a more effective advertisement than printed cards.

Hamburg's Eros Centre is eloquent testimony to the German talent for organization and efficiency. The centre is a four-storey structure of frosted glass and white brick with accommodations for 130 *schatzis*. Each bedroom in the house is decorated in contemporary motel-modern, with identical furniture, wallpaper, carpeting and draperies. On the walls different prints give each room its distinction, with seascapes the most popular. Should any customer prove obstreperous, help is summoned by a direct line to the nearby Daviswache police station. For the convenience of its customers, there is an underground garage for parking one's Volkswagen or Mercedes. For the convenience of the girls there is a twenty-four hour beauty salon and a recreation room for use during their idle hours. The centre's courtyard is heated by infra-red rays and on the whole has about as much sex-appeal as a drive-in bank. None the less, it has proved so successful that similar institutions have been inaugurated in Bonn, Cologne and Stuttgart. Munich, after banning public brothels in 1973, only to witness chaos in the trade, has gone back to the municipal bordello system on the grounds that as long as it cannot be wiped out it is better to try to maintain control. Across Germany's border to the south in Austria bordellos are legal. In Vienna alone there are 1000 registered whores, but because of awkward local laws, bordellos are *verboten* in Vienna while they are permitted in many provincial cities like Salzburg and Innsbruck. In his last film, *Lola*, director Rainer Werner Fassbinder gave an excellent portrayal of post-war Germanic bordello life as seen from both

Licensed Street of Prostitutes in Hamburg where Clients Barter through Windows
BBC HULTON PICTURE LIBRARY

sides of the trade.

On the other side of the Alps, in Italy, the bordellos were closed officially in 1958. They have less chance today of operating illegally in Rome than in the northern industrial centres such as Milan and Turin. For pre-war bordello life Italian-style, Lina Wertmüller's *Love and Anarchy* gives a vivid picture showing the bordel–political connection in Mussolini's heyday. It was another Lina, Senator Merlin, whose law closing the brothels in 1958 changed the scene in contemporary Italy. After ten years' work she finally got the anti-bordello law enacted, all the while protesting that she was not against prostitution *per se*, but rather was against the government acting as a kind of *procurator magnus*. Senator Merlin failed to highlight the fact that the Vatican owned much of the land on which the old bordellos stood.

Although there were some 300,000 known prostitutes in Italy in 1958, today's estimates put the figure at over one million, with perhaps ten per cent of these in Rome. Obviously with a whoring population of 100,000, accommodations

had to be found for them. In their halcyon days the better houses offered a choice among thirty girls or more. Today, the tourist in the vicinity of Via Veneto has a wider choice among streetwalkers, but his visit to the third-class hotel-bordello finds fewer of the old amenities. What with Rome's influence on all brothels in the Western world, thanks to the military commanders like Caesar, it is only fair that it was an Italian, Girolomo Fracastoro, who gave us the word 'syphilis'. In his sixteenth-century poem Fracastoro's eponymous hero is cursed with the disease for wronging the god Apollo.

As in Rome, the four-star bordellos of Paris are gone as well: the famed *One Two Two* on rue de Provence, the grand houses at 34 rue Pasquier, 6 rue des Moulins, 2 rue Saint Georges and the legendary *Sphinx* at 31 boulevard Edgar Quinet, near the Gare Montparnasse, have all disappeared. During its heyday *The Sphinx* employed sixty girls who accepted an average of 500 customers a day. During the annual Motor Show daily attendance multiplied nearly tenfold and

Scene from the House of All Nations
COURTESY OF LAWRENCE E. GICHNER

Mustang Ranch, Nevada, second
  half of 20th C
NEW YORK PUBLIC LIBRARY

additional girls had to be specially procured. As Detroit later discovered the
average male frequently confuses the horsepower of his car with his sexual
vitality. Fittingly, *The Sphinx* was run as a capital-venture enterprise and paid
divdends like any other well-run corporation.

Le Guide Rose, a reminder of the medieval romance and a forerunner of the
Michelin, was published in Paris every two years until the closing of the city's
bordellos in the post-war morality drive. *Le Guide* identified and described in
detail every Parisian brothel worthy of the name. Many of the better houses
provided live bands for dancing and between sets phonograph records supplied
the music, pre-dating by forty years the disco scenes found in many contemporary 'On Premises Swing Clubs'.

In the *House of All Nations*, called the 'International House' by Ruth (Madam
Sherry) Barnes who borrowed freely from it, one could repair after the dancing to
the Marine Room, which was outfitted like a stateroom on a transatlantic liner,
complete with portholes and a deck that pitched and rolled to induce the proper
sense of *mal de mer*; or one could choose the Wagon-Lits room which was
fashioned as a railway car with berths, into which was piped the sound of steel
wheels clickety-clacking along the track. This may seem an odd device to employ
in a bordello until it is remembered that during this period France was in love with
its railway system. Seemingly, half of all the French motion pictures of the time
dealt with the railroad, usually with Jean Gabin playing the part of the craggy-

Scene from the House of All Nations
COURTESY OF LAWRENCE E. GICHNER

faced engineer in and out of love with *les poules* at opposite ends of the line. Aside from its peculiar theme-chambers, the primary attraction in houses of this type was the staff, women recruited from a wide variety of ethnic groups. Blonde Nordic customers could have their African blacks and browns, swarthy Arabs their fair-haired Brunhildas. An attempt to imitate this exotic smörgåsbord is made in today's leisure spas where small-town American girls dissemble under names like Tanya and Nastasha in the big-city passion-pits, the disrobed business executives beguiling themselves with the idea that they are consorting with secret agents of the KGB.

Just as the *House of All Nations* idea was born in Paris and subsequently spread like wildfire around the world, so, too, the French invented the *partouse*, the orderly and reasonably priced *residences meublées* where a man paid the admission price for himself and his companion and both were granted the privilege of enjoying sexual congress with anyone else in the establishment who was similarly inclined. *Partouse* comes from *par tout*, 'by all', and fairly well describes the house philosophy. Visitors could be *partouseurs* or not as they wished; those not keen to participate served simply as voyeurs to the exhibitionists performing their gymnastics on the beds, rugs or dining-room tables. Although the *partouse* was an active business enterprise in pre-war France, it

The Sphynx Club, Paris, made particularly popular by the visits of the military who added to its lustre
COURTESY OF LAWRENCE E. GICHNER

would be another four decades before the concept was introduced to the United States.

In mid-1977 an enterprising New Yorker opened the now internationally famous *Plato's Retreat* in the basement of the Ansonia Hotel on upper Broadway and has enjoyed spectacular if uneven success ever since. Three years later *Plato's* moved to larger quarters on West 34th Street, just off 10th Avenue of 'Slaughter on 10th Avenue' fame. Here 600 to 1000 couples each week enjoy the retreat's amenities which combine the best of a Parisian *partouse* with those of a Jack LaLanne health spa. Couples, single women and lesbians are welcome; male homosexuals are barred, if detected. The club attracts chiefly couples who want to 'swing'.

According to students of the 'Swap Club' scene, anywhere from half a million to eight million American couples are into swinging. Its advocates point out that it is less time-consuming and emotionally demanding than having an old-fashioned affair. And it is less expensive. It also offers sexual variety for couples who have become bored with one another, and it is ideal for people who for one reason or another fear intimacy with their spouses. Moreover, it is in the best American tradition: it offers a chance to be 'popular', to make new friends and to keep busy. On the other hand, the swinger's life is not a long one. In a youth-oriented society everyone becomes less desirable with advancing age. Participants in the partner-swapping game must stay in shape, look and feel young. In this 'jogging and health-food' atmosphere nourishing fruit juices are served in preference to alcoholic beverages. The tradition of mixing sex and aphrodisiacs, however, continues unabated. Instead of ingesting oysters, cantharides or warm blood, today's orgiasts pop pills, methaqualone (quads) being the most popular. With this depressant, slurred speech and disoriented and drunken behaviour can be enjoyed without smelling of alcohol.

Happily, institutions like *Plato's Retreat* maintain a link with the past: included are an 'Arabian Tent fit for a Sheikh, a Jungle Habitat, Japanese Tea Room'. Keeping things up-to-date, there is also 'disco dancing with live DJs', 'electronic games, pool tables and backgammon room', plus two TV rooms for screening pornographic movies. Thirty-two 'lounge rooms' are offered for the actual business of the place. And there is a Mat Room where from five to 100 couples may go to the mat for an orgy or simply to observe the gymnastics of others.

Plato's Retreat and similar establishments represent a natural stage in the sequences of bordello history throughout the ages, from religious prostitution, through slavery, to medieval wantonness and the new slavery of the industrial revolution, to today's latest fad in whoring in an affluent society. Perhaps equality of the sexes has at long last been achieved. In swap-clubs one does not pay the woman for her services, nor she the stud for his attentions. The cash goes right into the coffer of the entrepreneur who offers nothing more than the premises with its hokey atmosphere. There is no demeaning passing of cash between customers and service attendants. One merely swaps one's wife, mistress or ladyfriend to husband, lover or boyfriend. An extra fillip has been added to the scene by the more traditional escort service, which will hire out the female companion needed by a single man for admittance to a couples-only club. As a result, an 'honest' or free from fraud husband can trade his wife to a stranger in return for the attentions of a bona fide whore, thus obtaining the same service he might have done if he had gone to a traditional whorehouse in the first place.

In keeping with the best all-American style, today's bordello is being marketed by all-new and improved methods. Like the fast food chains offering hamburgers, fried chicken and pizzas, the new institutions are being franchised nationally. Despite accusations of tax fraud, a *Plato's Retreat West* has already opened in Los Angeles. Plans have also been made to open similar franchises in other major cities in the South and Mid-West. Tied-in merchandise is offered for sale at the *Platos*, T-shirts and panties and bluejeans with the club's name and emblem emblazoned across breast or buttocks. There are banners and pillows, ashtrays and cocktail glasses, napkins and sex paraphernalia, all labelled to identify the owner as a tasteful swap-club visitor. Here is commercialized sex at its height.

Over the centuries the bordello has borne many names: angel house, angle house, ass palace, bagnio, bawdy house, beauty parlour, bird cage, brothel, buttocking house, cab joint, cat flat, cathouse, chamber of commerce, chippy house, coupling house, cunny warren, dame-erie, dirty spot, doll house, dress house, fast house, flesh factory, fun house, gay house, girl shop, goosing range, house of evil-fame, house of ill-repute, heifer den, hook shop, hot hole, hot-house, hot pad, house of joy, ice palace, intimaterie, jolly spot, kip, knocking joint, loose-love centre, ladies' college, leaping house, man trap, molly house, naughty house, notcherie, notch house, nunnery, old ladies' home, parlour-house, pheasantry, pushing school, red-lighterie, riding academy, scatter house, seraglio, service station, shooting gallery, sin spot, sporting-house, steer joint, stew, vaulting house, whorehouse, whoretel, window-tappery and zoo. To this time-honoured list may now be added in ascending order: massage parlour, rap shop, leisure spa, swap-shop and swap-club.

Do the unconventional wife- and girl-trading establishments presage the end of the bordello of old? Concerned traditionalists need look only to the example of New York city's ageing bathhouse, the Luxor, first a Turkish bath frequented by the likes of Walter Winchell, Jack Dempsey and Damon Runyan, then a popular homosexual hostelry. As noted earlier, a grand embroglio developed when plans were made to turn the building into a massive massage parlour. The City Fathers and a worried clergy were pitted against powerful real-estate interests and equally powerful organized crime factions. Much to the mayor's embarrassment it was learned that the property was owned by a staunch political supporter, who was also a member of the crusading citizens' committee organized to combat the area's sex business. For a while, the plans were shelved; the politicians and the public lost interest in the Luxor. Then, nearly a decade later, the Luxor Baths were back in business as what law enforcement officials called 'the largest and most lavish whorehouse in the United States'. It was equipped with an indoor swimming-pool, racketball courts and saunas. As estimated 300 prostitutes worked in the nine-storey building on a three-shift basis seven days a week. As a departure from the past, the working girls themselves ran the elevators.

Nevertheless, as zealous historians are quick to point out, many old traditions were preserved. This biggest bordello of them all maintained its connection with the stage thanks to the fact that it was in the heart of the city's theatre district and was just a few steps away from the High School of Performing Arts across the street. And its religious origins were not forgotten, with the church of St Mary the Virgin just down the block.

Conservatives need have no fear for the bordello's future. After more than 3000 years of service to the community there is little doubt that it will survive in one form or another for thousands more, or at least as long as it continues to be a moneymaking enterprise. City officials estimated that the annual take of the Luxor Baths was $5,000,000. As always, the bottom line tells the story. The working women end up with only a small share of the profits. The lion's share goes to their employers and managers. It was always thus.

SELECT BIBLIOGRAPHY

All titles listed published in Britain unless otherwise indicated

Acton, William *Prostitution* (F. Cass, 1972)

Alcock, Leslie *Arthur's Britain* (Pelican, 1973)

Alder, Polly *A House is not a Home* (Rinehart, New York, 1953)

Al-Nefzawi, Shaykh Umar Ibn Muhammed, *The Perfumed Garden* (Panther, 1967)

Armajani, Yahya *Middle East, Past and Present* (Prentice-Hall, 1970)

Ashe, Geoffrey *The Quest for Arthur's Britain* (Paladin, 1971)

Balsdon, J.P.V.D. *Roman Women: Their History and Habits* (Bodley Head, 1962)

Barnes, Ruth *Pleasure was My Business* (Lyle Stuart, New York, 1961)

Bauer, Max *Liebensleben in Deutscheur, Verganenheit* (Langenscheid, Berlin, 1925)

Bauer, Willi *Geschitchte und Wesen der Prostitution* (Weltspegel-Verlag, Stuttgart, 1956)

Benedict, Ruth *The Chrysanthemum and the Sword* (Routledge, 1977)

Billington, Ray Allen *Westward Movements in the United States* (Van Nost. Reinhold, 1959)

Bryant, Sir Arthur *The Age of Chivalry* (Collins, 1975)

Bukhsh, S. Khuda *Marriage and Family Life Among the Arabs* (Ashraf, Lahore, 1953)

Burckhardt, Jacob *The Civilization of Renaissance Italy* (Harper & Row, New York, 1958)

Burford, E.J. *The Orrible Synne* (Calder & Boyars, 1977)

Burton, Elizabeth *The Pageant of Georgean England* (Scribner, New York, 1967)

Burtt, E.A. (ed) *The Compassionate Buddha* (Mentor, New York, 1955)

Castelot, André *The Turbulent City : Paris 1783-1871* (Harper & Row, New York, 1962)

Chandra, Moti *The World of Courtesans* (Vekas, 1975)

Chaudhuri, Birad C. *The Continent of Circe* (Chatto & Windus, 1965)

Crawley, Ernest *The Mystic Rose* (Meridian, New York, 1960)

Crow, Duncan *The Edwardian Woman* (Allen & Unwin, 1978)

Davies, Hunter (ed) *The New London Spy* (D. White, New York, 1976)

De Becker, Joseph E. *The Nightless City* (Z.P. Maruya, Yokohama, 1899)

Dedmon, Emmett *Fabulous Chicago* (Random, New York, 1953)

De Leeuw, Hendrik *Cities of Sin* (Smith & Hass, New York, 1933

Dodds, John W. *The Age of Paradox* (Rinehart, New York, 1972)

Eberhard, Wolfram *A History of China* (Routledge, 1977)

Edme, Nicholas *Restif de la Bretonne* (Le Palais Royal, Paris)

Edwardes, Allen *The Jewel in the Lotus* (Bantam Books, 1977)

Ehrlich, Blake *London on the Thames* (Little Brown, Boston, 1966)

Evans, Joan *Life in Medieval France* (Phaidon, 1969)

Evelyn, John *Diary, 1620-1706* (Clarendon, 1955)

Fabienne, Janet *One, Two, Two* (Paris, 1975)

Fleishman, Hector *Les Demoiselles d'Amour du Palais-Royale* (Bibliothèque Curieux, Paris, 1911)

Flexner, Abraham *Prostitution in Europe* (Century, New York, 1914)

Franzius, Ennd *History of the Byzantine Empire* (Funk & Wagalls, New York, 1977)

Friedlander, Lee *Bellocq: Storyville Portraits* (Scolar, 1979)

Froissart, Jean *Chronicles* (Penguin, 1968)

Gentry, Curt *Madams of San Francisco* (Doubleday, New York, 1964)

Gies, Joseph and Frances *Life in a Medieval City* (Abelard-Schuman, 1975)

Grun, Bernard *The Timetables of History* (Thames & Hudson, 1975)

Haller, John S. and Robin M. *The Physician and Sexuality in Victorian America* (University of Illinois, Chicago, 1974)

Handlin, Oscar *The Americans* (Little Brown, Boston, 1963)

Henriques, Fernando *Prostitution and Society* (Citadel, New York, 1963)

Hogrefe, Pearl *Tudor Women: Commoners and Queens* (Iowa University Press, Ames, 1975)

Hsu, Cho-Yun *Ancient China in Transition* (Stanford, California, 1965)

Jeffrey, Julie Roy *Frontier Women* (Hill & Wang, New York,

1979)

Jusserand, J.G. *English Wayfaring in the Middle Ages* (Putnam, New York, 1950)

Kendall, Paul Murray *The Yorkshire Age* (Allen & Unwin, 1961)

Kimball, Nell *Nell Kimball* (Macmillan, New York, 1970)

Kubly, Herbert *Gods and Heroes* (Doubleday, New York, 1969)

Larivaille, Paul *La Vie Quotidienne des Courtisanes en Italie au Temps de la Renaissance* (Paris, 1975)

Laven, Peter *Renaissance Italy: 1464-1534* (Putnam, New York, 1966)

Lewis, W.H. *Sunset of the Splendid Century: 1670–1736* (Sloane, New York, 1955)

Lindsay, Jack *The Normans and Their World* (St Martin's, New York, 1974)

Longstreet, Stephen *City on Two Rivers* (Hawthorne, New York, 1975)

McGowan, Helen *Motor City Madam* (Pageant, New York, 1964)

Martin, Cy *Whiskey and Wild Women* (Hart, New York, 1974)

Mayhew, Henry *London Labour and the London Poor* (F. Cass, 1967)

Morris, Lloyd *Incredible New York* (Random, New York, 1951)

Muller, Herbert J. *Loom of History* (Harper, New York, 1958)

Nicolson, Harold *The Age of Reason* (Doubleday, New York, 1961)

Norton, W. Scott *China: Its History and Culture* (Lippincott & Crowell, New York, 1980)

Nutting, Anthony *The Arabs: Mohammed to the Present* (Potter, New York, 1964)

O'Connell, Marvin R. *The Counter-Reformation* (Harper & Row, 1974)

Page, Raymond Ian *Life in Anglo-Saxon England* (Batsford, 1970)

Petrie, Charles *The Edwardians* (Morton, New York, 1965)

Philby, H. St John *Saudi Arabia* (Praeger, New York, 1955)

Quale, G. Robina *Eastern Civilizations* (Prentice-Hall, Englewood Cliffs, NJ, 1975)

Reischauer, Edwin O. *Japan: Story of a Nation* (Duckworth, 1970)

Richardson, Joanna *The Courtesans* (World Publishing, Cleveland, 1967)

Romier, Lucien *A History of France* (St Martin's, New York, 1953)

Rose, Al *Storyville* (University of Alabama Press, 1976)

Runciman, Steven *Byzantine Civilisation* (Edward Arnold, 1966)

Sanger, William *History of Prostitution* (Harper, New York, 1858)

Seward, Jack *The Japanese* (Morrow, New York, 1972)

Silverberg, Robert *Empires in the Dust* (Chilton, Philadelphia, 1963)

Simon, Kate *New York: Places and Pleasures* (Davis-Poynter, 1973)

Smith, Page *Daughters of the Promised Land* (Little Brown, Boston, 1970)

Tabor, Pauline *Pauline's* (Touchstone Press, Louisville, 1972)

Thompson, Roger *Women in Stuart England and America* (Routledge, 1978)

The Travels of Marco Polo (Kestrel, 1980)

Trevelyan, G.M. *English Social History* (Penguin, 1979)

Vatsyayana *The Kama Sutra* (Panther, 1963)

Veze, Raoul *Le Baisier* (Bibliothèque Curieux, Paris, 1924)

Vogliotti, Gabriel R. *Girls of Nevada* (Citadel, Secaucus, NJ, 1975)

Waddy, Charles *Women in Muslim History* (Longman, 1980)

Washburn, Charles *Come into My Parlor* (National Library Press, New York, 1936)

Waterman, Willoughby C. *Prostitution and Its Repression in New York* (Columbia University Press, New York, 1932)

White, R.J. *Life in Regency England* (Putnam, New York 1963)

Wiley, William Leon *Gentlemen of Renaissance France* (Greenwood Press, 1954)

Wolsey, Serge G. *Call House Madam* (Beverly Davis) (Turondale, New York & San Francisco, 1943)

Erotic Enamel Miniature
Inside a Watch
Victorian
ASPREY, LONDON

INDEX